THE
PRODUCER'S
SOURCEBOOK

FOR THE INDEPENDENT FILM
& TV PRODUCER

Second Edition

RANDALL BLAIR

THE PRODUCER'S SOURCEBOOK
FOR THE INDEPENDENT FILM & TV PRODUCER

Cover design: Vila Design

TABLE OF CONTENTS

INTRODUCTION

There has never been a better time to be a Producer. Producers make content for theaters, television/cable and other media outlets, and the demand for that content is at an all-time high. For example, in the 2017/18 television season, there were over 1,300 scripted series on television/cable. In 2017, the global box office for feature films hit an all-time high of $40.6 Billion. And in the United States producers released 777 feature films. In 2018, Netflix plans to produce 700 original television series and release 80 original feature films. This is part of an estimated $8 billion they will spend on content in 2018. Less than ten years ago, Netflix did not produce any of its own content. Hulu is another recent entry to the original content game, and even though they continue to lose money, they plan to spend $2.5 billion on content in 2018. These are but some of the examples of how Producers are making content at an un-paralleled rate. And this trend not only helps Producers, but it supports the overall film and television industry, which provides 2.1 million jobs in the United States.

Producing is the heart of filmmaking. If you break down the tasks that are required to produce a piece of content (feature film, television show, documentary, educational video series, etc), the majority of them are what we call producing. Here's an illustration of this for a fiction film.

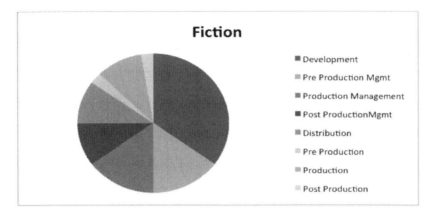

In this chart, Development, Pre Production Mgmt., Production Management, Post Production Mgmt, and Distribution are all producing functions and represent approximately 85% of the overall process or work of making this content. The other three sections, Pre Production, Production, and Post Production are all traditional production functions, which involve skills (camera, lighting, sound, and editing) that are typically taught in traditional filmmaking courses. And they represent only 15% of the overall process / work of making this content. Of course, it is an essential 15%, but it wouldn't happen at all without the work of the Producer.

This chart, which depicts the creation of nonfiction content, shows a similar breakdown with roughly 85% producing tasks and 15% production tasks.

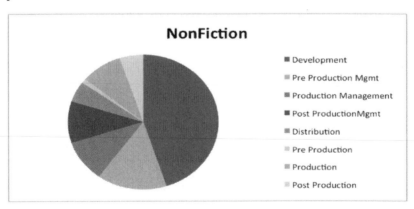

So before we go any further, let's clear up – as much as we can – what is "producing" and who is a "Producer" and what do they do.

A quick look in a dictionary will tell us that "Producer" is a noun and the simplest definition is that it is "someone who produces." Or in economic terms, someone who creates value or produces goods and services. Here is what the Merriam – Webster Learner's Dictionary (online) says:

DEFINITION OF A PRODUCER

1 : one that produces; *especially* : one that grows agricultural products or manufactures crude materials into articles of use

2 : a person who supervises or finances a work (as a staged or recorded performance) for exhibition or dissemination to the public

3 : an autotrophic organism (as a green plant) viewed as a source of biomass that can be consumed by other organisms

For our purposes number 2 seems good, but sometimes after an 18-hour day trying to raise money for a film or deal with agents, we might feel more like number 3.

This book focuses on the independent Producer, the ultimate entrepreneur and possibly the modern day Don Quixote. A person with an idea, a dream, who takes on the challenges and the risks of the modern media industry.

In film, television, and long-form video, the Producer is the person who controls and oversees all aspects of a production starting with the idea and ending with the speech at the awards ceremony. One illustration of this is seen when watching the annual Academy Awards show from the Academy of Motion Picture Arts and Sciences. Many Oscars are presented to the individual director, cinematographer, composer, editor, and costume designer for excellence in their particular crafts. But when they present the awards for best pictures – Animated Feature, Short Film (Animated), Short Film (Live Action), Documentary (Feature),

Documentary (Short Subject), and Best Picture - who gets those the awards? You guessed it. The Producers.

So if the Producer does all of that, then producing is all of those functions that the Producer does, keeping in mind that the Producer does not do all the other tasks, jobs, crafts that have their own Oscars. Here's a list of many, but not all, of the main functions/tasks/jobs of a Producer:

Generate ideas or acquire ideas/intellectual property

Develop the ideas/intellectual property into a script or treatment

Use the script or treatment to create a schedule and budget

Raise money to cover the budget

Hire the production and postproduction crew, particularly the director and editor

Manage the money during the production

Negotiate with agents for actors, if a fiction project

Negotiate with interviewees, if a documentary project

Manage the production and postproduction to make sure it is on schedule and on budget

Negotiate distribution contracts or supervise self-distribution

Prepare a strategy for and manage the marketing

Manage the social media presence of the project

So hopefully you noticed that nowhere in this list is there any mention of being able to direct actors, frame a shot, record sound, or make a split edit. Many Producers do not have any of what we call the traditional production skills that we require from a director, camera operator, sound recordist or editor. This is particularly true for feature films, especially those with budgets over $500,000. Now for low budget features and for documentary films, many Producers have some production skills and may even work that skill during the production phase of the project. One example of this is Barbara Koppel, who made the Academy Award winning films *Halen County USA* and *American Dream*. She was the sound person on those films in addition to being the Producer and director.

So a Producer who has production skills and experience is often at an advantage, particularly on nonfiction projects and on low-budget fiction projects. These days we see many Producers of nonfiction content who can also edit a film to a rough cut stage; then they turn it over to a profession post production house for the final edit, color correction, sound sweetening, and graphics. This trend has been a direct result of the proliferation of nonlinear editing systems that can live on a Producer's laptop. Now a strong word of caution – I don't encourage or condone the concept of a "one-man band." This is the filmmaker who thinks that they can do it all by themselves. They can't. Good films only come from a successful collaboration of craftspeople with different talents; and that collaboration, that team, is set up (selected and hired) by the Producer. And the Producer who has some experience with the different production crafts can often, but not always, make a better judgment when reviewing the resumes and the reels of different craftspeople.

Now a word of encouragement for those people who want to produce content but don't have a production background – never been to film school, never developed a production craft professionally. You can still become a successful Producer! A Producer's job is to take an idea and develop it to the point where they can raise money and then hire the best craftspeople they can afford. Many of these Producers rely on a director, who they hire first, to then hire the other craftspeople. The job of a Producer requires its own set of skills (ones that we will work on in this book), and there is no need to know how to white-balance a camera or select the right microphone or know that a "stinger" is grip-speak for an extension cord.

There is, however, one essential skill that all Producers need to have. Writing. I don't mean the particular skills of scriptwriting, although many Producers have at least rudimentary skills in that area. I mean the ability to communicate clearly and effectively in writing. For a Producer, it centers on the proposal that they will write to seek funding and distribution. This is a document that has to convey the power of the idea and the rationale for its success with a particular audience, in a specific market. It requires clean, concise language in simple sentences. It should read easily and build, word by word, a picture of what the film is all about.

PHILOSOPHICAL APPROACH

This book is the result of almost fifty years working in media, including twenty-five years teaching college students the basics of producing in the film, television and video industries. I wrote it because I have never found a textbook that approached producing in a way that made it accessible to someone starting in the industry and that offered sufficient details about the basic skills required to be a successful Producer.

My philosophical approach with this book is that a Producer can only be successful working in our industry if he/she knows the basics of how the industry works. There is a particular emphasis on the independent Producer, so the concentration is on producing television content for the networks that offer nonfiction programming (PBS and many of the niche cable networks) and on producing independent feature films. These are two areas where a new Producer can make an immediate impact; can get a meeting with a programming executive or a development executive; and with a great idea, can become an "overnight success."

Since the underlying assumption for this book is that the reader will be new to producing and the business of film and television, I have concentrated on the basics of how things currently work and then reference the changes that are happening. There is not enough room to explore all the many fascinating developments that currently impact our industry. My belief is that in order to understand the relevance and importance of changes, you first have to understand what is being changed. And not everything is changing radically, or changing at all. While there have been tremendous changes in the film, television and video industries over the past twenty-five years, many of the basic elements of the craft and the business have remained surprisingly unchanged. While some of the tools of producing have changed, the processes and the goals have remained the same. And we need to know and understand where we are coming from before we can appreciate where we are going.

ORGANIZATION

There are five parts to this book: Getting Started; The Television/Cable Universe; Feature Film Marketplace; Production Planning and Management; and Proposals. Within each part there are chapters that provide specific content. And at the end of each chapter you will find the following Supplemental Material:

Review Questions - to help reinforce what you have read.

Industry Speak – every industry has its own unique terms and definitions. These are some of the important ones that relate to each chapter. Be sure that you are familiar with them.

Further Activities – these are designed to expand on the material in the chapter. Also for the second edition, I have created a companion website www.theproducerssourcebook.com which contains resource material that will help you complete the further activities in the chapters on script breakdown, scheduling, and budgeting.

Further Reading & Research – for those eager to learn more, I present other books and sources for further information.

In this book I often use 'filmmaking' and 'film' as generic terms to reference making content in all formats, both analog and digital.

Link-rot: I try to make sure that all the web addresses and/or hyperlinks are accurate and still valid as of the publication date. I apologize if I made a mistake, or if there is any link-rot as these organizations are constantly changing their web presence. The organization name probably didn't change, so a simple google search should get you to the right place.

For this second edition, I have relied on great feedback from readers, teachers and students who have used the book. I have updated the industry statistics to include the most current information available. However, the film, television, and video industries undergo daily changes. Most changes are minor, but some are major, earth-shaking. After the publication of this edition, I will make every effort to update any part(s) of the book that have been impacted by major changes. These revisions/updates will be posted on the resource website www.theproducerssourcebook.com for readers to access. And, in the best "to err is human" tradition, there are probably some mistakes that will be found from time to time. With apologies in advance, corrections will be posted on the website as well. This will not include minor spelling and punctuation mistakes; but will focus on things of substance.

Supplemental Material – Introduction

Review Questions

1. What percentage of all the work required to make a fiction film are producing tasks? What is the percentage for nonfiction?

2. Describe who is a Producer in film, television and long-form video.

3. Who receives the Oscar for Best Picture?

4. Be familiar with the list of functions/tasks/jobs of a Producer

5. What is the production skill that many nonfiction Producers have?

6. Can you become a successful Producer without any production skills?

7. What is the one essential skill for all producers?

Industry Speak

Business plan - a written description of a proposed commercial activity, often used in obtaining start-up financing from investors and other sources of capital

Commercial potential - a subjective judgment about how a proposed movie project will do at the box office

Development - the initial stage in the preparation of a film; those activities relating specifically to obtaining underlying property, turning it into a finished screenplay or treatment, preparing a Producer's package, and raising money

Entrepreneur - a person who takes on the risks of starting a new business

Hook - something unique that will set a project apart, attract the attention or gain the interest of a target audience; this can be a story element or an individual involved in the project

Package - the total presentation of the basic elements needed to do a film; normally includes a script or treatment, schedule, budget and commitments by key talent

Producer - the person who carries the ultimate responsibility for the original shaping and final outcome of a film; generally, finds and develops a project; arranges for financing, oversees the production and post production and arranges and supervises the distribution of the film

Producer's fee - compensation paid to a film's Producer out of the budget of the film; also, the up-front payment to person who has developed a package and sold it to a studio for production

Producers Guild of America - an organization that tries to insure the correct application of screen credits for Producers; despite its name it is not a guild or union because the Producer is a managerial position

Producer for hire - a person who performs the services of a film Producer as an employee of a studio, production company or network

Royalties - payments for the right to use property such as copyrighted material; also, a share of the proceeds from the exploitation of the property

Target market - a specific audience segment that a Producer and/or distributor seeks to reach with a program and its advertising and promotional campaign

Trades - the daily, weekly or monthly newspapers and

magazines that specialize in reporting news and information relating to the entertainment industry

Treatment - an intermediate stage of writing between the idea and the shooting script for a feature film or the actual production of a nonfiction project; an essay style description of the story and characters; generally, 15 to 20 pages for a feature film or 5 to 10 pages for a nonfiction work

Further Activities

1. Write down five personality traits / strengths that you think a successful Producer would have.

2. Go to Wikipedia and search for 'Film Producer' and 'Television Producer'; you will see that the terminology and definitions get complicated; check out some of the individual Producers to see what were their backgrounds and how they started as Producers.

3. If you have the opportunity, go to a local film/television industry event and ask a Producer how he or she got started and what skills they value the most.

Further Reading & Research

Check out the Producers Guild of America
http://www.producersguild.org/

Get in the daily habit – read the industry trade papers to know what is going on in the industry. For film and television, I recommend *Variety, Hollywood Reporter, Broadcasting & Cable,* and *Current.* They are all available online. Another good resource for what's happening in television is the *Cynopsis.com* online newsletter. For documentary and nonfiction work, I suggest *Real Screen.*

PART ONE

GETTING STARTED

I t has to start somewhere – right? Maybe we should call it the Big Bang Theory – oh, wait, that's been done…

All good film and television projects start with a great idea - a great fiction story idea or a great nonfiction story idea. But ideas by themselves are not enough, and they cannot be protected, as we will read in Chapter 1.

Some Producers have a lot of their own great ideas, and the critical thing is to know what to do with them. For most Producers that means developing the idea into a script or a treatment. Some Producers have the skills and talent to do this themselves, but many need to rely on professional writers to make sure that the script or treatment is the very best. In these cases, the Producer hires the writer and uses a work-for-hire contract that insures that the Producer has the copyright, which otherwise would belong to the writer, even if the original ideas was the Producer's.

For those ideas that a Producer discovers, the first step is to determine if it's protected or not. If it's just an idea, then it's out there for a Producer to use and develop in the same way they would an original idea. However, most of the time Producers find ideas that have already been developed into what we call underlying property. What that is and how a Producer gets the legal rights to it is the subject of chapter 1.

Another basis for many films is the story of someone's life. Generally, everyone has some control over his or her life story, and a Producer cannot just tell it without what we call a Life Rights Agreement. That is the subject of chapter 2.

1

UNDERLYING PROPERTY

I t all starts with an idea. I know I'm repeating myself, but it's that important. The idea could be the Producer's own or one she got from another source. Whatever the source, the idea is exciting enough to engage her passion for storytelling. But there's a problem that is inherent with all ideas. What do you think that could be? Yes. The problem is that we can't protect our ideas unless we keep them to ourselves. The minute we share an idea we lose control of it and anyone can take it and use it. Ideas are not protected by copyright or other laws. To better understand this, a Producer needs to be familiar with the basics of copyright.

COPYRIGHT

According to the United States Copyright Office, which is part of the Library of Congress, a copyright is a "form of protection provided by the laws of the United States (title 17, U.S. Code) to the authors of 'original works of authorship' including literary, dramatic, musical, artistic, and certain other intellectual works."

The following are key excerpts from the document "Copyright Basics" issued by the U.S. Copyright Office.

What Is Copyright?

Copyright is a form of protection provided by the laws of the United States (title 17, *U.S. Code*) to the authors of "original works of authorship," including literary, dramatic, musical, artistic, and certain other intellectual works. This protection is available to both published and unpublished works.

Section 106 of the 1976 Copyright Act generally gives the owner of copyright the exclusive right to do and to authorize others to do the following:

- reproduce the work in copies or phonorecords

- prepare derivative works based upon the work

- distribute copies or phonorecords of the work to the public by sale or other transfer of ownership, or by rental, lease, or lending

- perform the work publicly, in the case of literary, musical, dramatic, and choreographic works, pantomimes, and motion pictures and other audio-visual works

- display the work publicly, in the case of literary, musical, dramatic, and choreographic works, pantomimes, and pictorial, graphic, or sculptural works, including the individual images of a motion picture or other audiovisual work

- perform the work publicly (in the case of sound recordings) by means of a digital audio transmission

Who Can Claim Copyright?

Copyright protection subsists from the time the work is created in fixed form. The copyright in the work of authorship immediately becomes the property of the author who created the work. Only the author or those deriving their rights through the author can rightfully claim copyright.

In the case of works made for hire, the employer and not the employee is considered to be the author. Section 101 of the copyright law defines a "work made for hire" as:

a work prepared by an employee within the scope of his or her employment; *or*
a work specially ordered or commissioned for use as:
a contribution to a collective work
a part of a motion picture or other audiovisual work
a translation
a supplementary work
a compilation
an instructional text
a test
answer material for a test
an atlas

if the parties expressly agree in a written instrument signed by them that the work shall be considered a work made for hire.

What Works Are Protected?

Copyright protects "original works of authorship" that are fixed in a tangible form of expression. The fixation need not be directly perceptible so long as it may be communicated with the aid of a machine or device. Copyrightable works include the following categories:

1 literary works
2 musical works, including any accompanying words
3 dramatic works, including any accompanying music
4 pantomimes and choreographic works
5 pictorial, graphic, and sculptural works
6 motion pictures and other audiovisual works
7 sound recordings
8 architectural works

These categories should be viewed broadly. For example, computer programs and most "compilations" may be registered as "literary works"; maps and architectural plans may be registered as "pictorial, graphic, and sculptural works."

What Is Not Protected by Copyright?

Several categories of material are generally not eligible for federal copyright protection. These include among others:

- works that have not been fixed in a tangible form of expression (for example, choreographic works that have not been notated or recorded, or improvisational speeches or performances that have not been written or recorded)

- titles, names, short phrases, and slogans; familiar symbols or designs; mere variations of typographic ornamentation, lettering, or coloring; mere listings of ingredients or contents

- ideas, procedures, methods, systems, processes, concepts, principles, discoveries, or devices, as distinguished from a description, explanation, or illustration

- works consisting entirely of information that is common property and containing no original authorship (for example: standard calendars, height and weight charts,

tape measures and rulers, and lists or tables taken from public documents or other common sources)

How to Secure a Copyright

Copyright Secured Automatically upon Creation

The way in which copyright protection is secured is frequently misunderstood. No publication or registration or other action in the Copyright Office is required to secure copyright. There are, however, certain definite advantages to registration.

Copyright is secured automatically when the work is created, and a work is "created" when it is fixed in a copy or phonorecord for the first time. "Copies" are material objects from which a work can be read or visually perceived either directly or with the aid of a machine or device, such as books, manuscripts, sheet music, film, videotape, or microfilm. "Phonorecords" are material objects embodying fixations of sounds (excluding, by statutory definition, motion picture soundtracks), such as cassette tapes, CDs, or vinyl disks. Thus, for example, a song (the "work") can be fixed in sheet music ("copies") or in phonograph disks ("phonorecords"), or both. If a work is prepared over a period of time, the part of the work that is fixed on a particular date constitutes the created work as of that date.

Notice of Copyright

The use of a copyright notice is no longer required under U. S. law, although it is often beneficial. Because prior law did contain such a requirement, however, the use of notice is still relevant to the copyright status of older works.

How Long Copyright Protection Endures

A work that was created (fixed in tangible form for the first time) on or after January 1, 1978, is automatically protected from the moment of its creation and is ordinarily given a term enduring for the author's life plus an additional 70 years after the author's death. In the case of "a joint work prepared by two or more authors who did not work for hire," the term lasts for 70 years after the last surviving author's death. For works made for hire, and for anonymous and pseudonymous works (unless the author's identity is revealed in Copyright Office records), the duration of copyright will be 95 years from publication or 120 years from creation, whichever is shorter.

Transfer of Copyright

Any or all of the copyright owner's exclusive rights or any subdivision of those rights may be transferred, but the transfer of exclusive rights is not valid unless that transfer is in writing and signed by the owner of the rights conveyed or such owner's duly authorized agent. Transfer of a right on a nonexclusive basis does not require a written agreement.

A copyright may also be conveyed by operation of law and may be bequeathed by will or pass as personal property by the applicable laws of intestate succession.

Copyright is a personal property right, and it is subject to the various state laws and regulations that govern the ownership, inheritance, or transfer of personal property as well as terms of contracts or conduct of business. For information about relevant state laws, consult an attorney.

Transfers of copyright are normally made by contract. The Copyright Office does not have any forms for such transfers. The law does provide for the recordation in the Copyright Office of transfers of copyright ownership. Although recordation is not required to make a valid transfer between the parties, it does provide certain legal advantages and may be required to validate the transfer as against third parties.

Copyright Registration

In general, copyright registration is a legal formality intended to make a public record of the basic facts of a particular copyright. However, registration is not a condition of copyright protection. Even though registration is not a requirement for protection, the copyright law provides several inducements or advantages to encourage copyright owners to make registration. Among these advantages are the following:

- Registration establishes a public record of the copyright claim.

- Before an infringement suit may be filed in court, registration is necessary for works of U. S. origin.

- If made before or within five years of publication, registration will establish prima facie evidence in court of the validity of the copyright and of the facts stated in the certificate.

- If registration is made within three months after publication of the work or prior to an infringement of the work, statutory damages and attorney's fees will be available to the copyright owner in court actions. Otherwise, only an award of actual damages and profits is available to the copyright owner.

- Registration allows the owner of the copyright to record the registration with the U. S. Customs Service for protection against the importation of infringing copies. For additional information, go to the U. S. Customs and Border Protection website at www.cbp.gov.

Registration may be made at any time within the life of the copyright. Unlike the law before 1978, when a work has been registered in unpublished form, it is not necessary to make another registration when the work becomes published, although the copyright owner may register the published edition, if desired.

FAIR USE

A concept related to copyright, fair use allows someone to use a copyrighted work without getting permission from the copyright holder and without violating copyright laws. There are no hard and fast rules to define fair usage, but the nature and amount of the use are key points. Traditional uses are for reviews and criticism, reporting and education. The following is reprinted from the Copyright Office. Be sure to focus on the four factors that are used to determine whether a use is fair use or copyright infringement.

One of the rights accorded to the owner of copyright is the right to reproduce or to authorize others to reproduce the work in copies or phonorecords. This right is subject to certain limitations found in sections 107 through 118 of the copyright law (*title 17, U. S. Code*). One of the more important limitations is the doctrine of "fair use." The doctrine of fair use has developed through a substantial number of court decisions over the years and has been codified in section 107 of the copyright law.

Section 107 contains a list of the various purposes for which the reproduction of a particular work may be considered fair, such as criticism, comment, news reporting, teaching, scholarship, and research. Section 107 also sets out four factors to be considered in determining whether or not a particular use is fair.

1. The purpose and character of the use, including whether such use is of commercial nature or is for nonprofit educational purposes

2. The nature of the copyrighted work

3. The amount and substantiality of the portion used in relation to the copyrighted work as a whole

4. The effect of the use upon the potential market for, or value of, the copyrighted work

The distinction between what is fair use and what is infringement in a particular case will not always be clear or easily defined. There is no specific number of words, lines, or notes that may safely be taken without permission. Acknowledging the source of the copyrighted material does not substitute for obtaining permission.

The 1961 *Report of the Register of Copyrights on the General Revision of the U.S. Copyright Law* cites examples of activities that courts have regarded as fair use: "quotation of excerpts in a review or criticism for purposes of illustration or comment; quotation of short passages in a scholarly or technical work, for illustration or clarification of the author's observations; use in a parody of some of the content of the work parodied; summary of an address or article, with brief quotations, in a news report; reproduction by a library of a portion of a work to replace part of a damaged copy; reproduction by a teacher or student of a small part of a work to illustrate a lesson; reproduction of a work in legislative or judicial proceedings or reports; incidental and fortuitous reproduction, in a newsreel or broadcast, of a work located in the scene of an event being reported."

Copyright protects the particular way authors have expressed themselves. It does not extend to any ideas, systems, or factual information conveyed in a work.

The safest course is to get permission from the copyright owner before using copyrighted material. The Copyright Office cannot give this permission.

When it is impracticable to obtain permission, you should consider avoiding the use of copyrighted material unless you are confident that the doctrine of fair use would apply to the situation. The Copyright Office can neither determine whether a particular use may be considered fair nor advise on possible copyright violations. If there is any doubt, it is advisable to consult an attorney.

FL-102, Reviewed June 2012

Fair Use is often misused by filmmakers at their peril. Always check with a good attorney if in doubt. There is a further discussion of this in chapter 24 Releases.

PUBLIC DOMAIN

Another important concept in this area is public domain. Public domain means, "owned by the public" and the use of this material is open and available for anyone. There are three basic ways that property is or can become public domain.

1. Facts or events are in the public domain; no one can own a "fact". But if you write about a fact in an original way, your original writing is copyrighted. A little confusing isn't it. It's often an area that needs a good attorney to keep a Producer safe.

2. Publications and other works created by employees of the U.S. or any other governmental (state or local) agency as part of their job are in the public domain. We the taxpayers pay them to create this stuff, so it belongs to us – makes sense, right?

3. Works that are old and have had their copyright expire are then in the public domain. The date when the copyright would expire is determined by two factors: the date of creation, and the applicable copyright law at that time of creation. A copyright lawyer is often needed to research and verify this.

Using these criteria, some things would be obviously in the public domain or not. Many things, however, are not so easily determined, and a good Producer should always consider getting a copyright report done by an attorney or special firm that handles copyright searches. Any money spent up front like this will prevent headaches and potential financial loses later on.

UNDERLYING PROPERTY

With this understanding of copyright, a Producer knows that the basis for her project has to be something in a tangible format. In general, we call this underlying property. Underlying property comes in many different forms, but there are some commonalities. For fiction projects - feature films or scripted television - underlying property normally takes the form of an original script, a novel, short story, comic book, play, fairytale, newspaper or magazine article, or nonfiction book.

A review of the underlying property of the feature films that have been nominated for the best picture Oscar through 2018 shows that 40% were based on novels, 30% on original scripts, 15% on theatrical plays, and 10% on nonfiction articles/books. However, if we look at all feature films released between 1995 and 2018, we see a shift. Of the 12,790 films in this group, 53% were based on original scripts, 23% on real life events (a person's life, newspaper/magazine article, or nonfiction book), 15% on a fiction book (novel, short story or comic book), 2% on a play, and .5% on a fairytale. Comparing these percentages to the percentage of the box office that these films made, we see some interesting, and in some cases depressing, results. Original scripts were the basis for 53% of the films and 46% of the box office. That correlation is okay. A better correlation comes from the 15% of the films based on a fiction book, which obtained 21% of the box office. But if we examine the 23% of the films that were based on real life events, we find that they took only 8% of the box office. What do you think might cause this?

In an average year, the major studios acquire the film rights to over 300 literary properties (not including original scripts) that would be underlying property. One of the larger acquisitions in past years is the approximately $9 million for an unpublished novel by Michael Crichton. Compare this to the reported $2 million paid by Warner Brothers for the film rights to the Harry Potter series. Another record is the $5 million for the original script, *Signs*, by M Night Shyamalan. Most of these properties obtained by the Hollywood studios will never be translated into a feature film, but the studios have a seemingly insatiable appetite for literary properties and other underlying property. Good Producers keep track of these sales and trends by reading the trade press every day.

Another big indicator of this appetite by the studios to control underlying property was the 2009 acquisition of Marvel Comics by Disney for $4.24 billion. And, that didn't even include immediate access to Spiderman, X-Men, the Fantastic Four or Iron Man. The rights to those properties had previously been licensed to other studios in long-term deals. DC Comics has been part of the Warner Brothers family since the 1970s.

There is often a cyclical pattern to Producers' and studios' interest in various forms of underlying properties. For example, in recent years the young adult novel or series has been very popular with studios – *Twilight*; *Harry Potter*; *Hunger Games*; *Divergent*; etc.

DOCUMENTARY AND NONFICTION FILMS

The underlying property involved with documentaries and other nonfiction projects often comes from the news media or from personal interests and contacts. *The New York Times* has had so many film projects come from its stories and articles that it hired a literary agent to work with Producers. Another big source of stories for documentaries and nonfiction is personal stories. We will look at the issue of life rights in the next chapter.

ACQUISITION OF FILM RIGHTS

Because underlying property is a tangible, legally protected thing, a Producer who wants to use it as the basis for a film or television project has to acquire the legal right to turn it into a derivative work such as a film. In order for a Producer to make a film from the underlying property, she has to obtain what we call the <u>Film Rights</u>.

For a Producer to acquire the film rights to a novel, for example, she has to enter into a written agreement with the author, or with the current copyright owner if the author has previously transferred ownership of the copyright. This agreement is called an Acquisition Agreement or a <u>Literary Purchase Agreement</u> (LPA). This agreement is a contract of sale and gives the Producer ownership and complete control of the film rights to the novel in regard to making a film based on the novel. For a Producer this is the first and most important contract in the process of the development a film. It is important to note that his agreement does not involve purchase of the copyright of the underlying property, the novel.

A good Literary Purchase Agreement will form the basis for a legally valid chain of title for the film that will carry forward to the sources of financing and the distributors of the film. A poor Literary Purchase Agreement that seems open to legal challenge will scare off any source of financing for the film or any distributor who may want to license the competed film. Because of the importance of this agreement, it should be clear to a Producer how critical it is to work with a lawyer who is experienced in these types of negotiations and contracts.

LITERARY PURCHASE AGREEMENT

In general, the Literary Purchase Agreement (LPA) gives the Producer exclusive and perpetual ownership of the film rights throughout the universe. The film rights include the plot, theme, title, and characters of a literary property. It gives the Producer the ability to change, modify and rearrange the plot and characters in any way she wishes. This is an outgrowth of the old studio system when the writer was normally an employee of the studio and the studio owned the copyright from the very beginning. A good Producer will not waste time and money on developing a literary property to which she does not have complete ownership and control of the film rights.

The normal LPA gives the Producer other rights as well, including a television show based on the film, music, merchandising and a novelization or stage play based on the film (as long as the original literary property was not in that format). Most Producers will also want to get the film rights to all sequels of the underlying property.

Because the Literary Purchase Agreement is a sale, an author with a good lawyer will often try to negotiate a reversion rights contract clause that brings the film rights back to the author if the Producer does not get a film made within a certain amount of time. This period normally varies from 2 years (sought by the author) to 10 years (demanded by the Producer). Under most reversion rights contract clauses, if the author gets the rights back and later sells them to another Producer, the first Producer is entitled to recoup her out-of-pocket development costs.

There is no standard price for a Literary Purchase Agreement. Some of the variables for a novel, for example, would include the book sales, whether it was on best-seller lists, and if it was a popular book club adoption (particularly Oprah Winfrey's book club).

The common method to determine a purchase price for the film rights is to base it on a percentage of the anticipated production budget of the film to be developed. A range of 2 to 5% of the anticipated budget is often used. Of course, from the point of view of the novelist, if the film's budget goes up, the price for the underlying property should go up as well. This is accomplished using an escalation clause, which contains a formula for the extra payment to the novelist in the event the budget goes up. An escalation clause can also be used to protect a novelist if the book gains unusual notoriety and book sales after the Literary Purchase Agreement is finalized. In this case there could also be an increase in the percentage of the budget given the author, ie from 2 percent to 3 percent.

The industry trade press is the best source of information on prices and trends in prices for film rights to literary properties. The sales are normally reported as the author receiving, for example "$250,000 against $900,000." This means that the author received $250,000 at the signing of the agreement and is entitled to receive an additional $650,000 at the start of principal photography on the film. If a film is not made, then the author keeps the $250,000 but does not get the balance. If there is an additional payment due because of an escalation clause, that additional payment is also made when the films goes into production.

The $250,000 used in the example above is not an unusual amount of money for the initial payment under a Literary Purchase Agreement for a popular novel. But it is an amount that is beyond the means of many Producers, especially those who are just getting started in the industry. This brings us to the concept of the new Producer's best friend, the option.

THE OPTION AGREEMENT

The Option Agreement is an agreement that is secondary to the Literary Purchase Agreement. It incorporates a completely negotiated LPA but states that the Producer has an exclusive right for a limited period of time to acquire the property under the terms of the Literary Purchase Agreement. The key point is that the Producer will pay a much smaller amount for the option. This is sometimes as low as several hundred dollars, if the property is not well known, and up to 10% of the total purchase price of the Literary Purchase Agreement. The option gives the Producer the time and authority to try to find the money to make the $250,000 (using our example) payment and validate the Literary Purchase Agreement. Please note that the Producer does not have to raise the money for the production budget, but just the money to make the down payment on the LPA. If successful, the Producer exercises the option, pays the amount called for under the Literary Purchase Agreement and that agreement is then valid and in force. If the Producer is unable to get the money, the option lapses and the Literary Purchase Agreement is never validated. The author is then free to deal with another Producer and owes nothing further to the first Producer, including not having to repay the option money.

NEXT STEP

Once a Producer has a valid LPA, the next step is to hire a writer to adapt that underlying property into a film script. The script is necessary to get the film funded, and it is also needed for the production management functions that are covered in part 4 of this book. The writer who the Producer will commission for this adaptation will probably be someone who has experience with the genre of the story in the underlying property. The Producer is careful to get a work-for-hire agreement signed with the writer before they start writing. This insures that the Producer owns the copyright to the script.

ORIGINAL SCRIPTS

Writers often write a script based on their own idea and then try to find a Producer to buy it. These "spec" scripts (written on speculation) are not based on underlying property but solely on the writer's imagination. It is imperative that the Producer purchases the copyright to the spec script before proceeding. This purchase agreement is often much simpler than a LPA, but the smart Producer still uses an experienced lawyer.

> A note to all scriptwriters: don't waste your time adapting a novel or other literary source into a script unless you have the film rights or the source is clearly in public domain. Without the rights, you are merely creating a writing exercise or sample that can never be sold or produced.

SUPPLEMENTAL MATERIAL - CHAPTER 1 - UNDERLYING PROPERTY

<u>Review Questions</u>

1. What type of underlying property was the basis for the most nominees for best picture Oscars through 2018?

2. What is the basis of many documentary and nonfiction films?

3. What exclusive rights does copyright give the author?

4. Who can claim copyright and when does it become the property of the author?

5. What is the problem with an idea as the basis for a film?

6. What works are protected by copyright?

7. What works are not protected by copyright?

8. How does an author secure copyright?

9. Is the notice of copyright required on new creations?

10. How long does copyright protection last?

11. How can copyright be transferred?

12. Is copyright registration required of new works?

13. What are the advantages of registration?

14. What are the four factors used to determine fair use?

15. What are the three basic ways property is or can become public domain?

16. What does the Literary Purchase Agreement buy?

17. What are the components of film rights?

18. What does a reversion right do for the author?

19. What is one method to determine the price for the film rights?

20. Why would an author want an escalation clause?

21. If an author is getting "$150,000 against $600,000" for film rights, how much do they get when principal photography begins?

22. Does the Option Agreement require a Literary Purchase Agreement?

23. What type of agreement does a Producer enter into with a scriptwriter for an adaptation?

Industry Speak

Literary Purchase Agreement - a contract used by a Producer to acquire the film rights to use another's literary work

Adaptation - a movie script, which uses and/or modifies a story that first appeared in another medium such as a short story, novel, theatrical play or magazine article

Agent - A person who acts for the benefit of another person or represents the interests of another to help them get work and to negotiate contracts on their behalf; in the film business, they are licensed by the states.

Chain of title - the successive conveyances or sales of a property commencing with the original source

Commissioned work - a work specifically ordered as a "work for hire" where the copyright belongs to the employer; most often a script but can also refer to an entire nonfiction project

Copyright - a bundle of rights for artists and authors giving them exclusive right to publish, copy, distribute or otherwise use their works or determine who may do so

Copyright infringement - the unauthorized use of copyrighted material

Fair use - the use of copyrighted material in a manner that does not constitute an infringement and can be done without the consent of or payment to the copyright holder

License - a right granted which gives a person permission to do something which they would not otherwise be entitled to do; generally characterized by a time limitation and conveys control but not ownership of such rights

Option - a contract in which the owner of a property agrees that someone has the privilege of buying the property at a fixed price within a stated period of time as clearly stated in a completed contract or other agreement; typically, one of the first steps in the development of a literary property into a film

Reversion right - a contractual ability to reacquire the film rights to develop, produce or otherwise exploit a particular literary property or development package

Sale - a contract or agreement by which ownership of property is transferred from the seller to the buyer; requires an offer and acceptance, parties dealing at independently, and payment of something of value

Speculation or spec script - a script that is written without compensation from or control by another party in the hopes of finding a purchaser for the finished property

Title - the registered name of a screenplay; also refers to a shorthand term of ownership and having the right to possess, use and exploit a property.

Underlying property - the literary or other work upon which rights to produce and distribute a film are based

Work made-for-hire - a copyright law concept that describes a creative work done by an employee where the employer owns the copyright; a contractual arrangement between a Producer and a freelance creative (often a writer) whereby the creative sells the copyright to the Producer in exchange for compensation

Further Activities

1. Read *Variety* and/or the *Hollywood Reporter* regularly to see what Producers are paying for underlying property.

2. Think of some of your favorite films and then investigate what was their underlying property. imdb.com is one source for this information.

3. Go to the Oscar website oscar.go.com and check out the films nominated for Best Screenplay Based on adapted material.

Further Reading & Research

For more information on the Literary Purchase Agreement read the article **NEGOTIATING THE LITERARY PURCHASE OPTION AGREEMENT (ABRIDGED, COLORED & FLAVORED VERSION) by Harris E. Tulchin.** http://www.medialawyer.com/article24.php.

The Center for Media and Social Impact publication on fair use. http://cmsimpact.org/code/documentary-filmmakers-statement-of-best-practices-in-fair-use/

The complete Copyright Basics document – US Copyright

office - http://www.copyright.gov/circs/circ01.pdf

Get in the daily habit – read the industry trade papers to know what is going on in the industry. For film and television, I recommend *Variety, Hollywood Reporter, Broadcasting & Cable,* and *Current.* They are all available online. Another good resource for what's happening in television is the *Cynopsis.com* online newsletter. For documentary and nonfiction work, I suggest *Real Screen.*

2

LIFE RIGHTS

LIFE RIGHTS AS UNDERLYING PROPERTY

A nother source for material to use as the basis for a film is the story of someone's life. The process and agreements used with this form of underlying property are very different from the literary sources. While this is primarily a concern for documentary Producers, it is also a factor for the many fiction films that are based on a life story.

The key concept in the area of life rights is that every person has the right to control the way they are presented in public and that they have the right to insist on the accuracy of any presentation. They also have the right to prevent the commercial exploitation of their name or likeness. One exception to this is the person who has placed himself or herself in the public eye such as a politician or possibly a celebrity.

There are three legal concepts that are at work here: the right of privacy; the right of publicity; and defamation. What follows are very general descriptions that would not stand up in a law course or a courtroom.

The right of privacy basically says that a person has a right to be left alone. You cannot "out" someone in any way or reveal private facts of their life. You cannot invade their personal space. This is true no matter how good your intentions may have been. The only exceptions are elected officials and criminals. The application of

THE PRODUCER'S SOURCEBOOK

this rule as it relates to celebrities is confusing and beyond the scope of this book.

The right of publicity means that people have control over the commercial use of their identity and image. You cannot use someone's face or name to sell your product without permission. This right holds true for celebrities and, because it is a property right, it extends beyond a person's life and may be passed on to their heirs or estate.

Defamation refers to the publication or saying of anything false which is injurious to the reputation of the person or which tends to bring them disrepute (dishonor or ill will). If the false thing is in print, it is called libel; and if it is spoken, it is called slander. There are some defenses against defamation. Truth is an absolute defense because defamation by definition refers to something that is false. Humor is another possible defense, but it must be very clear that it was meant to be a joke. And if it is clear that you are merely stating your personal opinion, then that can be a defense.

A corollary to this, that is important for filmmakers, is the concept of false light. This refers to the potential for taking material that accurately depicts someone in the context of the filming but then putting them in a false light by how they are edited into the film.

On one level, much, if not all, of this is covered by having a good appearance release signed by anyone who is in your film. These are covered in chapter 24 on Releases. But if you are going to base the entire film on someone's life story, then you need to get life rights.

There are three approaches to getting access to someone's story: public domain; published works; and the individuals involved. The public domain approach revolves around the part of public domain that has to do with facts. If you have facts that are based on independent research with interviews with two or more independent sources, you are good. You can rely on what is published in the newspaper because they theoretically have followed this approach. And the best of all are court records because people swear in court that they are "telling the truth, the whole truth and nothing but the truth." <u>Published works</u> are those magazine articles or books that have been written about the person. You need to be careful to determine what rights or research approach the author took for that published piece. And finally, if you are working directly with the real <u>individuals</u>, then you can get a Life Story Rights agreement, which parallels the LPA in many key areas.

One example to illustrate this is the Amy Fisher story. In 1992, Amy Fisher, a Long Island teenager, began an affair with Joey Buttafucoco. His wife, Mary Jo, found out about it, and Amy tried to kill her, shooting her in the head. Mary Jo fortunately didn't die, and the experience brought Joey back to his wife, abandoning Amy. Well, Producers were salivating for this story – drama, sex, betrayal, reconciliation, etc. Less than one year later, three movies-of-the-week aired in prime-time on NBC, ABC and CBS. December 28, 1992, NBC airs *Amy Fisher: My Story*. January 3, 1993, ABC airs *Beyond Control: The Amy Fisher Story*. And the same night, CBS airs *Casualties of Love: The Long Island Lolita Story*. All of the films drew good ratings, but the ABC film did the best probably because it had Drew Barrymore playing Amy Fisher. The basis for each film is the most interesting part. NBC purchased the life story rights from Amy. CBS purchased the life rights from Joey and Mary Jo (now reconciled). ABC relied on public domain, primarily the press and the trial transcripts.

Another example of the complex deals and relationships that can surround a true story is the following outline of the players and complex relationships involved with the story of Teena Brandon who was murdered in 1993 and ultimately became the basis for the award winning film *Boys Don't Cry*.

The players:

Teena Brandon aka Brandon Teena

Murdered in 1993

Lana Tisdel

> Real life girlfriend of Brandon
> Sues Fox Searchlight for unauthorized use of name and life

Aphrodite Jones

> Crime novelist
> Obtained life rights from Tisdel, Tisdel's sister, Teena's mother and sister
> Wrote book – All She Wanted
> Optioned book in 1996 to Blue Relief Productions
> Sues Fox Searchlight for holding up Blue Relief project in favor of *Boys Don't Cry* acquisition
> Settles with Fox Searchlight for undisclosed sum

Blue Life Productions

> Owned in part by Diane Keaton
> Optioned book All She Wanted
> Attached Drew Barrymore
> Set up deal at Fine Line Pictures
> Project in turnaround and winds up at Fox Searchlight
> Sues Fox Searchlight for holding up Blue Relief project in favor of *Boys Don't Cry* acquisition
> Settles with Fox Searchlight for undisclosed sum

Fine Line Pictures

> Put Blue Life Productions project into turnaround
> Picks up documentary *The Brandon Teena Story* for a feature project
> Neve Campbell attached

Fox Searchlight

> Lindsay Law, president
> 1997 - Picked up Blue Life Productions project
> from Fine Line
> 1999 – acquires *Boys Don't Cry* at Sundance for
> $5 million

Director Kimberly Pierce

> Developed script at Sundance Institute – *Boys
> Don't Cry*
> Originally different names and location
> Developed by Producer Christine Vachon
> Changes back to real names and place
> Film debuts at Sundance in 1999 and acquired
> by Fox Searchlight
> Film released to great reviews – wins Oscar for
> lead actress Hilary Swank

Susan Miska

> Documentary filmmaker
> Made the documentary, *The Brandon Teena
> Story*
> Picked up by Fine Line for a feature project
> Abandoned when *Boys Don't Cry* is produced

People today are very aware of the value of a good personal story or an interesting real-life character. Look no further than the reality shows based on duck hunters, junk dealers, and families with too many kids. There is money to be made by being odd and charismatic. And it's not all based on weirdness. Personal tragedies are also hot. In the summer of 2002, nine miners were trapped for 77 hours in the Quecreek Mine in Pennsylvania. During that time, they came to the realization that their story would have value after they were rescued (they had to stay optimistic). So they decided that they would jointly negotiate with Producers to have the best leverage to get the most money. Fortunately, their optimism was well founded, and they were rescued. By the end of that year, ABC had produced and aired a TV movie, *The Pennsylvania Miners Story*; and over the next few years there were at least two documentary films made about the dramatic rescue.

SUPPLEMENTAL MATERIAL – CHAPTER 2 – LIFE RIGHTS

Review Questions

1. What is the key concept behind the area of life rights?

2. What are the three legal concepts that can be involved in life rights?

3. What is the difference between libel and slander?

4. What are the three approaches to basing a film on someone's life story?

Industry Speak

Further Activities

Try to think of two people you know whose lives could make the basis for an interesting film or reality show. What approach would you use to get the rights to tell their story?

Further Reading & Research

Purchasing Life Story Rights by Mark Litwak. http://www.marklitwak.com/purchasing-life-story-rights.html.

Get in the daily habit – read the industry trade papers to know what is going on in the industry. For film and television, I recommend *Variety, Hollywood Reporter, Broadcasting & Cable,* and *Current.* They are all available online. Another good resource for what's happening in television is the *Cynopsis.com* online newsletter. For documentary and nonfiction work, I suggest *Real Screen.*

PART TWO

TELEVISION/CABLE UNIVERSE

Within the major conglomerates that own most of the industry, it is the television/cable operations that provide the most jobs, revenue and profits. Television and cable, as a whole, may not be as glamorous as the film studios and feature films, but it is a much more vibrant and important part of the industry.

In this book, the focus is on the nonfiction segment of the vast world of television and cable. This not because it employs the most people, which it does, or because it makes the most money, which it does not, but because it is the area where independent Producers can get a foot in the door. A brand new Producer with a good idea, that has been developed to meet the needs of a specific network, can get a meeting and make a sale. That does not happen in the world of fiction films or commercial television.

The Chapters in Part Two are:

Chapter 3 Television Industry Overview

Chapter 4 Audience and Ratings

Chapter 5 Public Broadcasting

Chapter 6 Cable Networks

Chapter 7 Advertising

Chapter 8 Sources of Funding

3

TELEVISION INDUSTRY OVERVIEW

T he history of television is a fascinating combination of technological discovery and development, the struggle between private enterprise and the government, and the growth of a new art form.

Going way back, the earliest discoveries and developments in radio and telephone were primarily accomplished by independent scientists, engineers and entrepreneurs such as Alexander Graham Bell and Guglielmo Marconi. The First World War, however, was instrumental in the development of wireless radio, accomplished by private industry, but funded by the government as part of the war effort. At the end of the war, the military sought to take control of radio in the interest of national security. Fortunately, the leaders of private industry, the equipment manufactures primarily, were able to stop this effort. That set the stage for the growth of the private radio and television industry in the U.S. into the largest and most successful in the world. The outcome of similar struggles turned out much differently in most other countries, which still have some government control of radio and television.

This is not to say that there isn't a logical and necessary role for government in the radio and television world. As early as 1927, the Radio Act brought some structure and sense to an industry that had fallen into chaos. The government stepped in and began to regulate the frequencies and the transmission power that local radio stations could use to broadcast. This created an orderly process that allowed for the development of standard receivers and for the clear separation of signals in a particular area. In 1934, The Communications Act strengthened this licensing process and created the Federal Communications Commission (FCC), which is still with us today.

Please spend some time and review the Industry Historical Timeline in the appendix at the end of this book. Pay particular attention to the development of technologies in the various areas of the industry and the regulation, or lack thereof, by the government.

One of the most important takeaways from a study of the relationship between technology and programming in the film, television, home video and VOD industries is that the ultimate success of a technological change has always been driven by the availability of content that is desired by an audience that is willing to pay for it. As audience demand increases, the price for the technology decreases and the process snowballs. This had been true with film, radio, television, VHS, and DVD. It has worked again with digital broadband Video on Demand (VOD), and with Subscription Video on Demand (SVOD); and it will work again with whatever is to come next.

The importance of content in this equation is great news for all Producers. We shouldn't fear new technology but see it as a new opportunity to get our films, television shows and other content to the audience. The manufacturers of the old technologies might have good reason to panic, but not us Producers.

The focus of this section is on producing programming for television and cable. To start, it is important to make sure that a Producer has a good sense of the overall structure of the industry and, in particular, the "players" who make the industry work.

THE PLAYERS

The Commercial Broadcast Networks.

The commercial broadcast networks are at the top of the food chain. We all know them: ABC, CBS, NBC, Fox and CW. These are for-profit enterprises that rely on large audiences and a lot of advertising dollars. All of these networks are owned by large conglomerate corporations, which also own the major film studios and other media as well. Here is a current lineup.

Walt Disney Co. –

ABC television network

Local television stations

ESPN, Disney Channel, Lifetime (partial with NBC) and other cable networks

Disney studio

Pixar; Dreamworks; Marvel; Lucas films

Comcast/NBC. –

NBC television network

Local television stations

Bravo, A&E, USA and SyFy cable networks

Oxygen and Weather channel

Universal studio

News Corp –

Fox television network

Local television stations

Fox News Channel; FX

20th Century Fox studio *

Major newspapers – WSJ; NY Post

MySpace

*this part of News Corp is being sold to Disney under a deal announced in December 2017, but not finalized at the time of this edition

Viacom –

CBS television network

CW (jointly with Time/Warner)

Showtime; Sundance

Local television stations

MTV and Nickelodeon cable networks

CNET

Paramount Studio

Time/Warner *-

CW (jointly with CBS)

HBO, TBS, TNT, Tru/TV and other cable networks

Warner Brother's studio

Time and Sports Illustrated magazines and other publications

AOL

*AT&T has signed a deal to buy Time/Warner, but it has not

closed as of the time of this edition

These relationships are a significant factor in the development and production of programming for the networks. And in most cases, the television operations of these conglomerates make much more money, both revenue and profit, than does the film studio operations.

Public Broadcasting

There is one non-profit public broadcast network, the Public Broadcasting Service, PBS, which relies on a large audience, audience subscriptions, and on the contributions of corporate sponsors. The interesting thing is that many of these corporate sponsors are the same corporations who are buying advertising on the commercial broadcast networks.

Cable Networks

On the cable side there are cable networks, many of them. And we still call them cable networks despite the fact that many people access them from a satellite service and not a cable service. Some estimate that there are over 1,000 cable networks, but there are really only a few hundred, maybe up to 300, that have enough coverage on cable and satellite systems to be serious players. We divide these networks into three types: general audience, niche audience, and premium.

The general audience cable networks have a programming strategy and target audience that is similar to the commercial broadcast networks. USA, TNT, TBS, and FX are examples of a general audience cable network.

The niche audience cable networks have a narrow programming focus that is designed to appeal to a particular segment of the overall audience. Examples of this would be the Cartoon Network, Discovery, the History Channel, the Travel Channel, the Home and Garden Network - you get the idea. The general audience and niche audience cable networks rely on advertising income as do the commercial broadcast networks.

The <u>premium</u> cable networks are primarily HBO, Showtime, Starz and their subsidiary networks. They require an additional subscription fee and do not carry any advertising.

The average household that has cable or satellite service has approximately 125 cable networks to choose from. Those who subscribe to digital cable have access to hundreds more networks including the HD versions of many of the networks.

<u>Digital Video on Demand</u>

For those of us who grew up with three commercial networks and rabbit-ear antennas, this is the brave new world. For most people, however, it's the norm; but the norm is evolving very quickly. Cable operators offer transactional video on demand of content to their customers with broadband service. Companies like Netflix, Hulu, and Amazon offer a subscription video on demand service. And these companies have developed large and successful production capabilities which produce original content.

THE LOCAL CONNECTIONS

How does the average person get their television programming delivered? Well, approximately 90% of TV Households get it from either a local cable operator or from a satellite dish provided by a Direct Broadcast Satellite (DBS) company. The other 10% or so get it the old fashioned way, by an antenna on their house which picks up the broadcast signals from local broadcast stations. But these households are then limited to just the broadcast networks. Of course, today we also get programming over the internet, and that broadband internet service generally comes from the local cable operator or the local telephone company.

Most of us live in one of the 210 <u>Designated Market Area</u> (DMA) television markets as measured by the A.C. Nielsen Company and used by the Federal Communications Commission (FCC) to describe the broadcast coverage of the radio and television licenses it issues. The number of stations licensed to local markets varies by the size of the population and the physical territory covered. For example, Los Angeles has just over 20 stations, while New York City has 15, Washington, D.C. has 13, and Davenport, Iowa, has 3.

The commercial broadcast networks have a station in each of the 210 markets, and these stations are either owned and operated (O&O) by the network or are affiliated with the network. The commercial broadcast networks have O&O stations primarily in the major markets but not all of them. From the very beginning of television, the FCC limited the number of stations that one company could own. Currently, Fox has the most O&O stations with 23, and ABC has the fewest with 10. The affiliated stations in the other markets are independently owned and have a contract with the broadcast network that creates a relationship between the parties. The local station owner gets programming and the ability to forge a local identity tied to the network's identity. The broadcast network gets its programming out to the local market and gets credit for the resulting audience. The networks sell most of the advertising spots or availabilities ("avails") during its shows and the local stations get a few avails during each show to sell to local advertisers. It's a good win-win situation, and there is only one station in each market that is either an O&O or an affiliate for each network. Both the O&O and the affiliate stations have a license to operate from the FCC and have a TV transmission tower placed somewhere in the area, normally on a high point of land. They also produce some of their own programming with a local focus such as local news, public affairs, weather, and sports.

The local situation for PBS is similar and different. PBS, as a national network, distributes its shows through local stations in each of the television markets. These stations, however, are neither O&Os nor affiliates. They are member stations, and PBS is actually a big cooperative organization. Unlike the commercial broadcast networks, PBS has more than one member station in many markets. For example, Los Angeles, New York City and Washington D.C. each have three PBS member stations. There are approximately 350 member stations in the country and they, like the commercial stations, have a license from the FCC, a broadcast transmission tower, and produce some local programming.

Cable television at the local level is very different from the local broadcasting situation. The local cable operator has a franchise from the local jurisdiction, normally a city or county, to build a network of cable lines in that jurisdiction. Most of these are exclusive agreements, which has led to a lack of local competition in cable services. The rationale for the exclusivity was that it costs the local cable operator a lot of money to string wires across the entire area and build the other infrastructure they need. Duplication of this investment by another company does not make financial sense, and cable companies would not have done it in the first place without the safety net of an exclusive license. The only competition to arise in recent years has been from telephone and power companies who already have their own wires into customers' homes.

Unlike local television stations, local cable operators do not do any programming. Their business is strictly to be a conduit for getting television signals into the home. They do, however, as part of their franchise agreement, provide a facility called a public access channel that allows the citizens of the local jurisdiction the opportunity to produce shows to air on that channel. The facility is paid for and managed by the cable operator, but the cable operator does not supervise or control the content that is produced and aired.

As is true in many industries, there has been a lot of consolidation in the cable business. Local cable operators, many of which started out as small companies with one franchise, have been acquired and consolidated into large Multiple System Operators (MSO) such as Comcast, Charter Communications, and Cox. Comcast is the largest MSO with operations in 40 states plus the District of Columbia and over 22 million total subscribers. And, of course, it also owns NBC and Universal Studios.

The other way that people get their television is from DBS or

Direct-Broadcast Satellite. DBS began in 1994 with Direct TV (now owned by AT&T); and the DISH Network came along in 2008. The industry has grown from seventy thousand subscribers in 1994 to over thirty-eight million today. This is about half as large as the number of subscribers to cable.

The process of digital delivery of content began with fiber optic cable provided by the cable operators or the telephone company. These same telephone companies also provide internet access via their cellular service to smartphones and tablets.

SOURCES OF PROGRAMMING

So those are the players and how they get their programming into your homes. Now we look at the sources for that programming. Where do the shows come from? These content providers are the primary focus for this book.

The commercial broadcast networks develop and distribute programs for several dayparts, which are standard blocks of time during the broadcast day that generally have some commonality in terms of types of shows and audience. The following are the standard classifications of dayparts used by the broadcasters.

Daypart Name From-To
Early morning 7 am - 10 am
Daytime 10 am - 4 pm
Early Fringe 4 pm - 6 pm
Early News 6 pm - 7 pm
Prime-time Access 7 pm - 8 pm
Prime-Time 8 pm - 11 pm
Late News 11 pm - 11:30 pm
Late Night 11:30 pm - 2 am

The three oldest commercial broadcast networks – ABC, CBS and NBC - provide programming for the Early Morning, Early News, Prime-Time, and Late Night dayparts. Fox and the CW offer programming only in prime-time. ABC, CBS and NBC produce the Early Morning, Early New and Late Night shows in-house with their own staff. For prime-time shows, all of the networks rely on the film studios for most of the shows they air. For example, NBC will license a show like *This Is Us* from the 21st Century Fox Television studio. It will also license a show from the NBC/Universal studio. The average license fee for a one-hour drama is between $1.2 and $1.6 million per episode. It's between $700,000 and $1 million for the average half-hour sitcom.

Since the focus of the book is on the independent Producer, we won't examine this any closer. Suffice it to say that an independent Producer has very little chance to get a show on a commercial broadcast network unless it is developed by a film studio or one of the very large independent production companies in Hollywood. A Producer who wants to produce this kind of television should move to Los Angeles and get started with a job at a network or a studio.

PBS is a broadcast network, but it operates with a much different purpose and a much smaller financial base than the commercial networks. It relies primarily on the member stations and on independent Producers for its programming. We will examine PBS in depth in chapter 5 Public Broadcasting.

On the cable side, the general audience cable networks are in many ways similar to the commercial broadcast networks in the sources of their programs. They buy a lot of shows that are coming off a successful commercial broadcast network run. These off-net syndications fill a large portion of the cable networks' schedules. In addition, most of these general audience cable networks produce original programs, which come from the same source as the broadcast networks – the film studios. Bottom-line is that these networks are not fertile ground for independent Producers either.

The premium cable networks air a combination of feature films that they license from the film studios and some original programming that is also produced by the film studios. It is no accident that HBO, the first premium channel, is owned by Time Warner, a conglomerate that also owns a film studio – Warner Brothers. The one type of programming that premium cable networks occasionally air that doesn't come from a film studio is documentary. These films are often produced by the network in collaboration with an independent Producer. This is a small but very prestigious market for independent Producers of documentary films.

The niche audience cable networks get almost all of their programming from independent Producers and small production companies. This makes them very fertile ground for new Producers and the focus of chapter 6 Cable Networks.

The digital providers like Netflix, Hulu and Amazon, get most of their programs by licensing content from the studios and production companies. They have begun original programming and have become a place where independent Producers can get a pitch meeting. This has not become a big market for independent Producers yet, but it has incredible potential.

SUPPLEMENTAL MATERIAL – CHAPTER 3 – TELEVISION INDUSTRY OVERVIEW

Review Questions

1. The critical period in the development of radio, which set the standard for television, happened after which world war?

2. What part has programming played in the success of a technological change in the media industry?

3. What networks are known as the commercial broadcast networks?

4. What are the five large conglomerates that own much of the television and film business?

5. What are the three types of cable networks? What is an example of each one?

6. Be able to describe the difference between an O&O station and an affiliate station at the local level.

7. What is the nature of the relationship between PBS stations and the PBS network? Approximately how many member stations are there?

8. Describe the ways that a local cable operator is different that a local television broadcasting station.

9. From what source do the commercial television networks get their prime-time shows? What are the average license fees for those shows?

10. Are the general audience cable networks more similar to the commercial networks or PBS?

Industry Speak

Affiliate station - a local television station which is independently owned but contractually affiliated with a commercial television network to broadcast the programs of the network

Basic cable - a group of cable networks and programming provided by a local cable operator for its lowest fee; does not include pay cable or "premium" networks

Broadcast - to send an electromagnetic signal through the air from a transmitter to a receiver

Cable franchise - a legal right issued by a local governmental jurisdiction, such as a city or county, to a local cable operator which allows the operator to provide service within that jurisdiction

Cable television network - a national corporation which provides scheduled programming to local cable operators and DBS companies in exchange for subscriber fees

Commercial television network - a national corporation which transmits regularly scheduled programs through television stations which it owns and operates or through independently owned television stations, which are affiliated with the network

DBS - direct broadcast satellite; a service to provide cable networks, pay-per-view programs and, in some cases, local television stations to subscribers by transmitting a signal from a satellite to a small dish on the subscriber's dwelling

Day-parts - a sectioning of the broadcast day into periods of time that are characterized by the demographics of the predominant viewers; used for scheduling decisions

First-run syndication - the initial licensing and first showing of a program in the off-network market which consists primarily of local television stations

Horizontal integration - a consolidation of business entities at the same level within an industry. For example, the film business has three levels - production, distribution and exhibition – and the Regal Cinema Group is a horizontal consolidation of businesses at the exhibition level.

Independent station - a local television station that is not owned by nor affiliated with a commercial television network or PBS

Local cable operator - a company which has a cable franchise to provide television programming over cables from the company office to the subscriber's home

Movie-of-the-week - a made-for-television film produced specifically for a slot in an ongoing series of film presentations or a film licensed for such a slot

MSO - multiple system operator; a company which owns a number of local cable operators in different locations or jurisdictions; an example of horizontal integration

O & O - owned and operated; a local television station that is owned and managed by a commercial television network

Off-net syndication - the process whereby programs which were first broadcast on a commercial television network are licensed and aired by a collections of buyers including local television stations and cable networks

Pay cable - in general, the system for transmitting television signals and programming by wire to the homes of fee-paying subscribers; also refers to the cable television networks for which the local cable operator charges an extra or premium fee over the basic cable rate

Pay-per-view - a cable television delivery method wherein the subscriber is billed only for specific programs as they are made available to and selected by the subscriber

Pay television - subscriber-paid-for television, generally the first pay television window for a film which is presented uncut and uncensored; includes cable and satellite delivered options.

Pilot - typically a ninety-minute or two-hour movie-of-the-week that is produced as a hopeful forerunner to a television series

Public access channel - a channel(s) the local cable operator provides to the residents of the local jurisdiction for the production and dissemination of local programs; negotiated as part of the cable franchise agreement

Subscriber - a person who pays a fee to a local cable operator or DBS operator for service; also, a person who contributes to a PBS member station

Vertical integration - the unified ownership of several different levels of production, distribution and/or exhibition. The same owner owns or controls at least two of a studio facility, production company, distribution entity, exhibitor chain, television network, cable networks or cable operators

Further Activities

1. One night during prime-time browse through as many different networks as you can and get a sense of what kind of programs they air. This works best if you have access to digital cable. If there is more than one PBS member station that you have access to, check to see if they are running the same schedule of programs.

2. Go online to the corporate website for one of the major media conglomerates and access their latest annual report; look into the report to find the breakdown of revenue and profits from their various divisions/operations. Look around to see what different companies, studios and networks they own/control.

Further Reading & Research

Get in the daily habit – read the industry trade papers to know what is going on in the industry. For film and television, I recommend *Variety, Hollywood Reporter, Broadcasting & Cable,* and *Current.* They are all available online. Another good resource for what's happening in television is the *Cynopsis.com* online newsletter. For documentary and nonfiction work, I suggest *Real Screen.*

4

AUDIENCE & RATINGS

T he basic concept that underlies the financial success of radio and television in the United States is the bargain between the advertisers and the networks. This bargain is as follows: advertisers will pay for ads in the shows that the networks air in exchange for the audience that the networks get for the shows.

In this chapter of the Sourcebook we will examine the key component of this bargain: the audience and how it is measured. Advertising will be covered in chapter 7.

THE AUDIENCE

We will look at audience measurement or ratings in a bit but first some general information on the audience and how it accesses programming.

According to the U.S. Census Bureau, there were 126.2 million households in the United States in 2017. Based on this and on its own on-going research, the A.C. Nielsen Company makes an annual estimate as to the number of households in the U.S. with at least one television in the home. These TV Households form the basis for all audience estimates and ratings. For the 2017-18 television season, which began in September 2017 and ends in August 2018, Nielsen estimates the number of TV Households to be 119.4 million. This represents approximately 95% of all households in the country. So pretty much everyone has at least one television. And many, of course, have more than one.

To review, there are four ways that households receive television programming: over-the-air with an antenna; by cable subscription and equipment; by satellite television subscription and equipment; and over the internet. 60% of TV Households subscribe to cable service. 30% subscribe to satellite service. And approximately 10% of the TV Households still access shows the old fashioned way – over-the-air with an antenna. In addition, almost 85% of households in the country have internet service which they use to access the websites that virtually all television and cable networks maintain. These websites offer current and past shows and are generally advertiser supported.

What about the access to the premium channels? We call this Pay Cable because subscribers pay for it in addition to the basic cable or satellite service that includes the broadcast networks and certain advertiser supported cable networks. There are, of course, different levels of cable or satellite service, and related costs. Approximately 45% of TV Households subscribe to pay cable and get one or more of the premium networks in addition to their regular cable or satellite service. The major pay cable services have also created subscription-based internet access.

A big factor in television programming and distribution is digital cable, which allows for Video On Demand (VOD). Today approximately 55% of TV Households subscribe to this more expensive and more extensive level of cable service – that's almost all cable subscribers. This is based on the popularity of the ability of digital cable to offer the many shows available on VOD, both free and paid. Virtually all of the cable operators now offer this service to all of their customers - it took a while for this infrastructure to be built. This development also allowed the cable operators to offer internet access to their customers.

Another factor that significantly impacts television is the Digital Video Recorder (DVR). Nationwide, approximately 55% of TV Households have a DVR capability. This is more in some cities; for example, in Los Angeles it is over 60%. This has caused a major shift in how networks and advertisers look at ratings.

Let's not forget the internet. Worldwide over 60% of homes have internet access and in the U.S. it is closer to 85%. Of those U.S. homes, the majority have broadband capabilities for streaming long form content. And significantly there are today over 4.5 billion cellular phone users worldwide, which is over 60% of the population. And in the United States almost 80% of those phones have broadband capability, which means they are capable of receiving programming. Cell phones are not yet part of the ratings equation, but that is currently being developed. Their future impact on the television world is inestimable, but it certainly will be huge.

And finally, there is the older technology of the DVD player, one of which is found in over 85% of TV Households and still accounts for a lot of viewing of past television seasons, vintage television shows, and films.

VIEWING PATTERNS

People watch a lot of television, and television viewing dominates media use. Recent studies show that the average TV Household in the U.S. uses its television(s) for 8 hours and 36 minutes per day. This is up from an average of just under 7 hours in 1990.

Studies also show that age is a factor in television viewing. Teens watch the least amount at an average of 23 hours per week. Then comes children 2 to 11, who watch an average of 26 hours per week. The most viewing is done by adults 65+, who watch an average of 49 hours per week – that's more than most full time jobs. The interesting thing is that this older audience is generally ignored by the advertisers.

Comparing media, another study reports that media users ages 2 and older (so everyone) spend 34 hours per week watching live television and VOD; 4 hours per week being online (Facebook, Google, other web work but not viewing television or films); 2 hours using a DVR (to watch television or films); and 30 minutes accessing video (television and film) online or mobile. The lessons here are the dominance of television as viewed in many ways and the continued importance of live television.

For live television, the viewing patterns are also studied on a nightly basis. The most watched night of the week is Sunday night. The least watched night of the week is Saturday night. And, the most important night of the week for advertisers is Thursday. Can you think of why? The reason has to do with the critical timing of a lot of advertising. An advertiser who wants the audience to go to their store for a weekend sale, or to the theater for a film that opens on Friday, wants to make as much of an impression as it can beginning on Thursday evening. Ads seen on Sunday night or earlier in the week are going to have much less impact on the response of the viewer for that product or service.

The viewing of commercial broadcast network shows versus viewing cable network shows is obviously of critical importance to those networks. If you recall, 100% of viewers can see commercial broadcast network shows, but only 90% can see cable network shows. In addition, there are only 5 broadcast networks while there are hundreds of cable networks competing for viewers. What this leads to is a great disparity between the number of viewers that a successful commercial broadcast network show will get as compared to a cable network show. A typical successful broadcast network show will get on average between 25 and 30 million viewers per episode. A typical successful cable network show, however, will only get between 7 and 9 million viewers per episode. That's a big difference. Another way to look at it is that in the 2016/17 television season, of the top 50 regularly scheduled shows (in total audience) on broadcast or cable, only one was on a cable network. #5 was Walking Dead on AMC. It is likely that Game of Thrones on HBO would have made the list, but it wasn't aired during that television season. These all regularly scheduled shows and did not include sports specials such as the World Series or the NFL playoffs, but it did include regularly scheduled NFL football on Sunday, Monday and Thursday nights.

The final point, and probably the most important one for the future of audience viewing patterns, is that the prevailing attitude among most viewers is that they want to watch what they want to watch, when and how they want to watch. The future of television programming has to deal with this new attitude and the ability for the audience to shift and to view programming in so many ways.

EVALUATING AUDIENCES – RATINGS

Advertising is still the foundation of television whether it is accessed over the air, cable, satellite, or the internet. Because of that, ratings are and will continue to be the industry's primary currency and the measure of success or failure. But ratings also serve as a cultural barometer of popular taste. We see it daily on blogs, Facebook "likes", Twitter etc. as people react to a show. And sometimes the comments that are made while the show is airing are incorporated into the show.

The show that had the greatest audience in terms of percentage of the potential audience was the 1983 finale of *Mash*. It had a rating of 60.2 which meant that over 60% of all TV Households in the U.S. watched that show live, which was the only way that they could watch in those days. Compare this to the second most watched show which was the 2015 Super Bowl watched by 47.5% of the TV Households. Now that 47.5% rating represented 114.4 million people whereas the *Mash* 60% rating represented 106 million people. But in terms of percentage of households, it is unlikely that any show will ever top *Mash's* last show.

When we discuss ratings for television there are two generic types: quantitative and qualitative. A quantitative rating gives us raw numbers based on age, gender and race. A qualitative rating provides data on income and educational levels, hobbies – lifestyle kind of stuff. They are both important for different reasons, but the ratings that most people hear about are the quantitative ratings. For television, these ratings are provided exclusively by the A.C. Nielsen Company. The Nielsen Company has a virtual monopoly on television ratings because no one else wants to invest the enormous amounts of money it would require to compete. And the fact is that the industry only needs one source, as long as it is confident that the one source is fair and accurate.

All ratings are broken up into different <u>demographic classifications</u> or demo sets that are used by television programmers and advertisers. These classifications are:

Persons	Men or Women
2+	
12 +	
18 +	18+
12-24	12-24
12-34	
18-34	18-34
18-49	18-49
21-49	
25-54	25-54
35 +	35-49
35-64	
50 +	50-64

Children & Teens

2-5
6-11
12-17

Every television show will use one of these demographic sets as its target audience; every television network, broadcast or cable, will have one as its target audience for a particular daypart; and every advertiser will have one as the target for its product or service. So anyone who wants to be a Producer for television has to know these standard demographic sets and use them in the development and pitching of a new show. It is not possible to over emphasize their importance.

Shows are evaluated on both the national and local levels. At the national level, we rate the shows that are in the dayparts programmed by the commercial broadcast and the cable networks; the most important of these being prime-time. At the local level, viewing is measure for the entire day. A major difference here is that the audience is measure at the national level for prime-time shows on a daily basis. The ratings at the local level, however, are only done four times a year during what the industry calls "sweeps" periods. Sweeps happen in November, February, May and July. They are normally characterized by some special programming done at both the national and local levels. It is no accident that the Super Bowl happens every year at the beginning of the February sweeps or that most prime-time shows end their seasons in May.

To understand ratings, we need to understand two concepts: potential audience and available audience. The <u>potential audience</u> is all the households in the U.S. with at least one television. That should sound familiar as it is what we have also been calling TV Households. So we know that for the 2017/18 television season Nielsen set the potential audience number at 119.4 million TV households. In addition, Nielsen sets a number for the potential audience of each of the different demographic sets. So for example, there is an potential audience number for Men 18-49 and for Women 18-34 and for Adults 25-54 and so on

The <u>available audience</u> is also called the HUT or Households Using Television. What do you think this number might be? Confused? That's okay, and I apologize because it's a trick question. That number will always be different, depending on the specific day and time of the day. It is measured as part of the rating process.

Now the goal for the ratings process is to determine <u>what is the size of the actual audience for a particular program at any point in time during the program</u>. The Nielsen Company uses several methods to accomplish this: diaries; passive meters; and people meters.

<u>Diaries</u> are little books with pages for each day of a week beginning with the most important day of the week for advertisers – Thursday. The pages are printed with the hours of the day, divided

into 15-minute segments. It is up to the viewer to write down in the diary what show he or she is watching at any time. They are encouraged to do this as they are watching and not try to remember after the fact. Diaries are used during sweeps months in all 210 television markets. The results are then keyed by hand into the Nielsen computers for number crunching. The whole thing is a cumbersome and tedious process that is fraught with potential for error. For one thing, human nature works against this process because most people soon forget to write down their viewing and try to remember several days later.

Passive meters came into use in the early 1980s, and it is a black box that attaches to the television(s) in a Nielsen television household. It records all activity on the television(s) and uploads that data every night to Nielsen's computer center. The passive meters were a major improvement over the diaries, and they also collected data all year round and not just four months a year. They also presented a major challenge in the sheer amount of data they dump each day. Some broadcasters complained after the passive meters were introduced because they suffered a drop in ratings. Others, of course, were happy with an increase in audience. The main problem with the passive meter, however, is that they are passive and do not record who is watching. The diaries at least have a spot to indicate who in the household was watching. So with passive meters we got household numbers but no good demographic breakdowns.

This problem was solved with the advent of the people meter, which is the same black box but with the addition of a remote control device. As each person in the household starts to watch a show they are supposed to enter their code number using the remote. If they leave, they should key out. Well, that works great as long as people comply and do it consistently. That is another of those human nature problems, particularly with younger viewers. Maybe that is why the 65+ group gets credited with so much television viewing.

One of the critical parts of this ratings process, and one that most people have the hardest time understanding, involves the concept of statistical validity. Until very recently Nielsen used a sample size of 5,000 metered households from which to make national ratings estimates for the entire country. Now to most people, a sample of 5,000 out of over 110 million seems awfully small. However, the trick is that it has to be a totally random sample. According to the statisticians, such a small sample can accurately reflect such a large universe as long as every household has the same random chance to be selected to be a Nielsen household for measurement. Nielsen has increased their sample size in recent years to 25,000 metered households and evidently plans to go to almost 40,000 households.

These 25,000 people meters are found in 56 of the largest markets and record over 10 million viewing minutes per day. Nielsen then gets scheduling information from the networks (broadcast and cable) that tells them what shows were playing at what times in each market. When all this data is matched up, it yields statistical samples of an average number of viewers at any moment for each show. All of this is also broken down into the demographic classifications based on who in each household was supposedly watching.

Finally, this data is calculated in two ways to give us two types of measurements called a rating and a share. The rating is a calculation of the measured audience as a percentage of the potential audience. The share is a calculation of the measured audience as a percentage of the available audience for that time and demo set.

Why do we need both, you may ask? The rating number is used primarily by advertisers because it is a calculation involving the constant of the potential audience. Remember that that number, potential audience, does not change during the television year. This allows the advertisers to make a calculation called Cost Per Thousand (CPM), which they use to compare the costs to advertise in different media.

The share, on the other hand, is used by programmers because it tells them how effective their show was in reaching, engaging and keeping the people who were actually watching television. Programmers don't really care about people who didn't have their television turned on.

Nielsen releases the measurement information in several ways. The networks, television stations and advertising buyers (advertising agencies) are subscribers to the measurement service and pay hundreds of millions of dollars a year for it. They get all the detail, including 15-second segmentation if they desire. Nielsen also releases summary information in various reports to the news media, and this is the stuff that the public sees. The first report is Live plus Same Day (L+SD) and contains all same day viewing and time-shifted DVR viewing up until 3 AM the next morning. It is at that time that the meters dump their data to Nielsen's central computers. This measurement is also called the "overnights". Many a programming executive or Producer has spent a sleepless night waiting for the overnights on a new show. This measurement does not include any web based or out-of-home viewing. Prior to 2006 the overnights were only live or real time viewing, but the increased use of DVRs forced Nielsen to change.

The next report is the most important report for the network sales people and the advertisers. It is called L3 or Live plus Three Days, which includes the same day viewing plus all time shifted DVR viewing for the next three days. Starting in 2008, this became the standard measurement for advertising, again as the DVR became a force in the industry.

There is a third report called the L7 or Live plus Seven Days, which includes the same day viewing plus time shifted viewing for the next seven days. This report is mostly discounted by advertisers but is looked at carefully by programmers to see if there is any possibility for a show that has been struggling in the overnights or L3s. Weak overnights and L3s but strong L7s will indicate to a programmer that there is an audience that likes the show, just not enough to put it as a priority in their viewing schedule. That can lead to story changes and/or changes in their promotional efforts.

SUPPLEMENTAL MATERIAL – CHAPTER 4 – AUDIENCE & RATINGS

<u>Review Questions</u>

1. TV Households represent what percentage of all households in the U.S.?

2. What percent of TV Households subscribe to cable service and to satellite service?

3. What age group watches the most television? The least?

4. What is the night of the week when the most television is watched? The least?

5. Why is Thursday called the most important night of the week for advertisers?

6. Can more people potentially watch a show on a commercial broadcast network or a cable network? Why?

7. What is the most important prevailing attitude among most viewers of television?

8. What is the difference between a qualitative rating and a quantitative rating?

9. What is the goal for the ratings process?

10. What is the main problem with the people meters?

11. What is the underlying premise of the ratings that leads to a statistical validity?

12. Why do we get both a rating and a share calculation?

13. What measurement report is now called the "overnights"?

Industry Speak

Diary - a written record of household television viewing for a period of a week that is sent to the ratings service

Demographics - the statistical characteristics of a specific human population, such as a television or movie audience; typically includes age, sex, and race

HUT - households using television; the number of households in the U.S. which are watching television at a particular point in time; also called the "available audience"

Overnights – the Nielsen rating that measures viewing of a program that happens the same day as the airing plus delayed viewing through 3 AM the next morning

Passive meter - a device that attaches to a television that indicates to the rating service whether or not the television is turned on and to what station or network

People meter - a device, similar to a remote control, that is used to tell the rating service not only that the television is on and to what station or network, but also who in the household is watching

Potential audience - the number of households in the U.S. with a television; also called TV Households; the number is revised every September by the AC Nielsen Company; this number is the basis for calculating ratings

Rating - the number of households tuned to a particular station and program expressed as a percentage of the potential audience or TV Households

Share - the number of households tuned to a particular station and program expressed as a percentage of the HUT

Target audience - a specific audience segment or demographic which a television or cable programmer seeks to reach with a television or cable program; expressed using the standard demographic sets established by Nielsen and used in their ratings reports

TV Households – an estimate made by Nielsen of how many households in the U.S. have at least one television

Further Activities

1. Check out TVbythenumbers.com and review the rating news. What was the show with the highest rating for the previous week?

2. Go to the A.C. Nielsen website – www.nielsen.com - and poke around – they provide research on a lot of different things.

   Access http://www.nielsen.com/us/en/solutions/measurement.html and read how they measure television.

3. Other interesting television related websites to check out are: tvinsider.com and tvguide.com

Further Reading & Research

Get in the daily habit – read the industry trade papers to know what is going on in the industry. For film and television, I recommend *Variety, Hollywood Reporter, Broadcasting & Cable,* and *Current.* They are all available online. Another good resource for what's happening in television is the *Cynopsis.com* online newsletter. For documentary and nonfiction work, I suggest *Real Screen.*

5

PUBLIC BROADCASTING

For independent Producers, one of the main places that is open to hear their ideas is the Public Broadcasting Service. If a Producer's passion is for high budget fiction films, then this is not normally the place for them. But public broadcasting has shown some increased diversity in recent years in the types of programming they offer. And there are many areas in the public broadcasting system that offer opportunities for Producers with good ideas.

HISTORICAL OVERVIEW

Public broadcasting has been around virtually since the beginning of radio. These first public broadcasting radio stations were mostly owned church groups who used the airwaves to spread their message. Then when commercial broadcast television developed in the mid 1940s, public television came right along. Various religious, educational, and philanthropic groups started local television stations in the early 1950s to broadcast their messages. They were generally small, independent, and constantly struggling financially. Many eventually sold their licenses to commercial networks, but others continued to operate to serve the public good.

In the 1960s, the three commercial broadcast networks (ABC, CBS, NBC) began to expand their news operations and focus a lot of attention on the burgeoning civil rights movement and on the undeclared war in Vietnam. Much of this attention was critical of the U.S. government, and the politicians in Washington began to wish for a system like their British counterparts had where they could control the news. In true political style, they formed a commission to study what could be done. The commission quickly determined that there was no chance to create a BBC-like ownership structure over U.S. broadcasting. Remember, that battle had been won by private industry after World War 1. The recommendation of the commission was that they could create a public system that would compete with the commercial broadcasters in the area of public affairs and news. As a result, in 1967, Congress created the <u>Corporation for Public Broadcasting</u> (CPB), which was charged with the creation of a viable public broadcasting system for radio and television that would offer a counter-point to the commercial networks. In 1969, the CPB launched the <u>Public Broadcasting Service</u> (PBS) as a programming and distribution cooperative that would work with member stations across the country. The member stations would pay dues to PBS based on the size of their markets. In return, the stations would get programs developed by PBS.

Ironically, the first programming success for PBS was not the news program that the politicians had hoped for but a kid's show that featured a big yellow bird. *Sesame Street*, a local show produced by WNET and the Children's Television Workshop in New York City, quickly found a national audience on PBS. News programming finally began during the Senate Watergate hearings in 1973 with the forerunner of *The McNeil/Lehrer Report*, a joint effort of WETA in Arlington, Virginia, and WNET in New York city.

For the next decade, PBS grew and developed a strong reputation for news and information, performing arts, and also for nonfiction and documentary programming. It developed a very loyal audience, but never an audience that challenged the commercial broadcasters for sheer numbers. It was popular with corporate sponsors who liked the image that came with helping public broadcasting. And it didn't hurt that the typical PBS viewer was very high on the qualitative research scale of household income and educational levels.

However, the next decade, the 1980s, presented PBS with a new challenge – cable networks that were created to offer the same programming for the same audience as PBS. In 1980, CNN started, and it offered comprehensive news coverage and analysis. Also in 1980, Bravo began offering performing arts programming. 1984 saw Arts & Entertainment begin with a clear mandate to provide a commercial counterpoint to PBS. Its signature show was Biography. And in 1985 the Discovery Channel premiered with a solid lineup of nonfiction and documentary programming.

The 1980s saw the explosive growth of cable with subscriber penetration jumping from 22% of TV Households to 54%. Quite a few of the approximately 280 cable networks that were available at the end of 1989 offered programming that cut into the PBS audience. Many of PBS's corporate sponsors moved to the cable networks as advertisers.

As it tried to compete with these new networks, one of the major problems that PBS had was the fact that it didn't offer a consistent national schedule. The commercial broadcast networks with their O&Os and affiliates would schedule a show for the same day and time in all markets across the country. The cable networks would schedule in the same way as their shows came across the wires of the local cable operators and, beginning in the early 1990s, the dishes of the satellite operators. PBS, however, had no control over its member stations, and they would air the PBS shows whenever they felt like it. This put PBS at a significant disadvantage when it came to promoting its shows to a national audience and convincing sponsors that their message was getting out there effectively. They, therefore, could not afford to spend as much money on production as could the cable networks. Better production values on cable then led to more viewers turning away from PBS.

In response to this challenge, PBS created the National Programming Service (NPS) in the mid 1980s. The NPS had a mandate to develop larger, more expensive shows with the agreement from the member stations that they would adhere to a standard, nationwide, prime-time schedule. The first big splash from the NPS was the creation and airing in 1990 of the *Civil War* series produced by Ken Burns and underwritten by General Motors.

Over the past years the NPS has continued and given PBS a fairly consistent image and programming focus. It is interesting to note that several of the cable networks, A&E and Bravo in particular, have significantly changed their programming strategy over the past ten years.

So, today the public broadcasting television world consists of approximately 350 member stations at the local level and PBS at the national level. PBS continues to get financial support from CPB, approximately 12% of its annual operating budget. CPB also gives out programming grants to PBS member stations and to independent Producers. The member stations pay dues that support the operating budget of PBS and create the pool of money that is used to create programming for the NPS.

SOURCE OF SHOWS

So where does PBS get its shows? We're addressing the national operation here and not the local programming done by each member station. PBS itself does not create programs. It selects proposals and develops ideas with other sources and then gives them money for production. It generally does not give all the money, and we'll address that need for additional money in chapter 8.

Considering the prime-time schedule of PBS's NPS, over 80% of the shows originate with the member stations. Most of these shows are found in the *program strands* that PBS/NPS offers, such as Frontline, American Experience and Great Performances. Some of the larger station contributors and their shows are:

WGBH, Boston

>   Frontline
>   NOVA
>   American Experience

WETA, Washington

>   Newshour with Jim Lehrer
>   Washington Week

WNET, New York

>   American Masters
>   Great Performances
>   Charlie Rose

If we consider the total schedule of PBS, then the percentage of shows that originate with the member stations drops to 60%, but that is still a very high percentage. And not all member stations are involved. In fact, only about one third of the member stations contribute shows to PBS.

The other 40% of the shows come from independent Producers who develop ideas and pitch them to PBS. In addition, independent Producers are often behind the shows that come from the member stations and the strands. So in terms of accessibility and scale of production, this is very fertile territory for the ideas of new independent Producers.

GETTING A SHOW ON PBS

We are going to look at two basic ways to approach PBS as a Producer:

1) with a proposal for a new show; and

2) with a show that is already completed.

Producer with a proposal.

For a Producer, the best method is to approach PBS, or any other network for that matter, with a proposal and get the money for the production. One of the primary goals of a Producer is to use other people's money for their productions. This is not easy to do, but it keeps a Producer's work on a professional level and keeps her from having to get a second mortgage on her house.

We are going to "follow" a Producer who has developed an idea for a prime-time show and believes that it is most suitable for public television. To reach this conclusion, they have exhaustively researched what type of shows public television offers, including ones that may be similar to their idea. This is part of an overall proposal the Producer creates (a more detailed discussion of this in in Part Four). PBS has clear guidelines for what they want in a proposal, and it can be found on their website www.pbs.org. A wise Producer will make sure that her proposal fits these guidelines.

Then there are four basic avenues to follow with a proposal:

1. submit to a program strand;

2. pitch to PBS National Programming Service;

3. submit to a member station; and

4. work with a national presenting entity.

The first consideration is whether or not this is the type of show that fits the programming strategy and philosophy of one of the program strands that dominate prime-time on PBS. If it does, then the Producer immediately goes to the producing member station and/or its production partner and pitches their proposal. If they like the idea, they will give the Producer all the money from their pool of production funds. These funds have come from PBS and from money they have raised directly from corporate sponsors. If it is an established Producer, they will work with her and her production company as co-Producers. If the Producer is new, they will probably bring the project in-house and "hire" her as a co-

Producer. Either way it's all good.

If the idea does not fit a program strand, then the Producer can pitch it directly to PBS in Arlington, Virginia. The Producer should see a clear spot in the schedule where her show would fit, but be aware that PBS sets their schedule a year or more in advance. Honestly though, this is a real long-shot. PBS receives over 2,000 proposals a year for only a few open hours in their schedule. If a Producer is successful, they will give her some money from their pool of programming money. It will almost surely not be all the money she needs, and she will have to raise money from other sources. More on that in chapter 8.

If rejected at the national level, or if the Producer doesn't really see where her idea would fit in the current national schedule, then her best bet would be to approach one of the member stations with her proposal. Which station would she approach? It could be the one in the area where she lives if they have some history of developing programs for PBS. Or it could be a member station that has a reputation and experience producing shows in the same content area as hers. For example, Maryland Public Television has a very strong reputation for shows on the environment. Oregon Public Television has a great history with shows dealing with Asian Americans. And, WETA in Washington, DC, has a strong public interest programming agenda.

One of the determining factors here is whether her story has a national focus or is simply a very strong local story. A local story is best done with a local station. However, some local stories with the right development can become national stories. And for those stories, a member station that is experienced with the development of national programming is her best partner. It may sound confusing, but basically a Producer has to follow the strength of the story.

Partnership or co-producing with a member station has a lot of advantages. They have the necessary contacts and experience within the public broadcasting system to help the show develop and find its correct program slot and audience. They also have facilities and equipment that can be used and help the budget and reduced the amount of money the Producer has to raise. And regarding fundraising, they have lots of contacts with corporate sponsors, foundations and others.

A final approach for a Producer is with one of the national presenting entities. These organizations were created in the late 1980s and early 1990s as a result of a study done by CPB at the request of independent Producers. These Producers felt that PBS was becoming too much of a closed club with 80% of its prime-time schedule controlled by the member stations and the program strands. The Producers argued that there was no way to get independent films on PBS that dealt with sensitive issues or portrayed under-represented groups of people.

In response, CPB created a fund that provides money to a national presenting entity for it to develop shows with independent Producers that will then be available to PBS for airing on an exclusive basis. Some of these national presenting entities were created to serve a particular group such as the National Black Programming Consortium, the Center for Asian Media, and Native American Public Telecommunications. Another one, the Independent Television Service (ITVS), was created with a more generalist focus in 1989.

A Producer who gets involved with one of these national presenting entities will receive all the funds for their project and keep 100% ownership in the program. In return, the Producer gives PBS an exclusive license for domestic television airing of the show for five years. This is all well and good, but there is no guaranteed that PBS will actually air the show. Unfortunately, PBS has continued to exhibit a reluctance to air shows that cover a number of sensitive topics. Consequently, these independent Producers are still frustrated with PBS, but they do get their shows produced, and they can distribute them in other markets such as home video and international during that five-year period. At the end of the exclusive period with PBS, they can take the show to other networks, but often the subject matter is no longer as relevant or "hot".

Producer with Completed Show.

If a Producer, probably a new one, is unable to get money in advance, then they can work hard and smart and get the show made on their own. It's tough, but it's done all the time. This Producer then has several avenues to follow with the completed show; all of which will sound familiar: the program strands; PBS; and the member stations.

One very important caveat here is the consideration that, if an idea in a proposal was not able to get acceptance for funding, then what is it about the actual program that will make it more attractive. Now it may be that it's just a matter of funds and with PBS that is always a major consideration. So, they might have loved the show on paper, but just didn't have the money, and will be very happy to consider it when done. The key is to make sure that the actual production follows the guidelines for financial underwriting, content integrity and production values that PBS demands. These are all found on the PBS website and in their Red Book (also on the website). If a Producer is unclear on any of that, I suggest that he consults with a Producer who has experience producing for PBS.

The Producer can take the completed program to the appropriate program strand. This is a long shot as they like to do their own shows or at least have control of them from the beginning. The objections they offer normally have to do with the content and the various technical aspects that are part of their "signature".

An approach directly to PBS nationally is also a very long shot for many of the same reasons.

Member stations are the best bet, and they are always looking for content to air, which they only have to license and not underwrite or produce. Submitting a show to 350 member stations is, however, a long, slow process and the expenses of it can more than absorb any license income. Fortunately, there are regional co-ops of member stations that review programs from independent Producers, negotiate license fees, and then make the shows available for the member stations. A Producer only deals with a few organizations and hopefully several large checks. License fees paid by the stations are calculated per program minute and run from a few dollars to hundreds of dollars depending on the size of the market of the member station that airs the show and the day part when the show will air.

SUPPLEMENTAL MATERIAL - CHAPTER 5 – PUBLIC BROADCASTING

Review Questions

1. What role did the CPB play in the creation of PBS and when?

2. What was the situation and the problem that led PBS to establish the National Programming Service?

3. What percentage of the NPS is comprised of program strands?

4. Approximately what percentage of the shows on PBS come from independent Producers?

5. What are the four basis avenues for a Producer with a proposal to follow?

6. What are the advantages of partnering with a PBS member station on a proposal?

7. What led CPB to create the national presenting entities?

8. What are the three avenues for a Producer to follow with a finished show?

Industry Speak

CPB – Corporation for Public Broadcasting – quasi-governmental organization that regulates and funds public broadcasting

National presenting entity - an organization that executive produces and provides programs to PBS; often organized to support films by and/or for particular groups within the society

NPS - national program service - programs selected and regularly scheduled in prime-time by PBS for its member stations in an effort to compete with the commercial television and cable networks

Member station - a local television station that is affiliated with the Public Broadcast Service; normally a non-profit organization, local government or university

Regional network - a co-op organization created by a group of PBS member stations in a region of the country to review and negotiate a license for independent programs

Sponsor or underwriter - an entity that provides tax deductible funds to a PBS member station or to the PBS National Program Service to help pay for the production of programs

Further Activities

Go to the following websites; try to answer these questions; but also browse around.

http://www.cpb.org/
About CPB
What is the Corporation for Public Broadcasting?
What does CPB do?
Does CPB produce programs?
When did CPB start?

Go to Financial Information (right side of page)
Operating Budget
For the latest fiscal year, how much did CPB allocate to television programming grants?
How much was given to the local television stations as direct grants?

Annual Reports / Annual Report (latest available)
Under Programs and Related Projects, browse the various

things they fund

http://www.pbs.org/
Producing for PBS (found at bottom of the home page)

About PBS
What is the PBS Mission?
How many people does PBS reach?

Content Priorities
What are the broad areas of PBS programming?

Submission Guidelines and Proposal Process
Does PBS produce the programs it airs?
How far in advance is the PBS schedule determined?
Review the Guidelines for Proposals.
What is required for completed programs?

Funding Standards
What are the 3 tests for funding acceptability?
What is the Program Challenge Fund?
Check the Additional Funding Resources
Check the Minority Consortia
PBS Plus
What is PBS Plus?

http://www.itvs.org/

About (top of page)

Check out the FAQs.
When did ITVS begin operations?
Who is eligible to apply?

Get Funded (top of page)
Check out the various funds

Check out Open Call
Who is eligible?
What are they looking for?
Who retains the copyright for projects that ITVS funds?
What rights does ITVS get for their money? How is PBS involved?
What does ITVS provide in addition to funds?

Further Reading & Research

Get in the daily habit – read the industry trade papers to know what is going on in the industry. For film and television, I recommend *Variety, Hollywood Reporter, Broadcasting & Cable,* and *Current.* They are all available online. Another good resource for what's happening in television is the *Cynopsis.com* online newsletter. For documentary and nonfiction work, I suggest *Real Screen.*

6

CABLE NETWORKS

HISTORY AND DEVELOPMENT

W hen commercial television took off in the mid 1940s, cable operators were right there as a vital component in the development of the industry.

World War Two had fostered the technological development of television as a military asset and at the end of the war the manufacturers of those components (RCA, GE and Westinghouse being the main ones) decided to turn their production toward civilian use. These same manufacturers created or soon controlled the nascent commercial programming networks that would provide the shows for the television sets they were trying to sell. Remember what we read in chapter 3, that the success of a new technology is always driven by available content.

One problem was that all the television sets received the television signals that were broadcast over-the-air from towers erected in the major urban markets. Households that purchased a television set from the local appliance retailer would install an antenna on the roof of their house to pick-up the signal from the television tower and then begin to watch shows (all in black-and-white). The problem came for appliance retailers who operated in rural or mountainous areas, far from the television towers. The households in their areas could not pick-up the signals, and the television sets were useless. They wouldn't even work in the retail store as a sales demonstration. So, some smart retailers got the idea that if they erected an antenna of their own, on a high mountain or closer to a city, then that could pick-up the signals. The signals would then be carried along on a cable to the appliance store and provide a picture that would help them sell television sets. It didn't take long, however, for a customer to get a set home and find that it wouldn't work for them and bring it back with some angry comments about a "rip-off" or "a piece of junk" etc. That same smart retailer then offered to allow the customers to splice into his cable and run a line into their homes and hook it up to their sets. And thus was born a community area television (CATV) system, or what we today call a local cable operation.

This was the cable industry for decades. It was primarily a local delivery technology with almost no programming or cable programming networks. Less than 10% of all TV Households had a cable hookup as of 1970. That all changed with the advent of HBO in 1972. HBO was the watershed because it provided something for a cable subscriber that was more than just clear reception of the local broadcast stations. It was a reason to subscribe for households that didn't need cable for reception. And, it was programming that was not available anywhere else. VHS and Betamax were still four years in the future. So companies that started in the mountains or in the rural areas to provide a signal now began to get franchises from local jurisdictions – cities and counties – to build a network of cable lines that could serve all the households in that jurisdiction. Now these operators began to look for more sources of programming.

In 1980, three big cable networks began, and they helped push cable subscription past 22% of TV Households. They were CNN, USA and ESPN. These three networks offered programming that appealed to a wide range of viewers' interests – news, dramas and comedies, and sports. They were followed in 1981 by MTV; 1983 Disney; and 1985 Discovery. More types of viewers were now attracted by programming that was interesting to them. By 1990 basic cable subscriptions had risen to 54% of TV Households; and they had access to about 60 cable networks.

The 1990s saw big shifts in technology with the beginning of direct broadcast satellite (DBS) and the rewiring of most cable systems with new fiber optic cables that were able to carry many more channels than the old wires. By 2000, there were over 280 cable networks competing for viewers. The cable networks were available in 65% of TV Households, but that included both cable operators and satellites. Cable subscription had fallen to 48% of TV Households as satellite grew to 17% of TV Households, many of which switched from cable.

From 2000 to 2010, the industry really exploded and there were now over 1,000 cable networks. Cable subscriptions rebounded and grew to 60% of TV Households, while satellite also grew and reached 30% of TV Households. Aggressive programming by cable networks was the driving force in this growth. The addition of Video on Demand (VOD) program offerings by Comcast in 2001 was also a big factor during this time. However, the cable/satellite industry then began to feel the effects of the web-based offering of programming being offered by the commercial networks, the cable networks, and the SVOD distributors like Hulu and Netflix. Subscribers began to drop cable as they began to rely only on the internet for their access to programming. One irony is that these "cord-cutters" often buy their internet service from the cable operators.

SOURCES OF REVENUE

Most cable networks are advertiser supported in the same manner as the commercial broadcast networks. In 2017, the total of advertising dollars spent on cable networks was estimated to be $13 billion. This was a fantastic increase from the $4 billion in 1995. Compare that to the $11 billion spent on advertising on the commercial broadcast networks. But don't rejoice for the cable networks just yet. The $11 billion for the broadcast networks is divided between only five networks (not evenly, of course). For the cable networks there are over 1,000 of them to divide up their $13 billion.

Cable networks do rejoice, however, over the fact that, unlike the commercial broadcast networks, they have an additional source of revenue. Each cable network receives subscription fees from the local cable operators or the satellite providers. From the monthly fee that a subscriber or customer pays, about 40% of that is given to the cable networks that the operator carries. The amount given to each network is based on a contract negotiated between the operator and the network. It varies according to the popularity of the network, which programming tier it is on, and its overall value to the business of the operator (primarily, how important that network is to keeping subscribers happy).

The average payment to the cable networks is $.15 per subscriber per month. Here is a list of the fees paid to some cable networks.

> ESPN- $7.21 (per subscriber per month)
> Fox sports- $1.36
> TNT- $1.48
> Disney- $1.21
> Fox news- $.99
> USA - $.83
> TBS - $.72
> Discovery- $.25
> Nat Geo - $.20
> TV Land - $.11
> Travel Channel- $.08
> Hallmark - $.06

As you can see, the sports related cable networks get a much higher payment than all the others. The reason for this should be obvious if we think of the costs they pay for their programming. The license fees for professional sports have gone to astronomical levels in the past decades.

This steady income for a cable network provides it with a solid financial foundation and keeps it viable in the face of a sometimes fickle advertising market.

The pay cable exception. There are some cable networks, however, that do not take advertising. These are the pay cable networks such as HBO, Showtime, and Starz. The deal between these cable networks and the cable and satellite operators is different than that with the advertiser supported cable networks. A subscriber pays an additional fee for each of these pay cable networks. That additional fee is divided 50/50 between the cable and satellite operators and the pay cable network. These pay cable networks then spend a lot of their money on programming because they constantly have to justify themselves to the subscribers that they are worth the additional fee. For example, HBO would see its subscriptions rise substantially when the new season of *The Sopranos* started and then fall back down when the show's season was over.

PROGRAMMING GOALS

We are going to look at three basic programming goals for cable networks, particularly the advertiser supported ones. The goals are:

to create a brand image;

to fill their dayparts; and

to leverage their assets.

For many years, the conventional wisdom of television programming was that people watched shows and not networks. This was true during the heyday of the three commercial broadcast networks when it would be easy for any of the three to carry any of the shows found on any other network. The shows just looked very much alike on all the networks. That changed with the beginning of the cable networks, which were often purposefully designed to carry a particular type of programming. In the broadcasting world, it also changed in 1986 with the start of the Fox Network, which had a distinctly edgy, and often masculine, image based on the type of shows it aired.

The big three commercial broadcast networks still operate on a show by show basis and they spend millions of dollars promoting their shows. Their goal is to capture a viewer for one show and then keep them for the following shows. This is also the approach of the general audience cable networks like USA, TNT and FX.

Most cable networks, however, primarily promote the network as a place to find a particular type of programming. They want to create a brand image the same way an advertiser does with a breakfast cereal. A recent poll of advertisers and viewers found that the best cable brands were ESPN, Discovery, the Food Network, and Comedy Channel. No surprises there. Their names alone describe their programming.

Once in a while we see a cable network drastically change their brand. This happened in 2002 when new management decided to overhaul A&E from Arts and Entertainment to airing reality shows (Duck Dynasty), strong off-net syndications, and original dramatic programming. One of the corner pieces of this effort was the licensing of *The Sopranos* from HBO for $2.5 million per episode. While some questioned the wisdom of this, it actually made a lot of sense. *The Sopranos* on HBO had a potential audience of 30 million TV Households (the total number of subscriptions to HBO at that time). On A&E the show had a potential audience of 90 million TV Households. That's a lot of new potential viewers who have never seen the show, which makes it much different from an ordinary re-run in syndication. In addition, the demographic draw of *The Sopranos* was much younger and that was a goal for the network as it looked to compete with TNT and USA. They struggled with their programming identity for a long time, and then in 2017, A&E reverted to exclusively nonfiction programming.

Court TV went through a similar transformation in 2008 and rebranded its prime-time programing with the new name Tru TV. Other networks such as Lifetime and Home and Garden have tried to shift the demographic focus of their programming to reach a younger audience that is more attractive to advertisers.

One interesting twist in the shows-versus-networks approach to programming is the growth of the DVR and VOD. Viewers are no longer as likely to just watch a network, but are more likely to program their own virtual network with the shows they like. This has created some incredible headaches and also opportunities for the networks and their programming and promotion departments.

The second goal for programmers is to fill their dayparts with shows that are appropriate for the demographic target audience and budgeted for projected advertising sales for the daypart. Shows have to meet both parts of this equation. They must interest the viewers that the network wants. And, they must be cost effective in relationship to the amount of revenue that comes from the advertising that the show attracts. This goal holds true for all television programming except for the pay cable networks. A show has to attract viewers for it to be valuable to the advertiser. And some viewers are more sought after than others. More on this in chapter 7 on advertising. For a Producer, this equation is very important. He must be aware of the target audience and make sure that his proposed show will attract that audience. In addition, he has to be sure that the budget for the show is realistic for the network and that daypart. Finding budget information from networks requires a lot of research, but it is possible. Careful reading of the trade press provides the basics for most networks. Many of them are also willing to share that information with Producers because they want them to come to the network with proposals that make sense for them and not waste their time with unrealistic budgets. One sure thing is that the cable networks, for the most part, spend a LOT less for an hour of prime-time programming than do the commercial broadcast networks. Some of the general audience cable networks might have a show that will rival the broadcast networks and their average license fee of $1.2 to $1.6 million per hour episode, but there are very few of those and not many per any one cable network.

The third goal is to leverage the budget for programming. They do this through co-productions and by licensing shows that are already produced. However, there is also a strategy that revolves around the acquisition of programs, normally by commissioning them, and thereby building a library of assets. These assets can then be re-purposed for other uses. Examples would be to use the show on a co-owned digital network, on an international network,

95

and for ancillary sales in the home video or educational markets. In this way, a show can pay for itself many times over.

SOURCE OF SHOWS

The general audience cable networks are now getting their shows from the same sources as are the broadcast networks – the studios. Therefore, that is not a logical place for an independent Producer to pitch.

The other cable networks, the niche networks, get much of their programming from independent Producers. That is good news for all of us.

TYPES OF DEALS

As an independent Producer ready to pitch a proposal to a cable network, what can she expect? Most cable networks have what is close to an open-door policy and welcome Producers with good ideas that have been developed with a cable network in mind.

There are three basic types of deals the most cable networks enter into with independent Producers:

a commission;

a co-production; and

an acquisition or license.

We will look at each one, paying particular attention to two critical points of each deal: how much of the budget the network will pay and how much of the show they will own.

The Commission Deal, also called a full commission, is the best, but the rarest of the deals. The Producer presents her proposal and the network loves it and wants to do it. It likes it so much that it will pay for all of it. That's the good news. The bad news is that they will want to own all of it. If someone pays 100%, then they want to own 100%. Logical. A newer Producer will not have much leverage to negotiate here, but an experienced Producer will be able to negotiate some ownership; maybe 5 to 10%. If a Producer has exclusive control over a person who is critical to the show, then their leverage obviously increases. Now some Producers will resist and not want to sell any ownership, but I suggest that this is foolish in most cases. If a Producer can get a network to come up with the entire budget, that means the network will also likely promote the heck out of the show and try to make it a big success. All of that is great for her reputation as a Producer. No one has to know about her deal. All they see is her credit as a Producer on a successful show on this network.

The second, and most common, type of deal is the Co-Production Deal. The network likes the show but they don't want to spend enough on it to cover all the costs. This is also how they leverage their production budget by working with a lot of partners. The percentage of ownership of the show will generally follow the percentage of money that each party contributes. Negotiating strengths also come into play here. This leaves the Producer with the task of finding money from other sources, assuming that they don't want to invest a lot of their own money. This search for money is made much easier because the Producer now has the network as a co-Producer. We will look at those other sources of money in chapter 8.

The final type of deal is the Acquisition Deal, or more properly called a license. The industry's use of the term 'acquisition' is unfortunate because it denotes a sale, and this is not a sale but a license. The license allows the network to air the show a certain number of times over a certain number of years; but the ownership stays with the Producer. There are few standards here because the networks are so different in their approaches to programming. This deal only happens after the Producer has produced the show and taken it back to the network. There are no guarantees up front that they will license it.

There are, obviously, many problems with this acquisition/license deal. But let's say that the show was budgeted for $250,000 when proposed to the network. After being turned down, the Producer went ahead and produced it for $125,000 - using all his tricks as a good Producer, probably including not paying himself anything. Now he takes it back to the network and screens it for them. They like it and want to license it. What do you think they offer as a license fee? Certainly not $250,000 which might be the average cost they pay for a commission for a show in this daypart. Not even $125,000 which would cover the Producer's costs; which, by the way, they should not know – they should think it looks like a $250,000 show. Unfortunately, the typical license fee would be between $25,000 and $50,000. To many Producers that doesn't seem fair, and it certainly doesn't go very far to cover his costs. Now the good news is that, since the network didn't put any money into the production, they don't own any part of it. The deal is a true license, which means it's not a sale. So, the Producer can sell the show in any other markets he can find: international television, VOD, home video, educational etc. Success in all of these markets might not recover all the costs, but that is the life of a Producer, particularly when starting out or with a show that they just have to make, even it means using some of their own money. And if he was able to get some foundation grants for the project, he doesn't have to pay them back – more on that in chapter 8.

Here is a handy grid to summarize the key elements of the different types of deals.

	% of budget	% of ownership
Commission	100%	100%
Co-production	Less than 100%	Less than 100%
Acquisition/License	None	None

SUPPLEMENTAL MATERIAL – CHAPTER 6 – CABLE NETWORKS

<u>Review Questions</u>

1. What is the problem with broadcast technology that led to the development of community area television?

2. What cable network led the big period of growth for cable and in what year did it premier?

3. What are the two revenue streams for most cable networks? How is pay cable different?

4. What are the three goals for cable television programming? Be able to describe them.

5. What role do independent Producers play in providing shows for cable networks?

6. What are the three basic types of deals that a cable network might make with an independent Producer? What are the advantages and disadvantages of each from the point of view of the independent Producer?

<u>Industry Speak</u>

Acquisition – a term misused by much of the industry to refer to what is really a license; properly used it refers to the purchase of a script, television program, or film

CATV – community area television – the industry term for the service that is commonly referred to as local cable

Commission – a deal from a cable network that provides a Producer with the money necessary for the production of a program. Normally refers to a full commission, which means the network supplies all of the money. Less than a full commission is more correctly a co-production.

Co-production – a deal with a cable network where the network and the Producer are partners and each contributes money to the production. There can be several or many co-Producers

DBS – direct broadcast satellite – the generic term used to refer to the delivery of television programming by satellite directly into the home

License – a right granted which gives a person permission to do something which they would not otherwise be entitled to do; generally characterized by a time limitation and conveys control but not ownership of such rights

Further Activities

Look at the network lineup for your cable or satellite system: how many networks are there? How many do you watch, even sporadically?

If you don't subscribe, then go online to one of the major MSOs such as Comcast or Media General and browse their schedule

Further Reading & Research

Get in the daily habit – read the industry trade papers to know what is going on in the industry. For film and television, I recommend *Variety, Hollywood Reporter, Broadcasting & Cable,* and *Current.* They are all available online. Another good resource for what's happening in television is the *Cynopsis.com* online newsletter. For documentary and nonfiction work, I suggest *Real Screen.*

7

ADVERTISING

In a free-market economy there is nothing that is more important than marketing. Anyone can create a product or think up a new service; but how do they make the potential customers aware of the existence of that product or service? Customers make choices based on their knowledge of products and services and on incentives to choose one over another.

The definition that I like best for marketing is: <u>getting someone to want what you have</u>. It's simple and says it all. The "someone" is your target audience, who will be your customer. The "what" is your product or service. The "getting" leads to a wide range of activities that comprise marketing and fall into the following components:

Advertising

Promotion

Social marketing

Customer service

This chapter focuses primarily on advertising because that is the financial engine that powers television. Promotion and social marketing are the stuff for another book. And customer service is a management challenge and a mindset that is best covered in a business school textbook.

ADVERTISING'S HISTORICAL HIGHLIGHTS

As civilization developed and became more complex with larger and larger villages and then cities, the need for advertising grew with it. Clear evidence of advertising has been found in ancient Greece and Rome. The town crier of old Europe was an advertising technique. The earliest ads in America appeared in the early 1700s in Boston and Philadelphia and were heavily influenced and enhanced by Ben Franklin. The first ad agencies appeared in the mid-1800s and they very quickly developed the concept of buying ad time for a client and getting a commission for it.

In 1914, the Federal Trade Commission, FTC, was created to regulate advertising practices; particularly the patent medicines of the day, which sometimes proved lethal. Advertising was a big factor in the growth of radio after the First World War and grew along with the success of the radio networks from the 1920s through the 1940s.

In the early days of television, advertisers produced most of the shows – soap operas, variety shows and dramas. The Hallmark Hall of Fame, the Kraft Suspense Hour, and the Bell Telephone Hour were a few of these. The soap operas got their name because they were produced by the companies (Procter & Gamble, for example) that made the household detergents advertised to the housewives who made up the audience. In the 1970s, the cost of production of programs grew too large for one company to justify, and the networks began to produce the shows and sell individual avails or spots to advertisers.

UNDERLYING BARGAIN

As we read in chapter 4, the basic concept that underlies the success of radio and television in the United States is the bargain between the advertisers and the networks. This bargain is: the advertisers will pay for ads in the shows that the networks air in exchange for the audience that the networks get for the shows.

Let's look at the advertisers' part of this bargain in more detail.

From the advertisers' viewpoint they agree to pay the networks to expose the audiences to the products and services as seen in the ads. What they will pay for the ads depends on how many watch the show and what demographic categories they are in. In addition, the advertisers agree that they will have no control over the content of the shows.

One of the most interesting facets of this bargain, however, is the fact that there is no provable direct correlation between an ad being seen on a network and a purchase or customer behavior. This is summed up nicely by a quote from John Wanamaker, a very successful Philadelphia merchant in the 1860s, and the man who is considered to be the originator of the department store concept. "I know that half of my advertising expenditures are wasted; the problem is that I don't know which half." Now this was before network television, but it is still valid today for most advertising. And it does explain the appeal of web-based advertising that allows for a direct measurement of customer action as a result of viewing an ad. But since web-based digital advertising represents less than 36% of all advertising expenditures in the U.S., Wanamaker's lament is still valid.

SOME BASICS

Total advertising media sales in the U.S. is in excess of $200 billion per year. In the most recent year it was divided as follows:

36.7% television/cable

36.7 digital

13 print

7 radio

6 Out-of-home & other

The percentage for television/cable has declined over the past several years as digital advertising has experienced strong growth. Trending consistently down is the use of print - magazines and newspapers; while radio advertising has remained steady.

As an example of the importance of advertising to television networks, let's look at an episode of a popular prime-time drama, in this case *The Blacklist* on NBC. In a typical episode there are 35 avails. Of these 28 to 30 are for the network and 5 to 7 are for the local affiliate or O&O station. If we use 30 avails nationally for this example and use the ad rate for *The Blacklist* from the 2017 upfront market, which was approximately $200,000, the total ad revenue for the network from one episode is $6,000,000. Under a typical license deal, the network can run an episode twice in a year, which means potentially doubling the ad revenue to $12,000,000. The license fee that NBC pays for the show is approximately $2,500,000. This means that the network has a net income of approximately $9,500,000 from this one episode of the show. Of course, the network has to pay all of its expenses from this revenue, and it has a lot of expenses – salaries, operational overhead, promotional costs, development costs, etc. But this is one illustration of why hit shows on the networks are so profitable.

The goal for all of advertising is to affect the actions of the target audience. Advertisers use three generic goals for most of their advertising efforts: brand awareness; brand loyalty; and brand image.

Brand awareness is to give new information to the audience on new products or services or to introduce improvements in existing products or services. This is critically important to advertisers who want to create buying habits in younger audiences. Studies show that buying habits are set in a person's teens and twenties and will stay with them the rest of their lives. Brand loyalty is to reinforce current behavior as it often addresses heavy users and tries to increase usage. Brand image is used to change a predisposition, to take on a competing product and change buying habits.

HOW ADVERTISING IS SOLD

Advertising is sold as a negotiation between the buyers, who are the advertisers represented by their advertising agencies, and the sellers, who are the networks represented by their sales departments. As in most negotiations, there are many variables and differences in the leverage of the parties. A network with the most popular prime-time shows has big leverage, as does the advertiser with a multi-billion-dollar advertising budget. Procter & Gamble is often the largest advertiser in the U.S. with almost $5 billion to spend each year.

There are two primary markets or times during which advertising is sold by the networks.

The first is the Upfront Market that happens in May and June. In this upfront market the broadcast and cable networks will sell approximately 80% of their avails for the upcoming season. In 2018, this represented $9 billion in revenue for the broadcasters and $10.4 billion for the cable networks. Remember, however, that the cable money is spread out among several hundred networks while the broadcasting network money is divided only five ways. In recent years, the broadcast networks share of the upfront money was approximately:

CBS $2.5 B

NBC $2.2 B

ABC $2.0 B

Fox $1.8 B *

CW $0.5 B

* the Fox number is particularly impressive because the network only programs 15 hours per week of prime-time compared to the 22 hours of the other big four networks. The CW programs 10 hours of prime-time per week.

During the upfront market each of the networks reveals its schedule for the following season, starting in September. This is normally done at big glitzy presentations followed by fancy parties where the advertising people get to meet the stars of the various shows. After the networks do their presentations, the ad agencies meet with the network sales people and begin to negotiate.

The ad agencies have developed a media strategy and budget with their clients. The media strategy could include advertising on television, digital sites, radio, magazines and billboards. For television, the strategy includes consideration of buying television ads, also called spots or avails (for availabilities), and for the production costs of the ads, which will be produced by the agencies. They have a target audience for the ads, which is expressed as people in a target demographic group (see chapter 4 Audience & Rating). This goal is also expressed in Gross Ratings Points or GRPs, which indicates how many people they want to reach with an ad. A GRP means one rating point of people in a particular demographic group. Please reread the ratings section of chapter 4 Audience & Ratings to be sure you understand what a rating point is. And the advertisers have a certain <u>Cost Per Thousand</u> (CPM) that they want to pay. The CPM represents what they will pay to reach one thousand people of the target demographic. And the strategy has a desired time frame for the ads, which could be annual (TV season), seasonal / holiday, monthly or weekly. There is also time sensitivity for some campaigns, meaning that they only want ads that run on certain times of the year or days of the week. They present all of this information to the network sales departments of selected networks and then wait for proposals.

The network sales departments create an ad rate for each show. They crunch the numbers using the ratings history of their returning shows and the ratings projections of their new shows. They also consider the type of audience that the show delivers with some demographics being much more attractive to advertisers than others. Advertisers historically have a hard time reaching Men 18-49, so any show that delivers that audience is very important to them. Another factor that goes into the ad rate is whether the show is one that people tend to watch live or do they tend to time-shift their viewing. A show that discourages time-shifting is much more valuable to an advertiser that has strong time sensitivity to their ads. This is one reason that the ad rate for sports is so high (the other is that they tend to attract Men 18-49). And finally, the placement of a show on the TV schedule has an impact on its ad rate. For example, shows on Thursday night are very attractive for advertisers who want to make impressions for products and services that people normally buy or consume during the weekends.

For each show, the assigned an ad rate or price per avail will then translate into a CPM based on the historical or projected ratings for the show. The average CPM for all of television (broadcast and cable) is estimated to be $14.50. The average CPM for the broadcast networks, except for the CW, is $35 to $40. The CPM for the CW is estimated to be $18.00. See the last section of this chapter, The Mechanics of Buying and Selling Ads, to see how CPM is calculated.

The network sales people will take a certain number of avails from different shows and then add up the ratings numbers to reach the total GRPs required by the ad agency. There is much more art than science in this as there are many, many different scenarios that the network sales people could come up with that would meet the ad agency request. And they have to do this in a way that keeps many different advertisers happy. Everyone wants ad exposure on proven popular shows – but not everyone can afford it.

The network sales people present their proposal to the ad agency and then the negotiations begin. Points of negotiation include: how long the advertiser is willing to commit – a month or two or the entire season; how the ads are spread over different shows, different days and time slots; and, of course, the ad rates per show. For example, an advertiser who demands avails only on Thursday prime-time during the fourth quarter is going to have less leverage than someone who is open to a run-of-schedule package, which allows for avails spread out over the entire prime-time schedule. Also a network is much more likely to negotiate ad rates for a new show then for an established successful show.

Finally, an agreement is reached that sets the price and placement of the advertisers' ads for the upcoming television season, September through the next May. In recent years this also incorporates the following summer schedule because more and more networks are programming original shows in the summer.

The second major market for ad sales happens at the start of the fourth quarter of the year (October 1) and is called the <u>scatter market</u>. At this time, the networks try to sell any time that was not committed in the upfront market. By now the networks and ad agencies have actual ratings results for the summer and fall shows, as most of them would have premiered by then. Shows that are doing well will get higher ad rates than they had during the upfront market and those that are not doing well will have lower ad rates. At this time, and also at the second opening of the scatter market at the beginning of the new year (first quarter), most of the 20% of avails that were not sold in the upfront market will be sold.

So, what happens if a network show is not meeting the rating levels as assumed in the network sales presentations? The networks do not make refunds, but they do give <u>make-goods</u>, which are additional avails at no additional cost. In this way the total GRPs are achieved for the agreed upon amount of money. This obviously cuts down on the number of avails that can be sold in the scatter market. On the other hand, if a show exceeds the assumed ratings, then the networks do not ask the advertisers for more money. The network will, however, raise the ad rate for that show in the scatter market and will have a positive point to use in their negotiations during the next upfront market.

The final consideration during the upfront and scatter markets has become the avails which happen when a network offers a show on their website. If the show is available contemporaneously with its airing (or within a day or two), it will normally contain the same ads as when aired. These avails are being added to the packages as developed between ad agencies and networks. These avails have also been used as a portion of a make-good package. Then after a few days, the ad package for the show changes, and these are new ad sales, often to different advertisers. The networks are not reporting big revenue here yet, but see it as a bargaining chip that will have more value in the future. Furthermore, the ads that appear during a VOD viewing of the show on a cable system are sold by the cable operator and not the networks, who may or may not share in that revenue.

There is one additional advertising market for television called the spot market. For the networks, this market opens after the first scatter market and involves sale of individual avails, mostly to smaller advertisers. The spot market also refers to the avails in the prime-time network shows that the networks give the local O&Os or affiliates to sell to their local clients. For the local stations, this market is open any time during the year for local advertisers.

THE MECHANICS OF BUYING AND SELLING ADS

The first step is to understand the method used to calculate the CPM or cost per thousand for an ad.

Let's assume that the television show *The Voice* has a rating of 4 in adults 18-49. According the AC Nielsen, each rating point in adults 18-49 is equal to 1,300,000 persons. As we know, the Nielsen Company makes this determination for every demographic group used in its ratings process. So *The Voice's* rating of 4 equals an audience of 5,200,000 people 18-49.

Calculation is: 4 rating points times 1,300,000 people per point = 5,200,000 people

Now we have to translate that audience into units of one-thousand to be able to do the CPM calculation. *The Voice's* audience translates into 5,200 units of one-thousand people.

Calculation is: 5,200,000 people divided by 1,000 = 5,200 units of one-thousand

Then we take the ad rate for *The Voice*, which is $265,000 per spot, and divide that amount by our units of one-thousand to get

109

the CPM of $50.96

> ## Calculation is: $265,000 divided by 5,200 units of one-thousand = $50.96 CPM

Now suppose that an advertiser wanted to get 50 GRPs on *The Voice*. We need to calculate how many spots that would mean. To do that, we divide 50 GRPs by the rating of 4 to get 12.5 spots.

> ## Calculation is: 50 GRP divided by 4 (rating points per spot) = 12.5 spots

If we assume that the advertiser will then run 13 spots on *The Voice* to get its 50 GRPs, then the cost to the advertiser for these spots will be $3,445,000.

> ## Calculation is: 13 spots times $265,000 per spot = $3,445,000

Another approach for an advertiser on a campaign is to determine that it wants a certain number of GRPs with a target audience and pay a budgeted CPM. If the goal is 100 GRPs of adults 18-49 and the budgeted CPM is $40, then the overall budget for the campaign is $5,200,000.

> ## Calculation is:
>
> ### 100 GRP times 1,300,000 audience per rating point = 130,000,000 people
>
> ### 130,000,000 divided by 1,000 = 130,000 units of one-thousand
>
> ### 130,000 unit of one-thousand times CPM of $40 = $5,200,000

SUPPLEMENTAL MATERIAL – CHAPTER 7 – ADVERTISING

Review Questions

1. Who produced the shows in the early days of television?

2. What is the bargain between advertisers and networks?

3. What is the amount of media advertising in the U.S.? What part of that goes to television/cable?

4. What are the three generic goals for advertising?

5. What are the two major markets when television advertising is sold?

6. Be able to describe the strategy between the advertisers and the networks during the upfront market.

7. What are the points of negotiation between the networks and the advertisers?

8. How has the growth of time-shifting of programs impacted the ad rates for shows?

9. What are make-good ads; when and how do networks use them to make advertisers happy?

Industry Speak

Advertising - all forms of paid media exposure and activities; includes the creation and dissemination of materials

Advertising campaign - a planned and related series of paid media exposure and activities designed to bring about a particular result, i.e. awareness of a film

Avail - a commercial advertising slot available for sale during a particular program

CPM - cost-per-thousand; a measure of advertising costs based on how many thousands of viewers a program attracts

GRP – gross rating point – one rating point in a particular demographic set; a goal of most advertising campaigns

Make goods – the avails given by a network to an advertiser to bring their CPM in line with the agreed upon amount

Marketing – getting someone to want what you have

Scatter market – the sale of avails that were not sold in the upfront market; begins in the fourth quarter of the year

Spot – another term for avail

Upfront Market – when the networks and advertisers contract for 80% of the avails for the upcoming television season

Further Activities

1. Watch a prime-time broadcast network show. Count the number of spots and categorize them by national, local and network promotions. Try to ascertain which of the three goals the advertisers are trying to achieve with each ad.

2. Think like a network sales representative

Using the following table of shows, try to pick some shows that would be appropriate for an advertiser that wants 100 GRPs in adults 18-49. They are advertising a new feature film that will premiere on Friday. For purposes of this exercise, don't be concerned if they are shows from different networks. What would your selection be for an advertiser who has a new sale of women's clothing over the upcoming weekend?

If you're really ambitious, try selecting a limited number (3 to 5) of shows and determine how many spots in each you would need to get to the target of 100 GRPs for the movie advertiser and for the clothing advertiser. And for the super ambitious, try to calculate the budget using the CPM of the shows you selected.

Don't obsesses over getting this correct. There are many "right" answers or approaches to this problem; and that's what makes this job so challenging and exciting.

Show	network		rating A 18-49	persons 18-49	Ad rate per 30 sec spot	CPM
Sunday Night Football	NBC	Sunday	8.4	10,920,000	$545,000	$50
American Idol	Fox	Wednesday	3.3	4,290,000	$356,000	$83
Big Bang theory	CBS	Thursday	5.3	6,890,000	$325,000	$47
Modern Family	ABC	Wednesday	4.1	5,330,000	$280,000	$53
The Voice	NBC	Monday	4.9	6,370,000	$265,000	$42
New Girl	Fox	Tuesday	3.8	4,940,000	$235,000	$48
The Simpsons	Fox	Sunday	2.1	2,730,000	$230,000	$84
Grey's Anatomy	ABC	Thursday	3.1	4,030,000	$206,000	$51
Family Guy	Fox	Sunday	2.6	3,380,000	$206,000	$61
The Blacklist	NBC	Monday	3.3	4,290,000	$201,000	$47
Scandal	ABC	Thursday	3.4	4,420,000	$200,000	$45
Two and half men	CBS	Thursday	2.4	3,120,000	$184,000	$59
the millers	CBS	Thursday	3.2	4,160,000	$175,000	$42
2 broke girls	CBS	Monday	2.5	3,250,000	$175,000	$54
once upon a time	ABC	Sunday	2.4	3,120,000	$173,000	$55
the crazy one	CBS	Thursday	2.9	3,770,000	$168,000	$45
how I met your mother	CBS	Monday	3.3	4,290,000	$166,000	$39
Person of Interest	CBS	Tuesday	2.4	3,120,000	$135,000	$43
Castle	ABC	Monday	2.3	2,990,000	$130,000	$43
Survivor	CBS	Tuesday	2.5	3,250,000	$120,000	$37
NCIS: LA	CBS	Wednesday	2.7	3,510,000	$120,000	$34
The amazing race	CBS	Sunday	2.4	3,120,000	$94,000	$30
dancing with the stars	ABC	Monday	2.1	2,730,000	$94,000	$34
Biggest loser	NBC	Tuesday	2.3	2,990,000	$92,000	$31
parks & recreation	NBC	Thursday	1.2	1,560,000	$92,000	$59
Parenthood	NBC	Thursday	1.4	1,820,000	$90,000	$49
Revolution	NBC	Wednesday	1.6	2,080,000	$88,000	$42
Trophy wife	ABC	Friday	1.6	2,080,000	$80,000	$38
shark tank	ABC	Tuesday	1.9	2,470,000	$80,000	$32
last man standing	ABC	Friday	1.3	1,690,000	$75,000	$44
The mentalist	CBS	Sunday	1.4	1,820,000	$74,000	$41
The good wife	CBS	Sunday	1.4	1,820,000	$71,000	$39
the neighbors	ABC	Friday	1	1,300,000	$70,000	$54

Further Reading & Research

Get in the daily habit – read the industry trade papers to know what is going on in the industry. For film and television, I recommend *Variety, Hollywood Reporter, Broadcasting & Cable,* and *Current.* They are all available online. Another good resource for what's happening in television is the *Cynopsis.com* online newsletter. For documentary and nonfiction work, I suggest *Real Screen.*

8

SOURCES OF FUNDING

I n chapter 5 on Public Broadcasting, we saw that in many, if not most, cases a Producer will have to raise money from sources other than PBS in order to complete their project. We found the same in chapter 6, Cable Networks, when we learned that most deals are either co-productions or financed without help from the cable networks. In this chapter we will examine the primary sources of funds for these types of nonfiction projects.

The primary sources that we will look at are:

individuals;
corporate sponsors; and
foundations.

INDIVIDUALS

Obtaining money from individuals for nonfiction projects is not as difficult as a Producer might assume. And it is much easier than raising money from individuals for fiction films, which we will discuss in chapter 14 when we look at the types of deals for feature film financing. The critical thing about raising money from an individual for a nonfiction project is to focus on their connection to the subject matter or issue covered in the film. With this kind of project, a Producer is not offering an investment opportunity that will bring anyone a profit. She is not even offering them an opportunity that will probably repay their money. The Producer is, however, offering them a way to contribute to the creation of a film about a topic which is important to them personally. People have all sorts of interests, personally and professionally, which cause them to be interested in a nonfiction film project. A project that touches on a certain disease or malady of the human condition is of strong interest to anyone who suffers from that disease or malady or has someone close to them who does. Many people are concerned about the environment. Many are concerned with protecting animals. Many are inspired by stories of courage, sacrifice, valor and overcoming obstacles. You get the idea.

So if these people are out there, how do we find them? Is there a list somewhere?

Well, in a way there are such lists, and we call them credits. A big part of developing a nonfiction film project is to research what films have already been done on that topic or area of interest. As a Producer conducts that research they pay attention to the credits that thank everyone who has contributed to the film. The assumption then is that if these people were interested in supporting a film once, they may be interested again. Another list can be found on the websites of any foundations or nongovernmental organizations or trade associates that are involved in the topic or interest area. They will have boards of directors and contributors who are prime targets for the Producer's fundraising efforts. There are undoubtedly social media sites that focus on the Producer's topic or interest area. Get active on them. Like and Friend everyone.

Another approach to individuals is through the crowd source funding sites like Kickstarter, IndieGoGo or Rockethub (to name only a few, but these have been used a lot by filmmakers). Producers who are successful in this area have developed a strategy that includes credits, gifts, receptions, etc. They are tireless in keeping their campaigns updated and keeping their contributors informed of their progress. It's a lot of work, but many Producers have raised significant amounts of money this way.

No matter how you find your individuals, a Producer has to be very careful as to how they characterize the money that they raise.

Do not in any way state or even imply that this money is an "investment" in the film project. To most people an investment is a way to make money, a profit. The vast majority, almost all, nonfiction film projects do not make any profit. Most do not even earn enough to repay the costs of production and distribution. Another characterization to avoid is that the money is a loan. Loans are typically paid back and normally with interest. Neither is appropriate here. Many filmmakers make a reasonable living this way, but they are not making their supporters lots of money, or even paying them back. People support these projects because they believe that the film will help the "cause" and that is what is important to them. Safe words to use to characterize this money are "gift" or "financial support".

CORPORATE SPONSORS

Watch any PBS show and there is clear evidence of the corporations that support nonfiction film projects. Some are found as supporters of a particular show and others support an ongoing program strand. In any event, they are there because they believe that an association with this program or strand or PBS in general will bring them certain benefits. These are clearly marketing benefits and such support comes from that corporation's marketing budget. If you recall the goals for advertisers – brand awareness, loyalty and image – then this sponsorship is much more aligned with brand image and possibly brand loyalty. It is not normally about brand awareness, which is the classic goal for advertising. Many of these sponsors are companies that do not offer goods or services to the general television public. The aerospace industry comes to mind. The average viewer is not going to buy a stealth bomber; but they are voters and they are opinion makers who can influence policies that impact these corporations. Many companies want to be seen as "good citizens" even if their products are often see in a different light – the tobacco industry comes to mind here.

These corporate sponsors have a variety of things that they can offer the Producer. They can, of course, give money to support the production. Nothing wrong with that. Some corporations can also provide services that can help. I've done a number of documentaries in the Czech Republic, and I always got terrific support from Czech Airlines in the form of free travel. Other times a corporate sponsor can provide products, like Patagonia giving a wildlife expedition parkas and other outdoor gear. The possibilities are almost endless for a creative smart Producer.

And these corporations are not thinking in terms of investment or loan. These are gifts that they put on their books as a marketing expense.

FOUNDATIONS

Foundations have proven over the years to be the largest and best source for funds for nonfiction film projects. There are thousands of foundations and many of them provide support for film and video projects. One source estimated this to be in excess of $100 million a year.

There are four general classifications of foundations: operating; public charity; general purpose; and special purpose.

Operating foundations and public charities are by their very nature not in a position to give money to a Producer. Their time is spent getting money to support their own work – feeding and sheltering the homeless or running a hospital or free clinic, for example.

A Producer should look at the general purpose and special purpose foundations as potential sources for funds. They are designated as such because of the nature of their mission.

Another way to classify general purpose or special purpose foundations is whether they are private, corporate, independent, or governmental.

Private foundations can be either corporate foundations or independent foundations, depending on their ownership. Corporate foundations are managed by their corporate parent and their missions coincide with the interests of the corporation. There are many arcane tax benefits for these corporations to have these foundations. Examples of corporate foundations are the General Motors Foundation, the Johnson & Johnson Foundation and the Nike Foundation.

Independent foundations are just that. Independent of corporate ownership, they are self-sufficient operations. Now sometimes this can be confusing. The Ford Foundation, for example, is an independent foundation created by the Ford family that started the Ford Motor Company. But it is not run by the Ford Motor Corporation. The Gates Foundation is a foundation that is independent of Microsoft. So many of these large independent foundations were created by the owners of large corporations and initially funded by their stock in those companies. Their missions follow the personal interests of these people.

Governmental Foundations can be found at all levels of government – local, state and federal. Of primary interest for Producers, at the local level there are often foundations that support the arts and humanities. They normally work with local Producers. At the federal level, there are three foundations that are of particular interest to Producers: the National Endowment for the Arts (NEA); the National Endowment for the Humanities (NEH); and the National Science Foundation (NSF). They all fund film and video projects.

GENERAL INFORMATION

No matter what type of foundation, the most important thing to all foundation is their mission. That is the reason they exist – to save the environment; to find a cure for cancer; to save the whales; etc. Some missions are more general. For example, here is the mission statement from The Ford Foundation website:

> *Our goals for more than half a century have been to:*
> *Strengthen democratic values*
> *Reduce poverty and injustice*
> *Promote international cooperation*
> *Advance human achievement*

Here is another, this one from the MacArthur Foundation website:

> *The John D. and Catherine T. MacArthur Foundation supports creative people and effective institutions committed to building a more just, verdant, and peaceful world. In addition to selecting the MacArthur Fellows, the Foundation works to defend human rights, advance global conservation and security, make cities better places, and understand how technology is affecting children and society.*

Foundations are very eager to share their mission. It is easily found on their website and in their publications.

When reviewing a proposal from a Producer, <u>the most important concern for a foundation is how will the project help to further their mission</u>. If a Producer cannot make a clear case that her project will help with the mission, then don't waste time with that foundation. This also means that the Producer must have a clear plan for distribution or dissemination of the film. How will it reach an audience in order to further the mission? How will people know about it? If it is an educational project, it has to be clear how it will get to the schools and there should be a teacher's guide as part of the process. This is where the involvement of either PBS or a cable network is often the difference between success and failure with foundations. A promise of PBS airing or the fact that it is a co-production with PBS or a cable network is a clear and powerful answer to the distribution and dissemination question.

The money that a Producer would receive from a foundation is called a <u>grant</u>. Grants are kind of the perfect thing because they are really a gift. The money does not have to be paid back and the foundations do not take any ownership or equity interest in the project. The only difference between a grant and an outright gift is that the money has to be accounted for. The Producer will have to file a Grantee Financial Report that details exactly how the money was spent. This is true for both private and governmental foundations, but the governmental requirements are much more onerous, and there are serious legal penalties for lying or fraud.

Most foundations will only give money to other non-profit organizations that have the 501(c)(3) tax exempt status from the IRS. There are some foundations that will give money directly to individuals or their for-profit organizations. The simple reason for this is that the foundations must generate a lot more paperwork when giving money to individuals or for-profit organizations. But a Producer does not have to have 501(s)(3) status to be able to work with the foundations who will only fund non-profits. A Producer can find a <u>fiscal sponsor</u> who will become the official recipient of the grant. A fiscal sponsor is a non-profit organization that is willing to work with Producers and become the conduit for the funds from various foundations. They do not take any financial interest in the project, but they do take a small fee (3% to 5% of the money raised through them) for their efforts. Generally, a Producer will look for a foundation that is interested in the project as a funder and then will ask them to serve as a fiscal sponsor to help the Producer get money from other foundations. There are also some film industry groups that work with Producers as fiscal sponsors. Women in Film and Video and the International Documentary Association are two such organizations.

Raising money from foundations is a time consuming process, and it often takes many grants to raise enough money for a film project. Most foundation grants are not very large; a few thousand dollars. Foundations must be comfortable that the Producer is going to continue to fundraise and produce the film no matter how hard it gets or how long it takes. The primary exceptions to this are grants from NEA, NEH and NSF. These governmental foundations and a few of the very large private foundations will fund an entire project with a budget of $200,000 or more.

Finally, and unfortunately, some foundations will not give money to film and video projects. This is true no matter how well the project meets their mission. There are several reasons for this. One is that the foundation does not believe that media will reach an audience in a way that will help the mission. It is a Producer's toughest job sometimes to convince people of the effectiveness of film. There is often not a direct correlation that can be offered as proof – sort of like the difficulty with advertising. This is fortunately changing slowly with the expansion of foundations use of video on their websites and the ability to track responses. Another reason for the reluctance is that many foundations have tried film and have been burned by a Producer who did not produce the project. Sometimes they just ran out of time and money and nothing was finished. Sometimes they finished but the final film was not what they had proposed and was no longer suitable for the foundation's mission. Most foundation that do not fund media will put that clearly on their website to warn Producers. If a Producer sees that, it is often best to just move on. It is very hard to convince such a foundation that their project should be the exception to their rule.

TYPES OF SUPPORT

Generally, a Producer tries to get a grant for the production of a film project including post production and distribution. That means that they have already done the work of research and development of the idea into a script or treatment before going out to foundations.

Other Producers will try to get a development grant from a foundation that gives them the money for their time and efforts to research and write the script or treatment. These grants are rarer, but they are done by the governmental foundations.

There are also grants out there that are limited to the distribution and dissemination of films that have already been produced. These foundations are taking the safest road because they can actually see the film and judge whether it should effectively further their mission.

HOW TO FIND FOUNDATIONS

There a three research approaches to finding foundations for a particular project: subject/mission; geography; and type of support.

The subject/mission match that a Producer looks for is, without question, the most important. As stated earlier, a foundation will not fund a project unless they believe it will further their mission. A foundation officer may personally love a Producer's proposal but will not fund it unless she believes it will further their mission. There are no exceptions to this.

Okay, then how do you find the foundations with a mission that matches? Many ways are very similar to the process used with individuals. Find out what foundations have supported similar projects or activities. A diligent web search based on key words from the subject will also uncover some foundations. And there is an organization called the Foundation Center that offers data bases to search.

Once you think you have a foundation that is a match, check their website for a list of projects that they have funded in the past. This will give you some idea as to whether they will be open to your proposal.

The geographical approach impacts private foundations and governmental foundations at the state and local levels. This is really a potential restriction on funding. Some foundations will only fund Producers and/or projects that are within a certain geographical area. A private foundation example is the 3M Foundation, which only funds within Minnesota. At the state or local government level, most grants are done only to residents of that jurisdiction. The governmental foundations are pretty strict on this. The private foundations are more flexible, primarily because they often do not get enough good proposals from within their stated geographic area. Because foundations by law have to give away a certain amount of money every year, these foundations then work with Producers from outside their area IF the proposed film meets their subject/mission requirement.

The type of support approach refers to whether a foundation will give money to individuals or not and to what pieces of the development, production, post production, and distribution they will fund. If they will not give grants to individuals, then a Producer can assume that she will use a fiscal sponsor and be able to work with that foundation. A Producer also has to carefully match the stages of their budget with the potential for grants.

HOW TO APPROACH FOUNDATIONS

The normal approach is for a Producer to send the foundation a query letter which gives a summary description of the project. It has to be carefully worded to be sure it clearly communicates the subject of the film. If the foundation finds the query letter interesting, it will request a proposal. Many foundations have a clear description on their website of what they want to see in a proposal. Be sure to follow that even if it means doing some reformatting of a "standard" proposal.

The proposal will be assigned to a program officer who will do some investigation and then prepare a report for his distribution committee. Generally, the only thing the program officer has is the Producer's proposal, so it has to be good. If the program officer likes the proposal he will try to sell it to the distribution committee, which may meet monthly, quarterly or semiannually (for the smaller foundations).

The distribution committee will approve or not. If not, the program officer will be able to communicate to the Producer what reasons the committee gave for its denial. The Producer can then revise the proposal and resubmit it. This can happen a number of times before the distribution committee is satisfied and says 'yes'.

Now the Producer can always say no to any revisions and move on to other foundations. Foundations can have strong points of view and their requests for revision can alter the fabric of the film in such a way that it is not what the Producer wants. Or it is possibly that certain revisions will create a film that PBS or a cable network will not air because it has too much of an advocacy approach.

SUPPLEMENTAL MATERIAL – CHAPTER 8 – SOURCES OF FUNDING

Review Questions

1. What are the three primary sources for funding that are covered in the chapter?

2. What is the main motivation for an individual to support a nonfiction project?

3. How should you characterize the money raised from individuals for a nonfiction project?

4. What benefits might a corporation realize from supporting a nonfiction program?

5. What are the four classifications of foundations? Which ones are of the most interest to Producers?

6. What is the most important thing to investigate about a foundation before approaching them for money?

7. What is an example of an independent foundation, a corporate foundation and a governmental foundation?

8. Be able to describe the attributes of a grant.

9. What is the value of a fiscal sponsor for a Producer?

10. Do all foundations support film and video projects?

11. What are the three research approaches to finding a foundation for a project?

Industry Speak

Annual report - a report issued by a foundation or corporation that provides financial data and descriptions of its grant-making activities

Beneficiary - the grantee receiving a grant from a foundation or other grantor program

Distribution committee - a committee responsible for making grant decisions

Fiscal sponsor - an existing nonprofit organization which works with an individual for the purpose of receiving grants from foundations that will only make grants to non-profit organizations

General purpose foundation - an independent foundation that awards grants in many different fields of interest

Grant - money made available from foundations, government agencies, special interest groups, educational research organizations or corporations for various purposes which match the stated mission of the organization

Grantee - see "beneficiary"

Grantee financial report - a report detailing how grant funds were used by a grantee

Independent foundation - a grant-making organization usually classified by the IRS as a 501(c)(3) private foundation, which includes a family foundation, and not a governmental or corporate entity

In-kind contribution - a contribution of equipment, supplies or other tangible resource, as distinguished from a monetary grant

Mission - the reason a grant-making organization exists; the stated goal(s) of the grant making operation

Operating foundation - an independent foundation whose primary purpose is to conduct research, social welfare or other programs; it may make grants but the sum is generally small compared to its other activities

Program officer - a staff member of a foundation or grant-making organization who reviews grant proposals and applications; also works with grantees after grant is made

Proposal - a written application submitted to a foundation or grant-making organization when requesting a grant

Query letter - a brief letter outlining the activities of a grantee and its request for funding, which is sent to a potential grant-maker

RFP - Request for Proposal - used primarily by the government to solicit proposals on a particular topic or initiative; seldom by foundations which prefer applications initiated by applicants

Special purpose foundation - an independent foundation that focuses its grant-making activities in one or only a few areas of interest

Tax-exempt - organizations that do not have to pay taxes such as federal or state corporate tax or state sales tax

501(c)(3) - section of the tax code that defines nonprofit, charitable, and tax-exempt organizations

Further Activities

1. Go to http://foundationcenter.org/improve-your-skills/fundraising and check out what they offer in the way of training.

2. Go to www.grantforward.com and see what they offer.

Further Reading & Research

Get in the daily habit – read the industry trade papers to know what is going on in the industry. For film and television, I recommend *Variety, Hollywood Reporter,*

Broadcasting & Cable, and *Current.* They are all available online. Another good resource for what's happening in television is the *Cynopsis.com* online newsletter. For documentary and nonfiction work, I suggest *Real Screen.*

PART THREE
FEATURE FILM MARKETPLACE

The feature film industry in the United States is vast. Some call it a "vast wasteland" but most others call it our most important and largest export, cultural or otherwise. Regardless of your position on its merits, the inescapable truth is that the feature film industry is a linchpin of our culture and our economy. In this section we will take a look at the industry, how it works now and the challenges it faces. While the majority of feature films are fictional stories, there are many feature-length documentary films made each year and a few of them get a theatrical release. Our discussions cover both types of films.

The chapters in Part Three are:

Chapter 9 - Film Industry Overview

Chapter 10 - Cash Flow

Chapter 11- Ancillary Markets

Chapter 12 - Distribution

Chapter 13 - Film Festivals

Chapter 14 - Feature Film Funding

Here is a schematic overview of the industry that we will use in our discussions in these chapters.

THEATRICAL MARKETPLACE

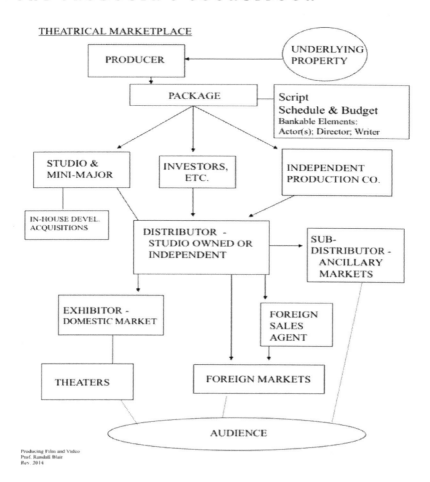

Producing Film and Video
Prof. Randall Blair
Rev. 2014

9

FILM INDUSTRY OVERVIEW

As I said when examining the television industry, one of the best ways to understand an industry is to start with the players – the companies, the people who make it work. So, let's look at the players in the feature film marketplace – who they are and what they do.

THE PLAYERS

Studios

The studios are the giants that sit at the top of the market. There are currently six major film studios in active operation: Sony, Universal, Paramount, Disney, Warner Brothers, and 20th Century Fox. In December 2017, Disney announced a deal to buy 20th Century Fox Studio from News Corp. So if that deal actually closes, then there will be five major film studios. Each of these major studios is part of a larger conglomerate that owns a number of major players in the media world in what economists and federal regulators call vertical integration. These conglomerates and their major holdings are already familiar to you from our look at the television industry in chapter 3.

Walt Disney Co. –

Disney studio
ABC television network
Local television stations

ESPN, Disney Channel and other cable
networks
Theme parks

Comcast –

Universal studio
NBC television network
Local television stations
Bravo, A&E, USA, SyFy and other cable
networks
Largest MSO in U.S.
Theme parks

Time/Warner –

Warner Brother's studio
CW network (co-owned with Viacom/CBS)
HBO, TBS, TNT, CNN, Cartoon Network,
TruTV, and other cable networks
Time and Sports Illustrated magazines and
other publications

News Corp –

20th Century Fox studio (going to Disney)
Fox television network
Local television stations
Fox News Channel; Fox Sports; FX/FXX
Major newspapers around the world

CBS/Viacom –

Paramount Studio
CBS television network
CW network (co-owned with Time Warner)
Local television stations
Showtime, MTV and Nickelodeon cable
networks

Sony Corporation - Sony Studio
Game Show network
Sony Electronics

In addition, each of these major studios owns smaller studios, also referred to as <u>labels</u>, which they have either created or acquired. Currently that list looks like this:

Disney –

Miramax
Touchstone
Pixar
Dreamworks
Marvel
Lucasfilm

Universal –

Focus
Rogue

Paramount –

Paramount Vantage
MTV / Nickelodeon

20th Century Fox –

Fox Searchlight
Fox Atomic
Fox Faith
These are also going to Disney

Sony –

Columbia
Screen Gems
MGM
Tri-Star

Sony Picture Classics
United Artists (through MGM)

And finally, all of the major film studios also have subsidiaries or divisions that produce television programs for the networks that are "sister" corporations and for the other nonaffiliated commercial broadcast or cable networks. These television divisions are the most profitable parts of the studios.

Independent Production Companies

Right below the studios on the feature film food chain are the large independent production companies that are capable of financing and even distributing their own films. The largest of these companies is Lionsgate which was founded in the mid 1990s in Vancouver, Canada. A publicly held company, Lionsgate produces films, including the 2005 Oscar-winning *Crash*, *The Hunger Games*, the Divergent series, and *La La Land*. In 2012 it purchased Summit Entertainment, which produced the *Twilight* film series. It also has an active television production business, which made *Mad Men* for AMC. When it began, Lionsgate was able to develop and produce feature films in large part because they had an output deal with one of the major studios. It now has a library of over 9,000 titles which generate some $200 million in annual revenues. Their production slate is now up to 20 annual releases with a projected $1 billion in revenue. This is a production and revenue level equal to most of the major studios. For this reason, some in the industry are now calling Lionsgate the seventh major studio; or maybe it will take the place of 20th Century if that studio gets absorbed by Disney.

Another example of such a company is Imagine Entertainment, which is owned and managed by Ron Howard and Brian Glazer. Imagine has a relationship with Universal Studios that goes back over 20 years and has encompassed more than 50 films that have grossed more than $12.6 billion worldwide. Some of the films created under this relationship are *Apollo 13*, *A Beautiful Mind*, *Cinderella Man*, *Liar Liar*, *The Grinch*, *Dark Tower*, and *American Made*. In similar fashion, Village Roadshow has an output deal with Time/Warner and

Spyglass has one with Sony. We examine these output deals in more detail as part of the chapter on Feature Film Financing.

The history of Hollywood is littered with independent production companies that have started, made a few films and then disappeared by either going out of business or, if lucky, being gobbled up by a studio. IFC, October, Atlantic, Arrow, First Look, Cowboy, Strand, Troma, New World, and Trimark are but a few of these. The common denominator for them is an ambitious slate of films under development, but no big, renewable, source of cash for production and no output deal to guarantee distribution of the films they make. The common cause of death is the lack of a consistent stream of successful films and the overwhelming costs of development, production and marketing.

A relatively new addition to the list of independent production companies are the production operations of the subscription on demand companies like Netflix, Hulu, and Amazon Prime Video. They are growing increasingly active in the production of feature films for their services, and some are even being released into the theatrical market. At the moment they are primarily working with established filmmakers but should be on an independent Producer's radar.

Distributors

Next are the distributors who take the films to market. We examine distributors in detail in chapter 12, but suffice it to say that there are three kinds of distributors: studio, independent and foreign. The major film studios all have a distribution operation that is owned by the studio. These studio distribution operations handle their films in the domestic and the foreign theatrical markets plus all of the ancillary markets. They will, of course, distribute all the films that the studio produces. In addition, they distribute some films produced by independent production companies, some with output deals and some without.

Some of the larger independent production companies like Lions Gate distribute their own films and also films which they license from independent Producers. Other independent distributors are only into distribution and do not produce their own films. They rely on acquisitions from smaller independent production companies and Producers. And, finally there are companies in most of the countries around the world which license and distribute U.S. made films, other than studio films. These foreign distributors generally work with the theatrical, television, cable and home video markets in their countries.

Exhibitors

Finally, we have the exhibitors, the owners of the theaters where the films will be screened. Today there are approximately 6,300 theaters in the United States with approximately 40,600 screens. This is an increase from only 17,000 screens in 1980. On the other hand, there were almost 7,700 theaters in 1995. During the late 1990s, a rash of bankruptcies among exhibitors, caused in part by overbuilding, led to a consolidation in the industry. Many single-screen theaters were closed as the industry went almost exclusively to multiplexes with 10 or more screens. Today the three largest exhibition companies control 50% of all screens in the U.S. AMC is the largest of these with more than 8,200 screens in 660 theaters. Regal and Cinemark USA, are the other two large companies. In 2012, the Chinese conglomerate, the Wanda Group, purchased AMC theaters for $2.6 billion; and it is now the largest movie theater company in the world.

An important development in the world of exhibitors has been the conversion to digital cinemas. At the end of 2017 there were approximately 39,500 digital (3D and non 3D) cinema screens in the U.S., which is almost 98% of all screens. This was an enormous increase from the 12 digital screens that existed in 1999. A 2008 financial agreement between the studios and the largest exhibition companies fostered a rapid increase in the conversion of analog screens to digital. We will discuss the importance of this development later in this section when we consider the cost of the film prints that distributors used to have to send to the theaters. Worldwide (including the U.S.) by the end of 2107, 98% of the almost 170,000 cinema screens were digital.

SIZE OF THE MARKET

Now, it's time to try to get a sense of the size of this marketplace. We are aided in this effort, to a point, by the researchers at the Motion Picture Association of America (MPAA), which is the trade association of the studios. Every spring, the MPAA releases an economic study of the industry from the previous calendar year. While some may argue that you can't trust any numbers from the studios, this report seems to be fairly objective, and it is the only thing we have other than expensive third party economic studies. When we try to go beyond the studio world, industry figures are either not available or are highly suspect.

For 2017, the latest MPAA study reports that the studios released 130 feature films. This includes films made by the main studios or their labels and any films that were licensed for distribution from outside Producers. The MPAA also reports that, in addition to the studio releases, another 647 feature films were released by other distributors. This total of 777 films released is the most ever, and represents an overall 22% increase in the past 10 years. By comparison, in 1995 the total number of films released was 370.

Up until 2008, the studios had averaged approximately 185-190 releases per year over the previous 12+ years. The high point was 205 films released in 2002. From 2008 to 2017 the number has dropped 23%. This dramatic decrease is a result of the industry labor issues in 2007/08, the Great Recession of 2008-2009, and the subsequent cost cutting measures undertaken by all studios.

Currently, the way the studios seem to be cutting back is to reduce the films that are in the mid-range of budgets ($35 to $70 million per film) and to concentrate on the more expensive tentpole films, which are way north of $150 million each. Then with their labels, they are focusing on the low end films, the $15 to $35 million range. This puts a lot more pressure on the larger independent production companies to take up the slack in the mid-range films. However, if these companies make too many mistakes with those films, they won't be in business for long.

The number of non-studio releases hit a peak of 470 in 2008 and then dropped to 399 in 2009. However, in 2012 it jumped back up to 550, and then to an all-time high of 647 in 2017. The ten-year growth as of 2017 has been 38%. These increases began in the early 2000s and resulted from the proliferation of independent feature films shot on digital cameras at a fraction of the cost of the typical studio film. The most sobering thing, however, at least to those producing the hundreds of independent feature films each year, is that while the studio films represent under 20% of the total number of films released, the box office from those studio films accounts for over 90% of the total box office.

In addition to the films released, there are films that are produced but not released in a given year. The MPAA reports that in 2017 there were 544 films, with a budget of $1 million or more, that were produced but not released into the theaters. The studios made 112 of these and the rest were produced independently. The total of 544 is up 20% in the past five years. While the studios occasionally produce a film and don't eventually release it, that is not common. It's a guess as to how many of the independent films will actually get released in 2018 or after. The further complication with this, however, is that there are many other films being produced with budgets under $1 million. The MPAA estimates that there were 277 of these produced in 2017 but not released. Then there are still other indie films being produced that do not find their way onto the MPAA's radar. How do we know that? One way is to look at the submissions to film festivals.

In today's film world, it is the goal of virtually every feature film Producer to have her film screened in competition at the Sundance Film Festival. Since the late 1990s this festival has become the number one event for Producers, distributors, critics, and people looking for good parties. It is interesting, therefore, to track the number of feature films submitted each year and see that it has gone from 250 films in 1994 to 1,000 films in 1999 and to approximately 4,000 films in 2017 (for the festival in 2018). As an interesting side note, there were over 6,000 short films submitted to Sundance for 2018.

Another approach to this game of trying to guess the number of feature films being made is to talk to distributors. A big part of a distributor's job is to keep track of what is going on in the industry. They all keep a tracking system for films from the first time they are announced. We will look at the process for a Producer to get his film into the tracking system in chapter 12 on Distribution. What we're concerned with here is that most distributors report that at any time they normally track over 10,000 film projects that are in various stages of development and production. That's a lot of films!

So what does all of this mean? It is clear that Producers are making feature films in record numbers. It is also clear that many of the films made outside of the studio system do not get released. That does not mean that they are all failures, however, as we will see in chapter 11 on the ancillary markets. For most of these films, an ancillary market becomes their primary market. The lack of a theatrical release does, however, substantially limit the realistic earning potential of a feature film.

TOO MANY FILMS?

One other important consideration is the impact on the theatrical market from having 700+ films released during a year. That's an average of over 13 films every week! Every year there are interviews with the heads of the studios who bemoan the number of films being made and released; and they say that they should all cut back on the number of films they release. And, they're just talking about the studio films, which compete the heaviest for the public's attention and interest. Yet even with the cutbacks in recent years the studios churn out their 130+ films. Why do they find it so hard to cut back as they say they want to do? Let's consider the following.

Better odds for a hit. No one knows which film will strike a responsive chord with the audience and become a hit. All the packaging of actors and directors, and all the promotion in the world can't guarantee it. So it becomes a numbers game, and the more times they play, roll the dice, the more chances of success they have.

Leverage with exhibitors. In the negotiations between studio distributors and exhibitors, the studios often have the upper hand because they have lots of films, many of which are highly anticipated by the audience. So the exhibitors have to take the studio's weak films to get the strong ones. A small independent distribution company does not have that clout.

Message to creative community. The last thing a studio wants is a reputation that it is not aggressively releasing films. It could be financial problems or a lot of creative problems, but whatever the reason, it scares away the Producers with new packages. That keeps the studio executives up at night. It also leads them to make the development deals that we will look at in chapter 14.

Bragging rights. The studio world is a male dominated, testosterone driven industry and bragging rights are important. A studio can't win the box office race without releasing a lot of films (and hoping that many of them are hits)

SUPPLEMENTAL MATERIAL – CHAPTER 9 – FILM INDUSTRY OVERVIEW

Review Questions

1. Who sits on top of the feature film industry market?

2. What is an example of an independent production company?

3. What do exhibitors do? How many companies control over 40% of the screens in the U.S. and Canada?

4. What percentage of screens in the U.S. are digital? What percentage worldwide?

5. What is the trade association for the studios?

6. How many films did the studios release in the latest MPAA report? How many were released by other distributors?

7. What percentage of the box office do the studio films take?

8. How many active independent film projects do distributors report that they normally track?

9. What are the four reasons that studios find it hard to cut back the number of releases the make every year?

Industry Speak

Audience - The group of people who see a film or to whom a film is generally directed

Buzz - The positive or negative talk regarding a film in production or in its initial showing

Conglomerate – a corporation that primary owns other

corporations, normally concentrating in a particular industry

Deal memo - a shortened version of a contract setting out the minimum negotiated terms between the parties; often used to get the film production process underway with the intent that the final contracts will be agreed upon later

Exhibitor – a company that own the theater(s) that screen feature films.

First-run - the initial exhibition of a film in a designated geographical area for a specified period of time

Independent feature film - any feature film that is not financed or made by one of the major studios

Independent Film & Television Alliance - a trade association that represents the interest of independent Producers and distributors of English language films in the international markets

MPAA - Motion Picture Association of America: an industry trade organization of the major studios founded in 1922 to promote the international dissemination of American films. One of their functions is the assigning of audience ratings to new films.

Further Activities

Check the local newspaper or Fandango to see how many new films are premiering in your area each week. How would you characterize the variety of genres and probable audience appeal? Which ones will compete with each other? How will they compete with the films already in the theaters?

Further Reading & Research

Go to the MPAA website http://www.mpaa.org and find the latest Theatrical Market Statistical Report, which is published every spring (March or April).

Go to the Independent Film and Television Alliance website http://www.ifta-online.org/ and see what they offer

Got to Box Office Mojo http://www.boxofficemojo.com and look around for the information it provides. Look at the release schedule for the next weeks.

Get in the daily habit – read the industry trade papers to know what is going on in the industry. For film and television, I recommend *Variety, Hollywood Reporter, Broadcasting & Cable,* and *Current.* They are all available online. Another good resource for what's happening in television is the *Cynopsis.com* online newsletter. For documentary and nonfiction work, I suggest *Real Screen.*

10

CASH FLOW

FOLLOW THE MONEY

E very business has a traditional structure and normal practices that control the flow of money – the cash flow. In addition to knowing the players of an industry, cash flow is an excellent guide for us to follow in order to better understand the economics of the feature film marketplace.

The following is an illustration of the cash flow path. We will examine some of these steps in detail here, and other parts will be covered in subsequent chapters.

It all starts with the Audience. That's why we produce films and video – to reach an audience, and one that is greater than our immediate family.

The first Audience that we want to reach with a feature film are the theater goers who pay their money at the local cineplex. Using the latest MPAA report, in 2017, there were 1.24 billion admissions to the domestic (US and Canada) theaters. That was down 6% from 2016 and way below the all-time high of 1.57 billion admissions in 2002. An interesting note is that the average admission (ticket price) in 2017 was $8.97 which followed an unbroken upward trend since 1993 when the price was $4.14. We can also compare this to the average of $2.69 in 1980.

The MPAA also reports that 76% of the population (ages 2+) in the U.S. and Canada went to the cinema at least once in 2017. The average of these moviegoers bought 4.7 tickets. And 12% of the U.S./Canada population are "frequent" moviegoers, meaning that they attend the cinema once a month or more. Of these frequent moviegoers, the largest age group was 25-39, and they were evenly split between male and female.

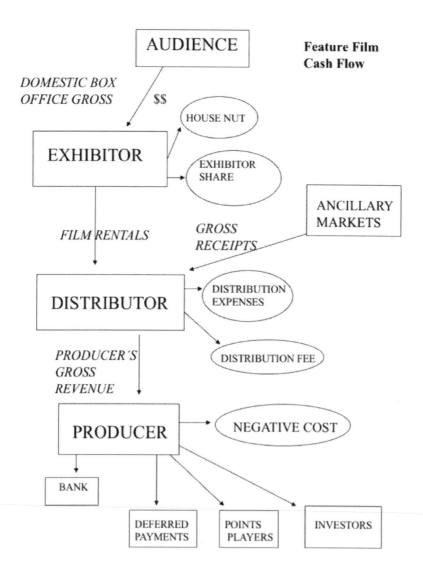

The money that the audience spends on tickets for these admissions is called the Domestic Box Office Gross. This was $11.1 billion in 2017, which was 2% below the record of $11.4 billion in 2016. For comparison, the total Domestic Box Office Gross in 2000 was $7.5 billion, in 1990 it was $5 billion, and in 1980 it was approximately $3 billion. The Domestic Box Office includes money spent to see all films released in the United States and Canada.

The *exhibitors* collect the Domestic Box Office Gross and then deduct from it according to contracts negotiated with the distributors for each film. In all cases the exhibitors deduct their *house nut*, which is a flat fee that covers some of their basic costs of operation. After that deduction, they take their share of the box office which is a negotiated percentage that changes each week that the film is in the theater. For the first week, the percentage is heavily weighted in favor of the distributor and can be up to 90%. The percentages move each week until finally it favors the exhibitor. The exact percentages are not that important. The most important thing to know is that, over the domestic theatrical exhibition life of the average film, the exhibitors will send the distributor an amount of money that is approximately 50% of the Box Office Gross. This money is called *Film Rentals*. While the box office gross numbers are used by the studios and others to brag about the performance of their films, it is really the film rentals that are the most important figure on the cash flow path to the Producer.

When we look at the overall life and cash flow of a feature film, we need to include the ancillary markets. We will discuss these markets in more detail in the next chapter, but suffice it to say here that they include foreign theatrical, home video/DVD (both domestic and foreign), video on demand, subscription video on demand, pay cable, television and basic cable (both domestic and foreign), and others. The money that comes to the distributor from these markets, less any fees and expenses of sub-distributors, is called *gross receipts.*

So our distributor now has the film rentals from the exhibitors and the gross receipts from the ancillary markets. According to the distribution contract, the distributor is now entitled to deduct its direct expenses. We will examine these in depth in Chapter 12 on distribution. For now, the most important expenses are the release prints (generic term used for both film or digital delivery) that the distributor makes of the film to send to exhibitors and the marketing and advertising expenses incurred to promote the film. Commonly these expenses are called P&A for prints and advertising. To get a general sense of P&A expenses, we can again look at MPAA figures, but unfortunately the last year they reported average costs was in 2007. For some reason they have stopped reporting such numbers. Can you think of why?

For 2007, the MPAA reports that the average P&A cost for members' releases was $35.9 million per film. This included film release prints that averaged $3.9 million per film and the advertising costs that were $32 million per film. For the studio subsidiaries, the marketing costs average was $25.7 million per film. And that was a very large increase from the $17.8 million per film in 2006.

After deducting the expenses which are allowed under the distribution contract, the distributor takes the negotiated percentage that is their distribution fee. While this is negotiated for each film, there are some industry standards for the different markets; for example, the standard distribution fee for domestic theatrical distribution is 35%. For foreign theatrical and television distribution, the standard fee is 45%.

After deducting their expenses and fee, the distributor sends what money is left, if any, to the Producer. In the case of a studio film, the studio is the Producer. The studio distribution operation functions as a profit center and will follow the same routine, sending the money from one accountant to another. This money is called the *producer's gross revenue.* From this gross revenue, the Producer has to cover the negative cost of the film. The negative cost is the total of the amounts spent on the production of the film from the original deal for underlying property through to the printing of the master negative(s) used to make the release film prints or the digital cinema prints on hard drives that are sent to the theaters. Negative costs also include overhead of the studio/production company plus any interest on bank loans used for the production. In 2007, the average negative cost for the MPAA studios was $70.8 million (up from $65.8 million in 2006) and for their subsidiaries/affiliates it was $49.2 million (up from $30.7 million in 2006).

The combination of the P&A costs and the negative costs on a film are called the Theatrical Costs. In 2007, the average studio film had a theatrical cost of $106.6 million; and for the studio subsidiaries/affiliates, it was $74.8 million for the average film. In 2000 those average theatrical costs were $82.1 million and $31.6 million respectively. In 1995 the theatrical cost for the average studio film was $54.1 million and for 1985 it was $23.3 million. The MPAA did not publish figures for the studio subsidiaries prior to 1999.

That means that the average theatrical cost for a studio film had risen by 350% over 22 years – far above the rate of inflation. A couple of significant reasons for this increase can be found in the enormous jump in fees paid to top talent, with film stars and even some directors now routinely getting $20+ million per film. Another factor has been the exponential rise in the number of expensive special effects in the typical studio film. An interesting discussion revolves around where these theatrical costs have gone in the ten plus years since 2007 – up or down?

If the studio or other Producer has received gross revenue, they have to first repay any bank loans associated with the film. That is always the first priority because a bank loan has to be repaid or they can seize the film. If there is any money left over, then it can begin to get distributed to the people who worked on the film on a deferred payment deal (for more information on this see the chapter 20 on Crew Deals). After this comes the people who have backend deals and are due net points on any net profits. These are often writers, directors and actors who don't have enough leverage to be able to negotiate gross points, which would come out of the gross revenue. Last in line would be the Producer and any investors who invested money in the film. While they might not get anything right away, they do own the film which might have a long term earning potential or value. For a Producer, as is the case with the studios and production companies, these films add to their libraries, which over time create a significant core asset value.

We will end this chapter with an intriguing and sobering calculation. If the studios release 140 films in an average year and the average theatrical cost is $117 million (assumes that 125 of the films are at the studio level and 15 are at the subsidiary level of theatrical costs; also assumes an overall rate of inflation of 15% between 2008 and 2017), then the total amount of money spent by the studios to make and market these 140 films is approximately $16.6 billion. Okay. Now what was the total of the domestic box office in 2017? Right, $11.1 billion. The studio share is approximately 90% or $10 billion. But wait, the studio distributors only get 50% of that in film rentals or $5 billion. Then the distribution division takes its fee of 35%. So the producer's gross revenue for the studios would be approximately $3.3 billion. By my calculations that leaves them a little more than $13.3 billion short! And, this doesn't include the many, many millions of dollars the studios spend each year on the development of film projects that never go into production.

Assuming that the studios are in business to make money (a very correct assumption), then where do they find the other $13.3 billion and more? The answer to that is coming up in the next chapter on ancillary markets.

SUPPLEMENTAL MATERIAL – CHAPTER 10 – CASH FLOW

Review Questions

1. What has been the trend recently with the number of film theater admissions and the average ticket price?

2. What is the definition of a frequent moviegoer?

3. What countries are included in the calculation of domestic box office?

4. What percentage of the box office gross comes to the distributor as film rentals on an average feature film?

5. What is the rise in the cost of studio films over the past twenty plus years?

6. Who is the last in line for the cash flow of a feature film, after all expenses are paid or recouped?

Industry Speak

Backend deal - a contractual arrangement providing for contingent compensation to be paid if certain revenue or profit levels are achieved; includes gross participation, net participation, bonus payments

Box office gross - the amount of money that has been paid by the public to an exhibitor for admission tickets to see a film, before any deductions for exhibitor expenses or fee

Film rentals - The money owed by an exhibitor to a distributor after the exhibitor's expenses and fee are deducted

Gross receipts – includes all the money coming to a distributor from the ancillary markets for a film

Gross points – a backend deal that provides a percentage of the producer's gross revenue

Negative cost – a calculation that includes all development and production costs spent to complete a film and make it available for distribution; does not include any marketing or distribution costs

Net points – a backend deal that provides a percentage of any profit realized by the film after all expenses, including deferrals, and costs of financing

Producer's Gross Revenue – the money that a comes to the Producer from the distributor

Further Activities

1. Search the industry trades and other sources to try to find budget costs for feature films. Can you tell whether this is negative cost or theatrical cost?

2. A little brainstorming – Why do you think the studios stopped releasing data on the cost of their films? Where do you think that studio negative costs have gone since 2007? Why?

Further Reading & Research

Check out the following:

National Association of Theater Owners
http://www.natoonline.org/index.htm

Indie Wire http://www.indiewire.com/

Box Office Mojo http://www.boxofficemojo.com/

Get in the daily habit – read the industry trade papers to know what is going on in the industry. For film and television, I recommend *Variety, Hollywood Reporter, Broadcasting & Cable,* and *Current.* They are all available online. Another good resource for what's happening in television is the *Cynopsis.com* online newsletter. For documentary and nonfiction work, I suggest *Real Screen*.

11

ANCILLARY MARKETS

I n chapter 10, Cash Flow, we discovered that the major studios spend over $13.3 billion more to produce the feature films that they release every year than they get back in producer's gross revenue. No business, not even in Tinseltown, can sustain that for very long. So there must be something more, and there is – ancillary markets.

Ancillary markets are all of the ways that Producers and the studios exploit and make money from their films after they are released in the theaters. And these markets get the films during a specific time period after the theatrical release, and we call this their Windows of Opportunity. The following diagram illustrates this flow of a film from one ancillary market to the next. And it forms the structural basis of this chapter.

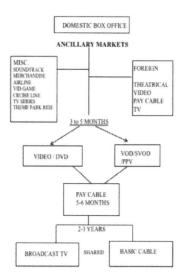

As you can see, it all starts with the domestic theatrical release. Think of that as the engine that then pulls the film into all of these other markets. Now it is, of course, possible for a film to start in one of the other markets without having had a theatrical release. Film are released straight to DVD or Subscription Video On Demand (SVOD) or to Pay Cable. But then their potential in the other ancillary markets is reduced or eliminated altogether. For example, a film produced by and released on Netflix (SVOD) will not be shown on HBO or NBC or AMC. But the economic model for Netflix is totally different from the studios and beyond the scope of this book.

OVERALL TRENDS

Before we investigate the individual markets, we should discuss some trends and issues facing the ancillary world in general.

The first big thing is that the industry and the world are changing and that leads to opportunities and headaches. For example, the growth of the domestic theatrical market has been pretty slow for many years now. The overall growth rate of the domestic box office over the past five years has only been 2% according to the MPAA. And if we look closely, virtually all of that growth has been a result of the increase in the average ticket price and not from an increase in the number of admissions. But the growth in the international box office has been much better – 18%. This has led to a very nice overall/Global growth rate of 13 %.

The studios are struggling with how to get the younger audience (12 to 24) into the theater, in much the same way that television people struggle to get them to watch television. There just seems to be too many alternative forms of entertainment and other distractions for this demographic. Meanwhile, the ticket prices have just about priced an evening at the movies out of reach for middle-aged parents and their families. And the older audiences complain that there is nothing being made for them. All of this puts more pressure on the ancillary markets.

The introduction of new technologies, at a seemingly ever increasing pace, can create new markets and damage or destroy others. We still call it home video but isn't it really home DVD? And now DVD is in decline with the advances in digital cable and Video On Demand (VOD); and VOD is battling SVOD over the internet. The mobility of screens also offers opportunities and challenges. You get the idea.

With all of these technologically driven changes, the competition has never been greater between the different markets. And that has led to changes in the traditional window structure of the ancillary markets. The windows are still there, but the timing continues to change. In the days of VHS home video, the window for home video was six to eight months. That meant that a film would be made available in home video six to eight months after it was released in the theaters. Now with VOD/SVOD bidding against DVD for an earlier shot at the films, the window has shortened to three to five month. And sometimes it is home video/DVD going first and sometimes it is VOD/SVOD going first. These companies spend big money to be the first to get a film in front of their customers.

The timing of the windows is also influenced by a few other factors. If a film doesn't do well in the theaters, the studio will often rush it into DVD/VOD/SVOD to take advantage of the marketing money already spent and whatever good word-of-mouth they may have. But successful tent-pole films can also be rushed. One reason is to take advantage of a holiday season if the studio thinks it might be a title that people will want to buy. The other reason is to counteract the international scourge that is piracy. Popular films will very quickly get pirated on the DVD market and through file sharing, and the studios want to head that off.

One strategy to get more money from families is called Premium Video On Demand. This means that a film is released in the theaters and on VOD at the same time or within a week or two. But the VOD price is very high - $50 to $60; and it's a 24-hour viewing period. The price is steep, but if a family of four goes to the theater, the tickets could cost $40 or more, and it's very easy to spent $20 or more at the concession stand. And many people have home entertainment systems with screens and sound systems that make it almost a theatrical experience. This has been tried a couple of times without too much success, with the main reason being the resistance or outright hostility from the exhibitors, who make most of their profit from those concessions.

So now let's look in depth at each of these ancillary markets.

INTERNATIONAL / FOREIGN

The international markets, also called the foreign markets, includes all countries except for the United States and Canada, which comprise what we call the domestic theatrical market. In 2017, the ten largest international markets in term of box office were China, Japan, the UK, India, S. Korea, France, Germany, Russia, Australia, and Mexico, in that order. None of them are the size of the domestic market, with China the largest at $7.9 billion and then Japan next at $2.0 billion. But all combined, the international box office in 2017 was $29.5 billion – more than two and a half times as large as the domestic box office of $11.1 billion. Up until 2001, domestic box office had always been larger than international, but that has changed in a big way.

You hopefully noticed that there is not a window specified for the international or foreign market. That is because there is no standard timing for this market. The studios distribution divisions make a film-by-film decision on a release date for the different foreign countries or areas of the world. The world is a big, complex place and each film needs a unique strategy to maximize its potential. For example, in broad terms, the summer is full of big, splashy, action/adventure, comic book based, high testosterone, blockbuster films. They are marketed to teenage males who are out of school and have plenty of time to see the same film five or six times – maybe each time with a different date. But is it summer at the same time everywhere in the world? Summer in the U.S. - what about Australia or Argentina or South Africa? Another factor is that every two years there is a summer Olympics or a World Cup. The summer Olympics dominate the U.S. media market and theater attendance suffers. The World Cup has an even greater impact on much of the world, but not as much in the U.S. Also, holidays are different around the world – you get the idea.

There is a release strategy called day-and-date, which means that a film is released in the domestic market and in select international market(s) on the same day. This happens fairly frequently. It also happens, but less frequently, for a studio film to be released in foreign markets before it is released domestically. The reasons are always fascinating if the studio divulges them, which it often does not. The advantages to this strategy is that it means that one marketing campaign is done for all of those territories – and with social media that happens quickly. The other advantage is that it counteracts the impact of piracy.

I mentioned earlier that the international box office is growing rapidly and that's great, but one issue for the studios is that these markets seem to be getting more fragmented. More and more locally produced films are taking over screens in each country, and some are even traveling successfully to other countries. Whereas we know that studio films make up 90% of the domestic box office, it is estimated that they make up only about 70% of the international box office. I should mention that this is our first encounter with the notoriously poor and unreliable reporting systems in many countries. It's just not like what we have here. While it's not so bad for the studios because they have the resources to monitor things, it is a huge problem for the distributors of independent films. The other issue at work here is what some call "cultural imperialism", meaning that some countries are afraid that films from other countries (the U.S. in particular) have too great an influence on their markets and viewers. And also, they want to encourage and support their own filmmakers. So they have quotas on the number of "foreign" films that can be imported. China is a great example; it only allows 24 foreign films per year – and those have to share their revenue with the Chinese government. France also has quotas but not as restrictive. And finally, there is an issue with censorship in some countries, primarily based on prevailing religious beliefs.

Concerning independent films, international distribution is normally thought of as a mix of markets and not just theatrical. A foreign distribution deal for an indie film normally includes all the markets within a specific country; not just theatrical as with studio films. The normal foreign revenue expectation is that 45% of the revenue will come from television, 35% from theatrical, and 20% from video/DVD / VOD.

A couple of things about films going international. Not all films do it successfully. Some are very successful and do better than their domestic performance. For example, in 2017, *The Fate of the Furious* did $1.2 billion in global or worldwide box office. 18% of that came from its domestic release and 82% from its international releases. Other films with in excess of 70% international box office were *Despicable Me 3*, *Coco*, *Pirates of the Caribbean: Dead Men Tell No Tales*, *Transformers: The Last Knight*, and *Kong: Skull Island*. On the flip side, box office for films like *Get Out*, *Lady Bird*, and *The Big Sick* were between 20% and 30% international. Even further down were *Girls Trip* at 18% international and *Tyler Perry's Boo 2!* at only 2%. Some things might be clear from this – big action films with lots of special effects and explosions tend to do better internationally. Comedy, however, can be a hard sell, especially if it's steeped in American culture. Romantic comedies and musicals also tend to suffer. The horror genre is interesting in that most don't travel internationally very well, with the exception of zombies. Zombies seem to be popular everywhere.

HOME VIDEO / DVD

VHS is dead. DVDs are soft. And Blu-ray has never taken off. That sort of summarizes the past twenty years of this ancillary market that we call Home Video. The estimate is that 86% of US Households have at least one DVD (including Blu-ray) player, and that doesn't count the DVD capability of most computers.

Historically the home video market has been a major factor in the growth of the film industry, particularly the independent film industry. Prior to the debut of VHS and Betamax machines in the 1970s, we had studio films and that was about it. A few indies got made but not many. Then this new market developed with an insatiable appetite for new films. Many independent films were even financed by the home video distributors. DVD came along in 1997 and continued this trend, and also brought network television series into the mix. Navigating between 22 episodes of a show on a VHS was incredibly cumbersome, but it's a breeze on a DVD.

While the home video market is under tremendous pressure from the competition of VOD and SVOD, it remains strong and a vital component of the ancillary revenue stream for a studio film. One result of this competition is that the window for the home video market has shrunk from a historical average of 8 months to less than 4 months today.

In the old days, home video came via the video store, which is no more. In the days of VHS people either rented a tape or bought it and the overall market was about 50% each – purchase or rental. It was a good business, and there were Blockbuster and Hollywood Video stores everywhere. But in 1997, the same year that DVDs came to market, a little company called Netflix was founded, and it would eventually kill off all the video stores. Sure it took the growth of VOD/SVOD to put the final nail in the coffin, but

Netflix was at the forefront of that as well. No one weeps for VHS or any other obsolete technology, but it is amazing how fast things can change.

So with DVDs we can also rent them or buy them. And with VOD we can rent (stream) or buy (download). So the strategy for the studio distributors has modified but also stayed the same. With each film, they try to figure out whether it is one that people might want to buy or just rent. That strategic decision will impact the pricing of the film and the marketing approach. Research has shown that we are a society that likes to own things, especially if it's a Disney film. But that does appear to be changing.

Some other things about the home video market that are important for Producers to know are:

1. more than 80% of rental or streaming earnings will come within 2 weeks after the opening of the home video release window;

2. 60 to 65% of sales and downloads come in the first 3 weeks;

3. the average film takes in more money from home video than any other market including theatrical and this can be up to three times as much;

4. home video can save a film that performed poorly in the theaters; but not always; and

5. films that do well in the theaters almost always do well in home video.

On final interesting fact about the home video market. That is the importance of the retailers of DVDs. Wal-Mart accounts for 40% of what the studios sell on DVD. But DVD sales are less than 1% of Wal-Mart sales. And Wal-Mart refuses to carry any R rated titles. It doesn't take much to see that Wal-Mart means a lot more to Hollywood than Hollywood means to Wal-Mart. The question is whether that gives Wal-Mart the ability to influence what the studios release.

The MPAA stopped releasing home video figures for studio films in 2001. Then in 2017, they brought it back to their annual market report. The numbers are impressive. But we will wait to discuss them until after we have looked at the digital aspect of home video.

VOD/SVOD

We find the origins of video on demand and subscription video on demand (VOD/SVOD) in the Pay Per View (PPV) concept. The earliest cases of PPV were boxing matches that were sent via satellite to theaters. A few other sporting events also used that strategy. But it was cumbersome and needed a really big event to be successful.

The cable industry began using the PPV approach as soon as the technology would allow it. But initially that technology was cumbersome and very limited. It took the advance of the industry to fiber optic cable to finally allow for the dramatic expansion of the PPV concept. Not only did the new cable technology allow for many more networks to be offered, but it allowed for two-way addressability and therefore individual transactions between the cable operator and the customer. The ability to push even more information/data over the cable, and at speeds that made for an acceptable viewing experience of a feature film, is the foundation of this market. In 2000, less than 1% of TV Households had access to PPV or VOD and by 2017, over 65% of TV Households had VOD capability.

There are different types of VOD deals that are negotiated between the cable MSOs and the studios. Some deals are done on a per-title license basis, that is film by film. And other deals are done to license entire libraries of films with no specific breakdown of money per film. The other important factor in the deals between MSOs and studios is that the cable company decides whether to charge and how much to charge subscribers for a particular film. They can charge per title or they can put a film on a "free" list, accessible to subscribers at any time for no additional money. MSO also allow subscribers to "buy" the film, but it is really a long term lease.

As this VOD market was developing between the MSOs and the studios, the internet and broadband and SVOD came along. Broadband penetration is estimated to be in excess of 85% of US households, even those that are not TV Households, and approximately 50% of TV Households subscribe to one SVOD service. Netflix got the ball rolling as an alternative or add-on to its DVD by mail strategy. It's a variation of the cable model but is based on a flat fee for a subscription that allows the subscriber access to any of the titles as many times or for as long as they want.

And finally we have retailers – primarily iTunes and Amazon – using the internet to mimic the old fashioned video store. You can buy or you can rent, but the rental is for some reason much more restricted. And Amazon Prime is really a SVOD service like Netflix. It gets very complicated, confusing.

The most interesting thing about all of this for Producers is that there are parallels to the old days of VHS and the growth of independent film. The SVOD services need fresh titles to keep subscribers happy, the same as the premium cable networks. So they are investing in the development of titles and independent Producers are right in there getting their films financed. They won't go to theaters, but they will get made and released in a vibrant market. And occasionally a SVOD service will release a film theatrically to qualify for an Oscar if they think it has that potential. In 2017 Netflix did this with *Mudbound*, which it didn't produce but picked up for distribution at the Sundance Film Festival.

Home Entertainment Spending

Home Entertainment is the label that the MPAA began to use in its 2017 market report for content released on disc and digitally in any form. So it combines the home video market and the VOD/SVOD market. In 2017, the global spending by consumers

166

on home entertainment was $47.8 billion, which was up 11% over 2016. This includes $15.7 billion for physical transactions (including rental and sales) and $32.1 billion for digital transactions (including electronic sell-through, VOD, and subscription streaming). The physical transaction revenue has trended down by more than 50% over the past five years, while the digital transaction revenue has more than doubled in the same period of time. Looking at just the United States (not including Canada as we do with box office), the overall spending is $20.5 billion, which was up 5% over 2016. As I hope you notice, this is almost twice as much as the domestic box office, which does include Canada. The physical transaction revenue was $6.8 billion and the digital transaction share was $13.7 billion. Both categories have changed in a similar pattern to the global revenue over the past five years.

The studio share of the domestic home entertainment revenue is estimated to be 95%. And even more important for the studios, they get roughly 80% of that revenue, after distribution expenses and royalties, which are not substantial. In fact, the minimal amount of royalties that are paid to the talent in the film is a major sore point between the industry unions/guilds and the studios. More on this in chapter 19.

PAY CABLE

Approximately 45 to 50% of all TV Households subscribe to one of the premium pay cable networks. HBO is the leader followed by Showtime.

There has always been a close relationship between the pay cable networks and the studios, and these days they are all part of the few conglomerates that control the industry. The reality is that these networks need films. Yes, they do produce series and sports and specials, but their bread-and-butter is films. And the studios have a lot of films. When these networks started in the early to mid 1970s, the studio had thousands of titles in their vaults collecting dust. Then these pay cable networks and VHS came along and the studios began to enjoy unprecedented profits from brand new markets.

Traditionally, the pay cable networks would negotiate an <u>Output Deal</u> with a studio. This deal meant that the network licensed every film that the studio made, and it was exclusive to that network. The studio had a licensee in place for all of its films, even the unsuccessful ones, and would benefit from a competitive negotiation between the pay cable networks. To some extent these output deals have been less lucrative over the past few years as the networks have done more of their own original programming. The other mitigating factor is that the networks are concerned that the films are getting too much exposure in the home video or VOD/SVOD window and that the availability on the pay cable network is not as much of an event as it has been in the past. It is estimated that the pay cable networks spent in excess of $3 billion to license films in 2017.

The interesting thing is that there has developed a standard pricing for these films. Generally, the pay cable networks will license a film for approximately 25% of the domestic theatrical box office. There are caps to this license fee in the case of a huge box office hit. But there are no minimums for the films that don't do well in the theaters. The really nice thing for the studios is that there are virtually no expenses involved, other than the royalties they have to pay to talent.

And the other nice thing is that these deals are not limited to the studios. Many independent Producers who have made films which failed to get theatrical release have found the pay cable market to be a great primary market. HBO has licensed in a year as many as 40 films that didn't get theatrical release.

These networks are also working with Producers to produce original content (film and television). And they have been very successful doing it. Producers have found these networks to be willing to take creative chances that the studios and the broadcast networks would not take. Just look at the Emmy Award Nominations over the past five years to see the impact of the pay cable networks on the industry. HBO has had almost twice as many nominations as did NBC, which had the most of any commercial broadcast network. Netflix also beat NBC.

BROADCAST TELEVISION / BASIC CABLE

In the early days of television, the film studios thought television was the enemy that would keep people from going to the theaters. That didn't turn out to be true. Then the studios found that television was a good customer, and all the major networks broadcast a movie-of-the-week (MOW) at least once and often on several nights of the week. It was great, ready-made programming at a time when broadcast television programming was still finding its footing. Then in the 1990s the broadcast networks began to cut back on airing theatrical movies. They were now producing so much original content that they didn't need to fill time with a film. Plus, the films were not proving as strong a ratings draw as a new drama or sitcom. And they had all the failed pilots of new shows to air as MOWs. The studios weren't too concerned or upset because by now they were all part of the same conglomerates, and the studios were making almost all of the television content, the new dramas and sitcoms, for the broadcast networks.

The basic cable networks followed a similar progression but with much older films because the pay cable networks had all the new stuff tied up. An enterprising Ted Turner actually bought the MGM studio in 1986 for the express purpose of getting its library of films for his superstation and then his cable networks.

There is a pricing standard for licenses in this market in the same way as there is for pay cable. The license fee is normally between 10% and 15% of the domestic theatrical box office. There is also a cap on the amount and the deal is normally for four years with a certain number of airings. The more airings, the higher the price. And again there is virtually no cost to the studio, except for the royalties.

Because this market has many networks, the overall amount spent in this market is estimated to be $3.5 billion. More and more of these deals are being done as shared windows between broadcast television and basic cable networks. This is particularly true when they are part of the same conglomerate. For example, ABC, the Disney Channel and ABC Family network combined to pay $130 million for the first two *Harry Potter* films. The CW and TBS shared a deal worth $160 million for 10 years of *The Lord of the Rings* trilogy.

For independent Producers there are also opportunities in this area, primarily with the basic cable networks. For example, Hallmark Channel recently announced that they have over 30 feature films in development, most of them from non-studio sources.

MISCELLANEOUS

So we've worked our way through the windows, but I'm sure you noticed that we skipped one – Miscellaneous. It's up there with foreign/international without a specific window. That's because it's varied and sometimes completely random, depending on the film and the strategy of the studio distribution team.

There really are no standards because each film presents different opportunities. Not all films have the plush toy potential of *The Lion King* or the action figure lure of *Star Wars*. Not all films have an award winning song or artist to put on a soundtrack. Some films are appropriate for airline viewing, but many are not. And of course, video games, TV shows, and theme park rides can inspire a film or can be based on a film.

Here are some interesting facts and figures to ponder:

1. Disney has sold over $2 billion in plush toys from *The Lion King*;

2. the first *Cars* movie did almost a $1 billion in merchandise sales;

3. before the second set of three *Star Wars* films came out beginning in 1999, Lucasfilms had collected an advance of $148 million from Hasbro for action figures AND $2 billion

from Pepsico for promotional rights with all their brands and their restaurants, including Pizza Hut and Taco Bell. The combined production budget for all three films was only $350 million; and

4. Universal had a deal with Walmart on the film *Hop* for over 100 licensed products tied to the film.

CONCLUSION

So we began this chapter looking for $13.4 billion to make the studios at least break even on their theatrical cost for the films they released in one year. To make this easier, we will follow one "typical" or 'average' film from domestic box office through the ancillary markets to demonstrated how this works. We will assume that our film is one of approximately 140 released by the studios in the domestic theatrical market and it made $100 million in domestic box office. That equates to $50 million in film rentals and a producers gross revenue of $32.5 million after distribution costs and fee. Our theatrical costs are estimated to be $122.7 million. That gives us a **loss of $90.2 million** on this film after domestic theatrical but before ancillary markets.

Using what we've learned about the ancillary markets we can project the following cash flow for our film.

Foreign / International markets – we will use the 2017 international box office of $29.5 billion; and a conservative studio share of 70% or $20.6 billion; the typical film rentals for foreign are only 40% and there is a 45% distribution fee; that leaves $4.5 billion coming to the studio. We divide that by 140 (the number of films released) and get $32.4 million for our film. In addition, we will estimate the foreign home video market to be $10 billion overall with $5 billion of that for the studios; after distribution expenses, fees and royalties, 80% of this goes to the studios; so the studio income for this average film is $20 million. That means that the foreign ancillary market contributes $52.4 million to our film. This still leaves us with a loss, but much less – **$37.8 million**.

<u>Home Entertainment</u> – Our overall domestic home entertainment market is estimated to be $20.5 billion; and the studio share is 95% or $19.5 billion. After expenses and royalties, approximately 80% goes to the studio, that means $15.6 billion to be divided by 140; giving $111.4 million for our film. That's a lot of money! More than domestic theatrical and more than foreign. It means that our film goes from a loss of $37.8 million to a **profit of $73.6 million**.

That's great, but we don't have to stop there.

<u>Pay Cable</u> – is next and the normal licensing fee of 25% of domestic box office means that we get an additional $25 million.

And finally, <u>Broadcast and/or Basic Cable</u>, generates another $12.5 million, using 12.5% of domestic box office as the licensing fee. Remember the standard range was 10% to15%.

So at the end of the initial exploitation of this film, it has a <u>profit of $111.1 million</u>. Everyone is happy. And it really doesn't end for many films because they continue to sell or rent DVDs, and they can go into second and third rounds of licensing in SVOD, Broadcast/Basic Cable. And then maybe a sequel comes out, and the original gets new energy and makes more money as people want to remember it or catch up before watching the sequel. Or if its Disney, they hide a film away for years and then re-release it to a whole new generation of viewers.

If we use the above as an average for the results of the films released by the studios, then we can see how they cover their negative cash flow coming out of the domestic theatrical market, and how they eventually make a substantial profit on their slate of releases. And that would not include those blockbuster films that would substantially raise the "average". All of this profit is more than enough to pay for their development costs, overhead, and lavish lifestyles.

SUPPLEMENTAL MATERIAL – CHAPTER 11- ANCILLARY MARKETS

Review Questions

1. What market sits on top of the chart for Ancillary Markets? Why is that market so important for the success of a film in the ancillary markets?

2. How would you compare the growth of the domestic theatrical market and the foreign market over the past five years?

3. What is happening to the timing of the ancillary market windows and what factors are influencing this change?

4. What is the largest foreign theatrical market? How does it compare to the domestic market?

5. What is the size of the foreign theatrical market and what percentage of it goes to the studios?

6. What are some factors that work against studio films in foreign markets?

7. What percent of US Households have at least one DVD player?

8. What is the estimated size of the home entertainment market and what percentage of that market goes to the studios?

9. What is the origin of the VOD market? And how has it grown over the past fifteen years?

10. What are the different types of deals between the studios and the MSOs for VOD?

11. How many US Households have broadband internet

access?

12. What is an output deal between studios and pay cable networks?

13. What is the standard pricing guideline for pay cable licenses?

14. What are some of the reasons the broadcast networks cut back on the airing of feature films starting in the 1990s?

15. What is the standard pricing guideline for broadcast/basic cable licenses?

16. What are some of the components of the Miscellaneous market and would they be good for all films?

17. Which ancillary market provides the most money to our sample film to help it make a profit?

Industry Speak

Ancillary markets- geographical or technological areas of demand for film which are generally supplemental to the domestic theatrical market; includes home video, VOD/SVOD, foreign, pay cable, and television

Ancillary rights - the right of a Producer to exploit the literary material or the film in the ancillary markets; also includes rights to sequels, remakes, television series, stage plays and sound recordings

Day-and-date – a theatrical release strategy that means releasing a film in domestic and foreign markets on the same day

Direct-to-video release - a feature film produced without any intention of seeking a domestic or foreign theatrical release or which goes into video release because it was unable to attract a theatrical distribution deal; generic phrase still used with the

DVD and VOD/SVOD markets

Premium VOD – a plan to provide a very expensive VOD for a film that is currently in theatrical release

Subscription Video on Demand, SVOD – a service where subscribers gain access to a library of film and video content that has been licensed from Producers or produced by the SVOD provider

Window - a limited time during which an opportunity should be seized or it may be lost. In film, the period of time in which a film is available in a given market (theatrical, home video, pay cable, television)

Video on Demand, VOD – a service provided by cable operators that allows their subscribers to access film and video content that has been licensed from Producers; content can be free to subscribers or there can be an additional fee

Further Activities

1. Think of some reasons that the international box office started to grow so large after 2000. What has happened in the world over the past almost two decades?

2. Do you think premium VOD has a future and why or why not?

3. As an independent Producer, do you have a feature film in development? Is so, draw up a plan of which ancillary markets you might approach for funding.

Further Reading & Research

Go to the MPAA website http://www.mpaa.org and find the latest Theatrical Market Statistical Report, which is published every spring (March or April).

Go to boxofficemojo.com and check out the Worldwide Grosses

for the latest year and see how the worldwide box office breaks down for the different films.

Check the most recent Emmy Award nominations to see the impact of the pay cable networks and the SVOD services on the television industry.

Get in the daily habit – read the industry trade papers to know what is going on in the industry. For film and television, I recommend *Variety, Hollywood Reporter, Broadcasting & Cable,* and *Current.* They are all available online. Another good resource for what's happening in television is the *Cynopsis.com* online newsletter. For documentary and nonfiction work, I suggest *Real Screen.*

12

DISTRIBUTION

WHAT IS A DISTRIBUTOR?

D istributors are very powerful gatekeepers in the film and video industry. They control the delivery of virtually all films and videos from Producers to almost every market, including theaters, television and cable networks, home video outlets, and foreign markets. Distributors are businessmen and women who have a sensibility for the creative world of the filmmaker and who also have an ability to manage a very competitive business venture. The distribution of a film or video often requires a substantial financial risk on the part of the distributor, and they are, therefore, very careful in their selection of which films or videos to distribute.

There are two essential truths about distribution.

1. Distributors need films and, therefore, need Producers; and

2. Distributors will not take on your project, no matter how much they love it, unless they are sure that they can make money from it.

It is not uncommon for a successful distributor to become a Producer or to enter into co-production deals with filmmakers. It is also possible for a filmmaker to distribute his or her own film or video, but this is a difficult and time-consuming job that takes the filmmaker far away from his creative work.

Distributors often concentrate in serving a specific market or markets. Very few distributors, other than the studios, cover all markets, although they will often try to get worldwide distribution rights from an independent Producer. If an independent distributor has worldwide distribution rights to a film per the distribution contract, they will often use a series of sub-distributors to market the film in areas where they have no expertise.

GENERAL CONCEPTS

Distributors need Producers. Distributors need a steady flow of new films to remain active in the various markets in which they operate. Since most distributors do not produce their own films, they rely completely on Producers for their films. One partial exception to this are studio distributors, who rely on their own studios for films. But studio distributors also distribute films that they have acquired or licensed from independent Producers or production companies.

Their need for product means that all distributors keep a close watch on the industry to find Producers with films that they may want to distribute. A large distributor may be tracking as many as 10,000 films in various stages of their development and production. We will discuss how a Producer gets on the distribution radar screen later in this chapter.

Distributors are in business to make money. Sure, the people who own and work for distribution companies love films, or you would hope so. But they are in business to make money and distributors will not take on a project, no matter how much they love it, unless they are sure that they can make money from it. I know this is repetitious, but it can't be stressed enough.

Leverage. Distribution is based on a contractual arrangement between Producer and distributor. As such, it is the result of often extensive negotiations between the parties over the terms of the distribution contract, which are discussed later in this chapter. As with all negotiations, the concept of leverage applies. Leverage basically means the ability to influence the negotiation process. The amount of leverage that a party has is directly proportional to their experience and to what assets they bring to the negotiation table. In general, the distributor has the most leverage in these negotiations. A first-time Producer with a feature fiction film that has played at film festivals but not won awards will have a lot less leverage than a first-time Producer whose feature fiction film has just won the top prize at the Sundance Film Festival. They both have a lot less leverage than the Producer whose first five films all made over $100 million at the domestic box office. Producers who are not experienced negotiators, and few are, should consider hiring a representative to conduct the negotiation. This could be their agent, attorney or Producer's rep.

TYPES OF DISTRIBUTORS

There are three general types of distributor: studio, independent, and foreign.

Studio Distributor

The major film studios all have a distribution operation that is either owned by the studio or co-owned by the larger conglomerate that owns the studio. These studio distribution operations will, of course, distribute all the films that the studio produces. Most of them are experienced and active in the domestic theatrical, home video/VOD/SVOD, television and cable, and all foreign markets. These are substantial operations with hundreds of employees, offices worldwide, and very large budgets. Most of them also distribute films produced outside their studio. They do this because their own studio production operation will probably produce 15 to 20 films per year, and this is not enough to keep the distribution operation busy and profitable. To obtain other films to distribute, the studio distribution operation will make contractual arrangements with independent production companies to distribute the films that these companies produce. These are normally companies that the studio management knows to be successful Producers of quality films. They are often owned by people who have previously worked for a studio. When a studio distributor agrees to distribute all of the films that an independent production company makes, this is called an output deal. Output deals are essential assets for independent production companies in

179

their on-going efforts to raise money for new films.

Studio distribution operations are organized as profit centers, and they charge a distribution fee to both their own studio and to independent production companies. It is not uncommon for the distribution operation of a studio to make money while the studio production operation loses money.

Independent Distribution Company

Film and video distribution in the domestic market is a business that has attracted many smart and aggressive business people over the years. They often start out by distributing one or two films that they believe will be successful in a niche market such as foreign language films, gay and lesbian films, or documentaries. If they are successful with the first film(s), they reinvest their profits in licensing and distributing more films. An example of a successful company that started this way is Miramax. Miramax was started in 1979 by the brothers Harvey and Robert Weinstein and named after their parents Miriam and Max. Their idea was to distribute foreign language films in New York and possibly other major East coast cities. The company began with one film and eventually got into producing, won awards, and in 1993 was acquired by Disney in a $60-million-dollar deal.

Because distribution involves a significant financial risk for these companies, a string of several unsuccessful films will often cause a distribution company, particularly a newer company, to fail. For this reason, it is essential that a Producer investigate distributors who express interest in their film to make sure that the distributor is financially strong and can fulfill the various commitments they make in the contract. Lawyers and accountants call this research "due diligence".

Foreign Distribution Company

The foreign distribution company is very similar to the independent distribution company except that it operates in one foreign market. These foreign markets are either defined as a single country, for example France or Germany or Japan, or as a territory which would include multiple countries, for example the Middle East, Africa or Latin America. A foreign distribution company might serve as a sub-distributor for a studio distributor if the studio distributor does not have its own operation in that territory. A similar arrangement would be done with an independent distribution company that has worldwide distribution rights to a film but does not have its own foreign operations. In addition, a foreign distributor can also enter into a distribution contract directly with an independent production company or Producer. This distribution contract can also be involved in specific types of financing - Negative Pick-up and Pre-sale - which are described in chapter 14.

WHAT DISTRIBUTION INVOLVES

Distribution is first and foremost a business. It is a business that takes films from Producers and gets them to the marketplace, which includes theaters, television, cable and all the other ancillary markets. All of this is done with extensive legal contracts between the parties, complicated financial calculations and oversight, and, ideally, a lot of good faith.

What do Distributors do?

There are six primary functions of a distributor:

> A. Know the markets
>
> B. Know the Producers
>
> C. Create a marketing campaign
>
> D. Have a backroom operation
>
> E. Collect payments
>
> F. Keep accurate and honest accounting records

A. Good distributors know their markets. It is their business to know who is buying, what they are buying, and how much they are paying. Distributors are generally on a first name basis with buyers. This is particularly true with theatrical distribution, which is still an intensely personal, one-to-one sales kind of business. Because of the variety and complexity of the various markets, a distributor will often specialize in one or in a few select markets. It is very uncommon for a single distributor, other than a studio distributor, to work in all markets. It is common, however, for a distributor to want to control all of the markets as we'll learn later when we look at the distribution deal.

Once a distributor and Producer have reached an agreement and the film is ready to distribute, the distributor presents the film to potential buyers. For most markets there are a number of potential buyers, and it is the distributor's job to find the one who will pay the most for the film and do the best job of exploiting the film in that market. For the domestic theatrical market, the buyers are the exhibitors who own the theaters. The exhibitors will enter into a competitive bidding process for a high budget studio film with plenty of star-power. But they are more reluctant to take on low budget, independent films with no recognizable actors. It is with these films that distributors' personal relationships with buyers can make the difference between a successful release and a failure. For the pay television market, buyers are the premium pay cable networks such as HBO, Showtime and Starz. And for the U.S. television market, buyers are the broadcast networks and the cable networks.

B. Good distributors also know the Producers. They keep track of which projects are in what stages of production, starting with development or pre-production. Films are the lifeblood of a distributor's business, and Producers are the driving force behind the creation of films. Therefore, there is a mutual need and dependency that generally works to everyone's advantage. In every situation, distributor and Producer enter into a Distribution Agreement, which is discussed in detail below.

C. The good distributor develops an overall marketing campaign using a variety of methods to get the Producer's film noticed by buyers and/or audience. This campaign will include an advertising and promotion plan, a festival and market strategy, and the production of various marketing materials. This campaign is often done with the advice of, and occasionally requires the consent of the Producer.

The advertising plan will include the use of television and radio spots, billboards, bus stop posters, print (newspaper and magazine) ads and internet ads. The promotional plan will include television and radio talk-show appearances by the key creative talent (director and actors), promotional tie-ins with retailers (particularly fast food chains), an internet site, and an active presence on social networking sites such as Facebook and Twitter. The distributor will also produce a theatrical trailer and a poster, for use by exhibitors.

The distributor's marketing strategy might also include a strategy for exposure of the film at the various film festivals and film markets in the U.S. and around the world. International festivals such as Cannes, Berlin, Toronto, and Venice will effectively showcase studio-made films, while domestic festivals such as Sundance will do wonders in raising the profile of an independent film. There are also film markets, such as the American Film Market, that showcase independent films. Several of the major festivals such as Cannes and Toronto also have film markets in addition to their film festival activities.

Another key component of a marketing strategy is the release pattern for the film. There are several patterns that are used. The goal of the strategy is to obtain the maximum audience for the film with the available marketing budget. There are a number of factors involved including: the genre, MPAA rating, availability of theaters, optimum season for release, anticipated critical reception and word-of-mouth, and the overall quality of the film (any award potential).

A studio film will normally get a <u>wide release</u> in more than 3,000 theaters nationwide. This is also called a <u>general release</u> and includes a major advertising campaign on a national level. A studio film with larger expectations than normal because of budget and star power is a called a <u>tent-pole film</u> and will be released in more than 5,000 theaters, or in some cases more than 10,000 theaters.

A low budget independent feature often requires special handling and is given a <u>limited release</u> which is generally under 100 film or digital prints in select theaters across the country. The marketing campaign for the limited release concentrates in the various cities by advertising in local newspapers and local television stations and with promotion using the same outlets. An <u>art-house release</u> is similar, but with only 5 to 10 film or digital prints, and even less advertising and promotion. If this type of film does well in the limited or art-house release, a distributor would possibly expand coverage to additional theaters in more cities and with more money for advertising. This strategy is also called a <u>platform release</u>, because it uses the success of a film in one set of theaters to justify, and pay for, the next stage or platform of the release. Studios occasionally use a platform-type strategy with a big picture by opening in 10 to 15 major cities and hoping to garner positive reviews before a general release the film.

Another variation on the limited release, particularly for independent films, is the <u>market-by-market release</u>, which has a few film or digital prints (10 to 20) concentrated in one city or region to take advantage of a limited advertising budget. These same prints are then moved to another city or region with local advertising targeted to that area.

<u>D</u>. Once a distributor has successfully sold a film or video to a buyer, the distributor turns to its backroom operation to handle the details of the transaction. The first task is to fulfill the order. For a theatrical buyer, this involves getting a print of the film – film or digital - and shipping it to the exhibitor. For a television/cable buyer, the distributor prepares a master digital file of the film from the Producer and ships it or sends it electronically to the network. If the buyer is from a foreign market, the distributor is also responsible for either dubbing the film or having it subtitled. If it is for the home video market, the distributor will

manufacture the DVDs and Blu-rays from a master tape or a digital file. A big part of this operation is to monitor the buyer to make sure that the film or digital print is returned or that the digital transfer is secure. Actual film prints and digital media are expensive to make and each set is used over-and-over again. Also, in a world where films are pirated and sold on street corners, access to prints or digital files has to be tightly controlled.

E. The distributor is also responsible for the all-important task of collecting payments from buyers. This is often a challenge, and a large distributor with an ongoing relationship with a buyer will obviously have more leverage when it comes to collecting the money that it is owed. Collecting money can be particularly difficult with foreign buyers, not because they are untrustworthy, but because they may operate in a country with strict rules and restrictions on foreign currency exchange. The critical thing for Producers to understand is that they will not get money from the distributor until the distributor gets money from the buyers.

F. The distributor must also keep an accurate and honest accounting of all the money spent and received related to the different films that it markets. This is the area where issues of direct and indirect expenses and the cross-collateralization of expenses and revenues are relevant (and discussed in detail below). As with any complex business arrangement, it is important for a Producer to consider a periodic audit of the distributor's books to maintain a satisfactory level of honesty and trust.

THE DISTRIBUTION DEAL

The distribution deal is a complex legal agreement that results from often arduous negotiations between Producer and distributor. The distribution deal represents a license and not the purchase of a film. This distinction is confusing because the industry insists on calling these deals "acquisitions", which would lead a sensible person to think of a purchase. The distinction is, of course, important to a Producer because a Producer always wants to retain copyright ownership of their film.

The relative leverage of both parties is determined by the nature of the film, the Producer's experience, and the distributor's current inventory of films. A good lawyer, with experience in these kinds of deals, is a must for even the most experienced Producer. In some areas of the country, particularly in major metropolitan centers, there are organizations of local lawyers who provide pro-bono or inexpensive assistance to artists. One such group is the Washington Area Lawyers for the Arts in Washington, D.C., www.wala.org,

> Critical items in the typical distribution deal are
> the following:
> Term
> Media and Markets
> Territory
> Advance
> Fees and Expenses
> Marketing strategy and commitments
> Delivery schedule
> Right to audit
> Arbitration

Term

The term of a contract is the number of years that the contract will be valid. For a distributor it seems like it can never be long enough, and they have a compelling reason for this. The reality of distribution is that it takes a long time for a film to work its way through all of the windows of opportunity for the different markets. As we saw in chapter 11, for most films, eventual financial success relies on it being exploited in most of the different markets. This can take up to five, even ten years. From a Producer's viewpoint, however, it will be very painful to have a long term contract with a distributor who they believe is not doing a good job exploiting the film. A new Producer will not have much leverage to negotiate on this point. So it is critical to investigate the distributor and ascertain its track record with similar films. If only one distributor offers a distribution contract, then the Producer often must sign and hope for the best.

Media and Markets

Media and Markets refers to the different areas of exploitation for a film, including domestic theatrical, home video/VOD/SVOD, television/cable, foreign etc. You should get the idea by now that the distributor will want the rights to all the media and markets, whether or not they specialize in or have experience in them. Generally, they get this because it follows the realities of the business. As we learned in chapter 11, it takes the cash flow from most, if not all, media and markets to allow the distributor to recoup its expenses and make a profit.

A word of warning to Producers – fractionalization. Fractionalization refers to agreements made by a Producer with different distributors for different markets. It is often a way that Producers obtain the financing for a film using either a negative pick-up or pre-sale type of financing arrangement. The danger for a Producer is that these existing agreements might cause another distributor to not want the film for a different market. The market we're most concerned with is the domestic theatrical market for a feature film. We know that most films do not make money in the domestic theatrical market and that they rely on the ancillary markets to finally make money. We also know that domestic theatrical release is often a major factor in the success of a film in other markets. So, if we approach a distributor for the domestic theatrical release of a film and tell him that certain other markets are already taken by other distributors, what do you think he will say? Right. The distributor might pass on the film because there are not enough ways to recoup the money they will spend on the domestic theatrical release. This is particularly true if the ancillary market that the Producer sold first was international or home video/VOD/SVOD, which are major revenue markets. A Pre-sale to one of these markets is often done, but it is not advisable to pre-sell both markets. Or if one of these ancillary markets has been fractionalized, the domestic distributor will probably cut way back on its upfront exposure for P&A, and forget about an advance.

Territory

This refers to the geographical coverage of the contract. The standard territories are: North America, which includes the U.S. and Canada; the individual countries in Europe; Eastern Europe; Australia/Far East; Latin America including Mexico; and "others", which includes China, India, Middle East, Israel, Turkey, and South Africa – generally taken as separate units.

For feature films, including theatrical documentaries, a distributor will often ask for world-wide distribution rights to give them the greatest potential for success. For a studio distributor with its own international operations, this is usually a sensible arrangement. With an independent distributor, however, it can present issues. Normally the independent distributor has strength in one or maybe a couple of territories. For the other parts of the world they work with foreign distribution companies or sub-distributors who specialize in a foreign territory. This process increases the cost to the Producer because the sub-distributor takes a fee and then the main distributor also takes a fee (but at a smaller percentage than they take when they are the direct distributor). However, it can be exceptionally time consuming for a Producer to negotiate individual distribution deals with all the different territories; and this is time the Producer could spend on developing her next project.

Advance

An advance is always the sexy part of a distribution contract. That's because it's so desirable and so hard to get. When it happens, it is normally for a Producer with a feature fiction film that several distributors want and are prepared to bid for. A Producer might gain this kind of leverage with a film that has won a major festival award or has a major star acting in it.

An advance is money that the distributor pays to the Producer in advance of the actual distribution of the film. It is money that would ordinarily have come to the Producer in increments over a long period of time as the film works its way through the various markets and territories. The distributor then pays itself back from the distribution proceeds of the film. If a film is very successful, the Producer would get additional money from the film after the distributor recoups the advance. As a businessperson, the distributor will calculate the amount of the advance on: (1) how much she believes the film will make in distribution and (2) how competitive it will be among distributors to secure the distribution rights to the film.

For a Producer, an advance does not have to be repaid no matter how poorly the film performs in distribution.

Many independent Producers will use the advance to pay for the licenses for music rights and other copyrighted elements in the film and to pay crew deferrals and other debts. The amount of an advance is not directly related to the production cost of a film, so there may be a handsome profit for the Producer of a low-budget film that is the subject of an aggressive bidding war among distributors.

Fees and Expenses

The general flow of cash for a feature film from the audience through the distributor to the Producer is described in chapter 10. To review, the distributor collects film rentals from exhibitors and gross receipts from the various ancillary markets. No money goes to the Producer without having first gone through the distributor. This is designed by the distributors to make sure that they can first cover their expenses and take their fee. It is part of the contract and reflects the overall leverage of the distributors. There are no exceptions.

There are two general types of expenses that distributors incur: direct expenses and indirect expenses.

Let's deal with indirect expenses first. These are expenses for the general overhead of the distributor such as office rent, staff salaries,

THE PRODUCER'S SOURCEBOOK

business insurance, etc. A distributor is not allowed to recoup these kinds of expenses from the money generated by a Producer's film. They must cover these expenses with the distribution fees that they earn.

Direct expenses, on the other hand, are those expenses that are incurred by the distributor in the course of distributing the Producer's film. Direct expenses are recouped from the money earned by the film.

Most direct expenses fall under the industry designation of prints and advertising - P&A. Film prints are the physical copies of a film that are manufactured and sent to theaters for screening. For a 35mm print of a 2-hour feature film, the cost is approximately $10,000 per print. Digital media is not as expensive but does run several thousand dollars per hard drive unit, which is good for one screen. At any one point in time, a film might have anywhere from a hundred to several thousand prints running around the world. Some feature films go into ultra-wide distribution with 10,000 prints. Film or digital, this is an expense that the distributor pays before ever getting a penny of revenue back from a film.

According to the Motion Picture Association of America, the studios spend an amount to market a film that is approximately 50% of the cost of making the film. This includes advertising a film using such media as newspapers, network TV, the internet, cable TV, radio, billboards and magazines. The highest percentage of advertising money goes to network TV. Marketing expenditures include production/creative services for trailers and posters. They also include market research (which is standard for studio releases) and promotional and publicity efforts on behalf of films. These are all costs that the distributor incurs up-front.

Hopefully it is clear that the distributor, particularly an independent one, takes on a very large financial risk with the P&A expenses. Of course, the studios own their films and this investment is part of their doing business, but it certainly increases their risk. For other distributors who license films and spend a lot of money up front, it should be obvious why they demand that they be paid first; remember it is the Producers who maintain copyright ownership of the films.

In most cases, it is clear whether an expense is direct or indirect, although distributors have various names for them. Most distribution contracts will have or should have a clause that specifically lists what is allowed as a direct expense, or an expense that is recouped from the cash flow from a film. There are, however, some expenses which fall into a gray area. These include the expenses to attend a film festival or market by a distributor who is representing several films from different Producers. Should the costs be divided equally among the films being represented? This would seem logical/fair from a Producer's point-of-view. Distributors, however, are worried that not all of the films will generate activity or income. They are then inclined to cross-collateralize, which means that they will deduct all of their expenses for the festival or market from the film(s) that generated income. Some distribution contracts specifically mention this practice and others are silent on the matter.

While it may not seem to make sense for a distributor to spend more than she thinks she can recoup from a film, it does happen. Distributors are only concerned that a film generates enough revenue to recoup its expenses and pay their fee. A Producer is advised to have in the contract a cap or a maximum amount that the distributor can spend on the film. This cap can fluctuate and increase if the film is more successful than originally forecast.

All distributors charge a fee for their services. This is always calculated as a percentage, but the amount of the percentage and manner in which the percentage is calculated can vary. Distribution fees are fairly standard within a market. For example, the standard distribution fee for a domestic theatrical feature film release is 35%. A common distribution fee in the foreign markets is 45%. Normally the fee is applied to the amount of money that remains after the distributor has deducted the direct expenses from the money or revenue that the film has generated. This is called a net deal, which relates to the term that accountants use for this deduction of expenses from revenue. This is the most common type of deal and is preferred by Producers over the gross deal, which allows distributors to take their percentage from the revenue amount before the deduction of direct expenses. This gross deal method obviously results in a larger fee for the distributors. In either of these types of deals, distributors then deduct their own indirect expenses from the fees they receive, and what's left is their profit.

Marketing strategy and commitments

Producers look to the distributor for their expertise in marketing films. It is their track record of success with similar films that the distributor uses to sell the Producer. It makes sense that a Producer of a romantic comedy might not select a distributor that only handles horror films. A distributor will generally describe the strategy they anticipate for the release of the film in the various markets and territories.

The discussion of this strategy includes negotiation over a release commitment by the distributor. This means simply that the distributor commits to release the film in a certain market by a specified date, or a certain period of time after the final film is delivered to the distributor. There are reasons for a distributor to not rush into releasing a film immediately upon delivery. There are certain times of the year when certain types of films seem to do better. For example, the traditional wisdom is that big action films do best in the summer months while relationship dramas are better released in the spring and fall. And distributors wish to avoid competition with other films with similar themes, story lines or actors that are already in release or scheduled for release. Occasionally, however, a distributor will get cold feet on a film and not want to risk any money on a release. Several films involving urban terror were not released in the year or so after September 11, 2001. There have been similar responses after most tragic events if the film in any way contains material that is comparable to or relates to those events. Films that deal with difficult social, religious or political issues might cause a distributor to try to avoid release. Having a release commitment from the distributor insures the Producer that the film will either get released or the distribution contract is voided. The Producer can then try to find another distributor.

If the initial release of a film is in the domestic theatrical market, then the release commitment also includes a P&A commitment and the release strategy for the film. As we have seen earlier in this chapter, there are a number of standard release patterns and strategies for theatrical releases which depend on the nature of the film and the size of the marketing budget.

Delivery schedule

All distribution contracts will contain a delivery schedule which lists the material that the Producer must give the distributor before the contact is final. Generally, advances are not given until this point. These deliverables include the technical requirements for the master film negative, legal records including chain-of-title contracts, copyright registration and releases, proof of insurance, and publicity materials such as still photos taken during production of the film. Some distributors will ask for accounting records such as bank statements and canceled checks; but smart Producers know that they only need to provide these types of records if the distributor invested money in the production of the film.

As will be further discussed in chapter 23, the important thing for Producers to know is that they should be compiling this material from the very beginning of the development of the film.

Right to audit

President Reagan had a phrase for his dealings with the Soviet Union prior to its breakup in 1989. He said he would "trust but verify". That phrase is certainly appropriate for a Producer when dealing with a distributor.

While most distributors are honest businesspeople, there are some exceptions. Producers need to be diligent in watching after their own interests. Even with the typical honest distributor, there is reason to be cautious. Distributors typically handle large numbers of complex transactions and large amounts of money, and mistakes can happen.

A distribution contract must include a clause that allows a Producer the right to conduct a periodic audit of the distributor's book and records as they relate to the Producer's film. This is typically done by a Certified Public Accountant (CPA) hired by the Producer who visits the distributor's office during normal business hours. Even if the Producer does not suspect any problems, it is advisable to conduct an audit just to let the distributor know that the Producer is on top of things.

Arbitration

In the event that a dispute arises between the Producer and distributor, most distribution contracts require that it be settled by an arbitrator in an arbitration proceeding rather than in a court with a judge and possibly a jury. This can save both parties time and money, but it also limits the ability of the Producer to appeal an unfavorable decision.

HOW TO FIND A DISTRIBUTOR

If a Producer play her cards correctly, she lets the distributors find her. This is called "generating a buzz". The culmination of this process is the finely orchestrated unveiling of a film at a major film festival. We'll talk about the general strategy of festivals in the next chapter. Here we concentrate on hooking a distributor's interest with the goal to get a distribution deal.

At the risk of sounding like a broken record (or CD or digital download for a more current metaphor), distributors need films. Where can they come in contact with a lot of new films? Film festivals. The major film festivals are crawling with distributors looking for the next breakout independent film. Most of them come with their checkbooks in hand and ready to deal. The trick for a Producer is to make them think that her film is the one they have to have out of the hundreds at the festival.

If a Producer has done his homework properly, the distributors should know that his film exists long before the festival begins. He wants them to put him on their tracking radar and begin to anticipate his film. But that's all, just anticipate, not see. Never send a rough cut or any screening material to a distributor prior to the grand unveiling. No matter what they say, no matter how they beg, do not do it. They will say that they can "visualize the film" from a rough cut, but don't believe them. A rough cut is a rough cut, and it will never get a Producer the best deal for his film. Build the anticipation. Many Producers have a hard time saying "no" to someone who is so eager to see their film. It's human nature. In that case they should consider hiring a Producer's rep who will not only guide him through the process, but will deal with the distributors and be the 'no' person. Having a Producer's rep also sends a message to the distributors that the Producer knows what he's doing and is a very serious Producer with a film to be anticipated. Many Producer's reps are also attorneys and they will be there for the legal negotiations and contract work that has to be done once a distributor is hooked.

To get on the distribution radar, a Producers creates a professional looking press release on his letterhead, which he should have for many uses, and sends it to the trade press. That's really all he needs to do. The trade press will put it into their listings of projects, and the distributors will see it. Then they will call him and become his newest BFF. Keep the press releases going out as the project moves from development to preproduction to production and post production. If a big star or famous director gets attached to the project, send a special press release.

Some Producers send the first press release at the beginning of development and others wait until they have money and are moving into preproduction. For brand new Producers, it's probably better to wait until preproduction for the first release. After he has a track-record, then the fact that he's begun development on a new project will be newsworthy.

The Producer finishes his film, and it gets accepted for competition at Sundance. Now the calls intensify. The distributors will try to get a look before everyone else. That's their job, and they can be very persistent and persuasive. Hold out – get a Producer's rep or attorney. What the Producer wants is to have all the interested distributors together at the screening of his film in the theater with an audience. The better the audience reaction, the more the distributors will want the film, and the more afraid they will be that their competitor will get it first. This begins a bidding war that the Producer's rep or attorney should handle. This little, low budget film may then be the headline news in the trade press the next day.

Some distributors are known for making "pre-emptive strikes" on a film, sometimes sight unseen. They will offer a lot of money to keep the film off the bidding table. The Producer is told that he can take it or leave it within a very short time period before the screening. He takes it, and he's set. He leaves it, and he may get a lot more money in a bidding war. Or, if the audience reaction is not so strong, he may get a lot less money or possibly nothing at all. Producing is not for the faint-of-heart.

And speaking of little, low budget films, a Producer should never brag about how little he spent on making the film. Now don't start with the Robert Rodriguez *el Mariachi* legend. That was a marketing ploy, and it worked for him, but don't expect it to work for anyone else. In most cases, actual negative costs are very hard to estimate from what's on the screen, and that is to the Producer's advantage if he keeps quiet. Let's say that he wants to license his film to a distributor for millions of dollars. But what if he lets it be known that he only spent $100,000 making it. That seriously compromises his bargaining position with the distributors. They know that he doesn't need to have a huge advance to break even or make money. This positioning is especially important if there is only one distributor interested in the film. And don't be concerned that a distributor will find out how much was spent. They do not have any right to inspect the accounting books and records to see how much was spent on the film.

If your film is ready and the timing is not good for the major film festivals, don't panic. A Producer's rep, agent or attorney can arrange a screening for distributors in a theater or screening room. Don't send out DVDs or web access (password protected) viewers. There is no control over how the film will be watched, and almost certainly the viewing will be full of interruptions for phone calls and meetings or screaming kids and needy spouses. Get all the distributors in the theater, same as a festival, and pack the seats with friends and relatives who will laugh or cry in all the right places. Don't invite the crew if this is the first time that they have seen the finished film because they will laugh in all the wrong places.

So what happens if the distributors don't pursue a Producer, and he doesn't get into a major festival? Is he out of luck? It depends on what is his definition of "luck". If it means getting a theatrical distribution deal, then he may be out of luck. If it means getting a distribution deal for the ancillary markets, then there is hope. He probably won't have a Producer's rep or attorney so he will do all of the work but, hey, it's his film.

The Producer takes each market starting with the largest one after theatrical, which is home video/VOD/SVOD, and investigates the distributors. He creates a list of films that are similar to his in terms of genre, star-power, budget, etc; then finds out who distributed those films. They become his primary contact or attack list. Find out how the other films fared in distribution. This information might be tough to find, but he really needs it. If the distributor had a good experience with the similar film, then they will be more open to his film. The reverse is obviously true as well.

If the Producer doesn't have any success finding a distributor in the home video/VOD/SVOD market, then go to the next level of ancillary markets and repeat the process. At whatever level he gets a distribution deal, the distributor will probably want to tie-up all rights to further markets. They want to do this to maximize their potential to make money. For most Producers it is a sensible way

THE PRODUCER'S SOURCEBOOK

to go and will probably result in maximum money for him as well. He can spend a lot of time and money trying to get distributors at each level of ancillary markets when he could be working on his next film.

SELF DISTRIBUTION

This brings us to the topic of self-distribution. Producers make films to be seen by an audience greater than their family and friends. A distribution deal is necessary to achieve a greater audience, but what happens if a Producer fails to find a distributor?

Two critical traits for a Producer are eternal optimism and entrepreneurship. Those traits lead many of us to say, "What the heck, I'll do it myself." There's no magic to distribution. It's just hard work and cash. And even more hard work can often compensate for a lack of cash. We'll discuss some successful techniques for self-distribution, but before that, a word of caution. A Producer should take a moment, a day, a week and decide what are her priorities. She can distribute her film, but it's at the cost of not working on her next project. She has to be brutally honest with herself. Is the current film really worth the time and money? Would that time and money be better spent on the next film, which will be much better because of what she learned making the last one? This is obviously not always an absolute either/or situation. She can try to balance both, but she must be careful that the balance is right for her future.

There are several important components of self-distribution to discuss.

Identifying the audience. The Producer should know this cold, at least from a theoretical POV, but now we need to figure where they are. Where do they live? What theaters do they frequent? How often do they go out to see a film? What SVOD services do they subscribe to? What pay cable networks do they pay for?

Advertising and promotion. Once we know where the audience is,

198

then we have to let them know about the film and motivate them to go see it. Most of us are very familiar with advertising because we see so much of it. But it's a different story when it comes to designing it and placing it. PR people make a lot of money as do advertising people, and it's because they have special skills and experience. Things that a Producer normally does not have. Most Producers today do have experience with social media, but using social media effectively for marketing is a different story.

Four-walling a theater. Dealing with exhibitors is not for the faint of heart. Their multiplexes are designed for maximum profit by putting many butts in many seats. The Producer who is self-distributing normally approaches the small art-house theater and negotiates a deal where they rent the theater for a flat fee, and they keep all the admission dollars. The theater keeps the concessions. It means that the Producer's advertising and promotion had better pay off with lots of people coming to the theater.

Internet distribution. Many Producers today use the internet for distribution and there are several approaches. It is possible to self-release on Amazon through their CreateSpace program. They will make and ship a DVD of the film as it is ordered and pay the Producer a royalty. It's a very good program, but it still requires advertising and marketing by the Producer to get people to know that it is available. Netflix might make a deal to carry the film as part of its SVOD service. Same issue for the Producer to let people know it is there.

DISTRIBUTING DOCUMENTARIES

The nonfiction world is harder to describe in terms of markets and distribution. Some Producers make feature length documentaries that are meant for theatrical release. Others produce 60-minute documentaries for television. And then there are those who create nonfiction films for educational and home video distribution. Then, of course, there are the many, many nonfiction projects that are done on contract for clients – corporate, nonprofit, and government. For now, we will stay with the passion projects that are developed and seek funding for general distribution.

Many Producers who work in this area will develop a proposal for a new film and then share it with a distributor to get their feedback. The distributors know the market, and they are sources of valuable information that can help a Producer shape the project to give it the best chance to succeed. Don't worry, the distributors are not likely to steal the idea – it's in a proposal form so its protected. And they can also be a source of funding if they like the idea and want to get involved.

MARKETS FOR DOCUMENTARIES

Theatrical. Of course, many Producers want to see their documentary in the theaters, big screen and lots of people. Each year there are a handful of feature length documentaries that achieve theatrical distribution. Some years there are fewer than 10 and other years more than 50. But cumulatively they never gain even 1% of the domestic box office. The most successful documentary to date has been for *Fahrenheit 9/11* in 2004, which grossed $119 million domestically and $100 million international. *March of the Penguins* did well in 2005 with $77 million domestic and $30 million international. Only three others in the past twenty-five years have barely managed to go over $20 million domestic.

Television/Cable. This is really the primary market for most documentaries and other nonfiction work. The broadcast networks, except for PBS, don't do much nonfiction anymore, but the cable networks have more than picked up the slack. And there is a niche cable network for almost any interest that is open for a documentary that relates to that interest. Sports docs for ESPN, women's rights for Lifetime, travel for Travel Channel, etc. And then there is HBO, which has a very active documentary division and has won many industry awards with their films, all of which come from independent Producers.

Home Video – VOD/SVOD. This can be a secondary market for those that find a primary release in theaters or on TV/Cable. And it is a primary market for many, many documentaries and nonfiction films. Success in these markets requires a lot of marketing from the Producer to get people aware of the film – very similar to self-distribution. This is a royalty based market with royalties between 5% and 25%.

Educational video. Another secondary market, but one that has actual distributors. These companies have libraries that include feature length documentaries, television/cable film, and lots of self-produced smaller projects. They pay Producers royalties of between 15% and 30%.

GENERAL CONCEPTS FOR NONFICTION

It is not terribly hard to get in the door of a programming executive at PBS or a cable network if there is a strong, clear, story line and a good proposal. This is true even for brand new Producers. These executives need material that will appeal to their audience, and they don't really care where it comes from or who makes it. But they don't respond to pitches the way the fiction film people do, especially not from new Producers.

One mistake that Producers make is that they believe that, if they make a film, a programming executive will buy it, even if that same executive passed on the film in the proposal stage. Sure it sometimes happens for new Producers, but very rarely. What is it that will be in the finished film that wasn't in the proposal? If it is something important, then it should have been in the proposal in the first place. Successful Producers always use other people's money, and that comes from a good proposal.

Festivals and film markets are great for exposure but not always wonderful for selling documentaries or other nonfiction. If a Producer is using a festival or film market to sell their film, that means they have probably made the film using their own money, taken creative shortcuts to save money, and are desperate to get a deal, any deal. That is not a good formula for success. Better to use the festivals and film markets to pitch a proposal, make connections, establish relationships, and just learn more about the different parts of the industry.

SUPPLEMENTAL MATERIAL – CHAPTER 12 - DISTRIBUTION

Review Questions

1. What are the two essential truths of distribution?

2. Be able to discuss the leverage between Producers and distributors with different levels of experience and success.

3. What are the three general types of distributor and how do they differ?

4. Why is it important for a Producer to verify the financial health of an independent distributor that they are considering working with?

5. What are the six primary functions of a distributor?

6. What are components of an advertising campaign?

7. What are components of a promotional campaign?

8. What does the backroom operation entail?

9. Is a distribution contact a license or a purchase?

10. Be sure you know the critical items in the typical distribution contract.

11. What is the danger with fractionalization?

12. What are the two factors that a distribution might use to calculate the amount of an advance to offer a Producer?

13. What is the difference between a distributor taking his fee in a net deal versus a gross deal?

14. How does a Producer create a buzz about his new film?

15. What two traits lead a Producer to consider self-distribution?

16. What are the important components of self-distribution?

17. What are the different markets for documentaries and other nonfiction work? How likely is a theatrical release for a documentary?

18. Will programming executives work with new Producers?

Industry Speak

Acquisition/distribution agreement - The written licensing contract between a Producer and distributor which sets out the terms and conditions under which the distributor will license and distribute the film. This type of contract does not cover a case where the distributor provides financing for the project

Acquisitions - films that have been independently financed and produced by independent Producers which distributors have acquired a license to distribute

Advance - money obtained up front in anticipation of profits; money paid by a distributor to a Producer prior to the release of the film.

Arbitration - a non-judicial method for resolving disputes; the submission of a controversy, by agreement of the parties, to persons chosen by the parties for resolution

Assignment - a written agreement which is used to transfer some or all of the right, title and interest in a specific property to a purchaser

Audit - an inspection of the accounting records and procedures of a business by a trained accountant for the purpose of verifying the accuracy and completeness of the records

Boilerplate - the terms and conditions found in most contracts, normally in small print, which a party to the contract, such as a distributor, might say are "standard"

Breakout - A significant expansion of a films bookings after an initial period of exclusive or limited engagement; generally, for a film that is a surprise hit

Cap - A ceiling, upper limit or maximum to a provision in a contract

Contingencies - Pre-conditions to a contract, particular events or circumstances which must occur before other obligations are owed

Cross-collateralization - an accounting practice whereby distributors offset their costs and/or losses in one market against their income and/or profits in another market; the offset can also be on one film against another

Day-and-date - a release strategy whereby a film is released in the domestic theatrical market and one or more foreign markets at the same time; can result in a film being exhibited in over 10,000 theaters at one time (*Spiderman 3* – 16,700 theaters)

Deliverables - a term refers to a delivery schedule in a contract, which lists the physical items that are to be provided by the Producer to the distributor before a film will be released

Direct distribution expenses - all costs and expenses in connection with the distribution, advertising and exploitation of a particular film

Display advertising - advertising in newspapers and magazines, which features art work or other information relating to a specific film

Distribution - the licensing of a film in various markets along with the marketing of the film; includes: negotiating with exhibitors and licensees, ordering prints from the lab, planning and implementing the advertising and promotional campaign, transporting the prints to the exhibitors, collecting film rentals and other revenue, accounting for revenue and costs, paying the Producer

Distribution fee - the contractual amount which the distributor charges for its services, does not include direct distribution expenses

Distributor's gross receipts - the total amount of money received by the distributor from all sources for the exploitation of a film

Domestic theatrical market – includes all the exhibitors and theaters in the United States and Canada

Foreign sales agent - person authorized by a Producer or distributor to license rights to the film and exploit the film in a foreign market

Four-wall - A distribution technique where the exhibitor gets a pre-set price for the use of the theater and the Producer keeps all the box office proceeds; concession sales are negotiable

Fractionalized rights - the separating out of various markets or media from the distribution agreement

General release - a release strategy in which a film is exhibited in a large number (1,000 +) of theaters and throughout the country in most of the major U.S. markets at the same time; also called a "wide release" when it goes to 3,000+ theaters

House allowance or "nut" - negotiated dollar amount which represents the estimated operating expenses for an exhibitor during the course of a week

Laboratory access letter - letter signed by the Producer authorizing the film lab to deliver the film negative to the distributor

Leverage - the power to control or influence others during a negotiation

Limited release - a release strategy in which a film is exhibited nationally or in a small, specific area with a limited number of prints (less than 100); sometimes used for test marketing

Marketing campaign - an overall plan or strategy to sell the film and promote audience awareness and anticipation for the film; includes advertising and promotion

Narrow release - a release strategy in which a film is released in a few theaters (+/- 10) in the hope of favorable word-of-mouth reaction that will allow for a wider release in the weeks ahead

Ninety/ten deal - a common distributor/exhibitor deal for split of box office gross; after deduction of the exhibitor's house allowance from the box office gross, the distributor takes 90% and the exhibitor takes 10% for the first week; the distributor's percentage drops 10% with each week to a negotiated minimum percentage (can be as low as 35%)

Platforming - a variation of a narrow release strategy in which the film is opened in a single theater or a small group of key theaters in a major city with the specific intention of widening the run to numerous theaters either in one step or in phases after the film has established itself

Prints and ads (P&A) - The film prints actually distributed to theaters for exhibition and the advertising which promotes the film; also used to refer to the digital assets used for distribution

Promotional activities - part of the marketing campaign, geared toward gaining free media attention and public interest such as interviews, screenings for critics, public appearances by director and/or stars, sneak previews, etc.

Release pattern - the general exhibition plan in which a film is exhibited in a predetermined schedule of territories and number of theaters; the goal is to obtain the maximum audience with the budget available for prints and advertising; factors include: budget, genre, MPAA rating, quality of the film, availability of theaters, optimum season for release and anticipated word-of-mouth

Release strategy and schedule - the plan and timing for the release of a film to the theaters and to all other markets

Residuals and royalties provision - agreement by the distributor that it will pay any residuals or royalties required by guild or other agreements connected with a film

Rollout - a release pattern with scheduled, usually weekly, phases of expanding theatrical exhibition

Saturation booking - a release strategy which schedules a film for exhibition in a large number of theaters in a limited market or area, and supports it with a strong advertising and publicity campaign

Special handling - film marketing strategies for what may be a quality film but one which does not have obvious broad commercial appeal; includes a limited or platform release strategy, a highly targeted advertising campaign and extended runs to build word-of-mouth

Worldwide rights - the right to distribute and exploit a film in all markets and territories throughout the world and the universe

Further Activities

1. Look at the Wikipedia article "List of Film Distributors by Country" and browse through to get a sense for how many

there are in the U.S. and worldwide. Some names you will recognize (the film studios) but most you won't. Click on some of the links to get a further sense of who they are. Try a few from the different countries.

2. Pick a topic such as Environmental Film Distribution or Travel Film Distribution and do a google search. Check out a few of those companies. Look through their catalogue of films. See if they have a part of their website that discusses how they work with Producers.

Further Reading & Research

Get in the daily habit – read the industry trade papers to know what is going on in the industry. For film and television, I recommend *Variety, Hollywood Reporter, Broadcasting & Cable,* and *Current.* They are all available online. Another good resource for what's happening in television is the *Cynopsis.com* online newsletter. For documentary and nonfiction work, I suggest *Real Screen.*

FOR THE INDEPENDENT FILM & TV PRODUCER

13

FILM FESTIVALS

T here are thousands of festivals that actively look for films. The big trick to the festival routine is to carefully select the right festival for a film. Sure it's great to get selected by Sundance or Cannes or Toronto, but does the film have a realistic chance against so many others. And the numbers are daunting. For its recent festivals, Sundance typically receives over 2,500 dramatic feature films and over 1,400 documentary feature films. They selected fewer than 50 for competition and an additional 65 for screening. When the festival started in 1994 they received a total of 250 submissions.

The unfortunate fact is that the big festivals are almost closed shops. The majority of films that are selected are tracked in advance by the festival directors based on their knowledge of what's going on in the industry and on the input they get from trusted sources. These sources are usually Producer reps who work for filmmakers or talent agents representing actors and/or directors. This unfortunately makes it much harder for that unknown "little gem" of a film to make it.

Many of the festivals also conduct a film market where there is an active trading in film projects. Many films are accepted for the film market which were not accepted by the festival. The organizers believe that these films are commercial enough to have a chance to be licensed. These films may be screened in the market for buyers but not for the public. A screening at a film market is not considered a premier by most festivals so it doesn't hurt a Producer's chances to be accepted in a festival elsewhere.

ADVANTAGES

The advantages for a Producer from a festival or even a film market showing are several.

1. Gain exposure to people in the industry as a new or developing talent;

2. Acquisition executives from the distribution companies and the studios might be there to see the film and to meet the Producer;

3. Might even make a deal with a distribution company;

4. Directors of other festivals might be there and will invite the Producer to their festival;

5. Gain a sense of what others are doing and how a Producer stacks up.

Finding festivals is as easy as keeping up with reading in the trade publications. *Variety* publishes a special feature each year on the major festivals. To supplement that, spend some time on the Internet searching for festivals. All festivals have a web site. For example, check out:

http://www.sundance.org/ http://www.slamdance.com/ http://www.berlinale.de/ http://www.sxsw.com/

Film markets are also covered in *Variety*, and they also have web-sites. Check out: The American Film market at http://www.americanfilmmarket.com/ and the Toronto Festival and market at http://www.bell.ca/filmfest

ENTERING FESTIVALS

Here are a few tips on strategy for entering festivals. This assumes that a Producer doesn't have a Producer's rep or an agent. Have a plan of which festivals are best for the film and a schedule of when they happen and their submission deadlines.

One important tool to know about is the web site www.withoutabox.com, which is owned by IMDB, which is owned by Amazon. A Producer simply registers their film on the site and begins using the search engine. The really cool thing about Withoutabox, however, is that it is directly linked to thousands of festivals and makes the process of entering these festivals very simple.

Don't wait until the final deadline to submit. As soon as the festival issues its call for entries get the film submitted, if it's ready. The review process is on-going and early submissions often have a better chance of selection.

Festivals love to premier films. Be careful with festival criteria especially for the larger festivals which may not accept an entry if it has been in another big festival or had a premier in their territory or region. For example, Sundance requires that to be in competition the film must be a U.S. premier and not have played at more than two international festivals.

Make sure to have adequate publicity support materials including a one-sheet, flyers, postcards, posters etc. The one-sheet is a standard 81/2 x 11 sheet with the basic facts of a film including plot summary, key talent, production company contact and a photo or graphic. The flyers and postcards have a good production photo with the logline for the film and the date and time of the screening(s). A Producer must make sure to have taken some good production stills during production.

STRATEGIES FOR WORKING A FESTIVAL

It's hard work.

   A. Make sure to have time and hopefully some money. Make festivals, film markets and overall promotion a part of the budget. The entry fees when submitting to a number of festivals and film markets can add up to hundreds of dollars.

B. If a Producer is accepted to a major festival, then hire a publicist.

C. Have marketing materials ready. They should be available in electronic form to easily e-mail to an interested party. Have some good production stills.

D. A Producer needs to create a "buzz" or awareness of their film. This can come from promotional materials, poster, awards or reviews at another festival, or just talking to as many people as possible.

E. A good, dynamic web-site is essential. A full social media campaign is also a good thing to have. A series of tweets or blogs from the festival can generate interest.

F. Don't show up just for the screening and leave. Spend as much time at the festival as possible, especially before the screening. Use the time before the screening to promote it - there are a lot of other choices for people to make.

G. Try to get others from the cast and/or crew to attend AND work. Treat it like a political campaign, and the goal is to get people to the screening. A Producer will need to be able to work the crowd like a politician. If they can't do it, then make sure to have someone there with them who can.

H. Make sure to have a clear set of goals for the festival. Is the Producer looking for a distributor? Is she looking for funders for her next film?

I. Don't be crushed if nothing happens at the festival. Response from distributors often comes after the festival is over.

J. Be fun, be original, but don't be a jerk.

SUPPLEMENTAL MATERIAL – CHAPTER 13 – FILM FESTIVALS

<u>Review Questions</u>

1. What are the advantages to being in or going to a festival?

2. What are the strategies for entering a festival?

3. What are some of the things to do when at the festival?

<u>Industry Speak</u>

One sheet - a standard size (27" x 41") color movie poster which is used for display at theaters and other locations; also, a standard 8 ½ x 11 sheet with the basic facts of a film including plot summary, key talent, production company contact and a photo or graphic which is distributed to the press and at festivals and markets

Press kit - part of the marketing campaign designed to be offered to the media; generally, contains ad mats, synopsis of the story, cast and crew list, narrative biographies of the director and stars, copies of the reviews of the film and 8 x 10 photographs; an electronic version of the press kit is essential

Press tour - a director and/or stars are made available for the media in the major cities in which the film opens

Producer's representative – a person, normally with industry experience and contacts, who works on behalf of a Producer to secure festival screenings and distribution; can be a lawyer who also negotiates for the Producer

Promotional tie-ins - combines the promotion of a film with a product such as a soft drink or food product

Publicist - the person responsible for promotion and publicity of a film or a person (usually the director or star) through all media

Publicity - any act designed to attract public interest or editorial content as opposed to paid advertising

Trailer - a short (normally less than 3 minutes) promotional film exhibited in theaters as a preview of coming attractions

Further Activities

Further Reading & Research

Go to the web site www.withoutabox.com, which is owned by IMDB, which is owned by Amazon. "The best start here. Sundance, TIFF, SIFF and other world renowned festivals use Withoutabox as their first source to discover talented indie filmmakers. In fact, over half of the festivals on Withoutabox have celebrated 10+ years on the circuit. Each festival on Withoutabox is vetted for filmmaker value prior to going live for submissions."

Check out https://www.filmfestivals.com/. "Since 1995 we connect films to festivals and document the world of festivals worldwide. We offer the most comprehensive festival directory of 6 000 festivals, browse festival blogs, film blogs...and promote yourself for free."

Chris Gore's Ultimate Film Festival Survival Guide, 4th edition, Watson-Guptill Publications

Get in the daily habit – read the industry trade papers to know what is going on in the industry. For film and television, I recommend *Variety, Hollywood Reporter, Broadcasting & Cable,* and *Current.* They are all available online. Another good resource for what's happening in television is the *Cynopsis.com* online newsletter. For documentary and nonfiction work, I suggest *Real Screen.*

14

FEATURE FILM FUNDING

F or a Producer there is nothing more challenging and more rewarding than funding a film. Each genre of film has its unique approaches to funding and related challenges – funding a documentary feature is much different than a television documentary, and funding an independent fiction feature is much different than a studio film. This chapter focuses primarily on the Producer who is funding independent feature films.

OVERVIEW

First thing to know is that there is no such thing as a "standard" deal. And there is no one kind of deal that fits all Producers or all films. All deals are a hybrid of different funding techniques and sources that a Producer normally spends years working to put together. And as a Producer gains experience, she gains access to more funding options that are not available to a new, inexperience Producer. And finally, the different funding techniques can be cyclical in nature, often tied to the health of the economy, the availability of money for investments, and the advantage of tax write-offs.

The overall goal for a Producer as he funds different films, as he gains experience and credibility, is to gain ownership of some or all of a film. It is almost guaranteed that a Producer will give up some ownership, but the ultimate goal is to do as much as possible with other people's money and not have them own most of the film. A new Producer, however, can't afford to be greedy, and it's more important to get the first few films made than to worry about a big percentage of ownership.

Two essential elements for success when seeking funding are information and passion. Information is necessary in order to know the markets and the potential investors, lenders, etc. Know what makes them excited about a film and what scares them – what can get them fired or lose a lot of money. And passion is needed because it is very difficult to do this, and a Producer's passion has to keep them going. Remember that no one in the deal being putting together has as much to gain as the Producer does, even if she's not able to retain much ownership.

THE PACKAGE

It all starts with a package that contains the basic ingredients for success. But what makes up a good or successful package? It's a rhetorical question because the answer is - whatever it takes to get the deal done.

Here are some critical considerations of a good package.

A. A great script. Nothing works without that. Don't spend a second trying to raise money for a script that is not done and the best it can be. That doesn't mean that it won't change as its made but don't ever apologize that the script needs work. This could be all that a Producer has in a package, and it can be successful.

B. Money or material. Directors and actors, even the great ones, all respond to one of two things when a Producer tries to get them attached to a project. If a Producer promises to pay them their going rate for a film, they'll do it. Or if it's a really low/no budget, a Producer needs them to fall in love with the script and feel like it is something they have to do to be a complete artist, even if they are going to be paid SAG or DGA minimum, or sometimes even less. For obvious selfish reasons, their agent will help a Producer with the first approach but will try to shut the door on the second.

C. To succeed, a package has to have a critical mass but what that is will differ from project to project. It can be as simple as a great script. Or it could be a great script and other things we call <u>bankable elements,</u> such as a well-known actor attached to the film. Or a well-known director. Or a great script and two up and coming actors and a hot new director. Generally, script writers don't count for much as a bankable element; not unless the script writer is the best-selling author of the underlying property.

D. It's a business of relationships and anyone, everyone, can prove valuable. The PA on a set could be the daughter of the head of the studio. The studio executive's son is on a soccer team with a Producer's son. A college classmate is the son of a famous actor or Producer. The barista is poised for a breakout role. You never know. So it pays to be nice to everyone and then to remember your friends on your way up the ladder of success. I'm sure you've heard the old adage – be nice to people on the way up because you'll meet them again on the way down. And all of us have ups and downs in this business.

Another other part of the relationship discussion concerns agents. All actors and directors will have them as soon as they get a taste of success. It is always best to not try to circumvent them. They won't be on the Producer's side because they represent the talent, and they make their money when the talent gets paid. But most agents, especially as they start, need clients and need films for their clients. Why not the Producers?

E. Be genuine and honest. A Producer should not try to be someone with more credits and experience than they really have. It's too small an industry to be able to get away with a puffed-up or dishonest resume. And there are plenty of people and companies that are eager to help the newcomer.

F. And finally, keep open to opportunities. There are no rules that a Producer has to follow other than common sense and decency. Understand the standard ways things are done and what the different people have invested in them; but then don't be afraid to try something unique.

TYPES OF DEALS

To examine the different types of deals that Producers make for feature films, we are going to follow a Producer from the beginning of her career to a stellar finish. At each level of her growth, our Producer will have access to new types of deals but will not give up the ability to do deals the way she had done in the past. And the most important thing to remember is that a Producer is judged on getting a film made, not on the artistic merit or even the box office success. A Producer who builds a reputation that they get films made on-time, on-budget, and on-spec (meaning it is very similar to what was proposed) will almost always find work and funding. If the films happen to be successful at the box office, then their career rise is that much faster and further. But a reputation for not getting films finished, or going over budget, or films turning out substantially different than promised, will derail a career before it gets started.

New Producer.

Our Producer is making her first film. It has a budget of less than $500,000 and no-name local talent – good actors but no big credits. Where does she go to get the money?

Her first stop will be family and friends. They know her, believe in her, got her through film school, and want to see her succeed. Now not everyone has a rich relative in the family, and the amount of money that can be raised this way is often small. But small amounts from everyone in a large family can add up. The most important thing, however, is that this is never characterized as a loan or as an investment in the film – it is an investment in the Producer as a member of the family. The other and even more important thing is that the Producer has to be ABSOLUTELY

SURE that the family member can afford to never get that money back, because they never will. If they need the money the next month for rent, DON'T TAKE IT! I cannot emphasize that too much – therefore the capitalizations. 105% of these kind of films never make any money. Accept that and don't tell anyone or promise anything else.

Our Producer then remembers IndieGoGo, Kickstarter (owned by Amazon), and RocketHub. They are a few of the hundreds of crowd funding sites that help people raise money for good causes and creative projects. They are co-op funding operations and not investors or lenders. Think of it as donations or better yet as gifts. In return, the Producer gives them a trinket or other suitably insignificant but meaningful gift. A good crowdfunding campaign has many levels of support possible and each one gets different stuff – a poster, a DVD, an invitation to the cast party… This approach can work very well and has even been used to raise millions of dollars – but by someone with a name and/or for a property with a name ie. *Veronica Mars* the movie based on the television show.

Our Producer's next idea is to go to the bank. After all, that's where the money is. So she marches down to the branch of the local bank or savings and loan and asks for a loan. "What do you have for collateral?" is their question. Local banks make loans involving hard collateral – houses, cars, etc. That's the stuff they understand. So if the Producer wants to take out a second mortgage on her house or borrow against her car title, the local bank is the place. But I hope it is quickly apparent that this is normally a BAD idea. The only way this works is if the Producer has a day job that earns enough money to afford the extra debt service.

The Producer then gets an offer in the mail for a new credit card with no interest for a year and a big line of credit. Perfect, right? WRONG. Credit card debt is the worst – extremely high interest rates. To use them our Producer has to know where the money is going to come from to make the monthly payments.

And finally our Producer can <u>barter</u> for goods and services. Barter is older than money and there are very sophisticated barter networks (BarterNetworksInc.com) around that help people use their professional skills to barter for something else. Craigslist also has a barter section. Sometimes the barter is for credit in the film, and then it's easy. But not many people or vendors really need that. If, however, our Producer is a wiz at website development, and the vendor needs a website – presto, a barter.

<u>Nascent Producer.</u>

Sorry, just a fancy word for beginner but not brand new. Our Producer is now on his second or third film, and his budget has grown to between $1 million and $1.5 million. For actors, he is now in the market for TV faces – those actors who have recurring roles but not starring roles on television shows. His first films went to festivals but none had theatrical distribution.

He is probably way beyond the capacity of family and friends or second mortgages or barters. But by this time he has the beginning of a very nice track record because every project he has done was completed on-time, on-budget, and they looked a lot like what was promised. So he has two new avenues open for him.

<u>Private Investors</u> are not family and friends; they are probably not even someone the Producer knows. Nor are they the people who contribute to crowd funding sites. There are all sorts of private investors from Warren Buffet and his many billions to a local doctor or lawyer or businesswoman who has a small portfolio of stocks, bonds, and other investments – probably real estate. We are talking about people who are called <u>accredited investors</u>, which is a Securities and Exchange Commission (SEC) term that designates someone who is wealthy enough and supposedly smart enough to understand an investment and make a rational decision about one. To be an accredited investor, a person must have a net worth of at least $1 million, not including their primary residence, and make at least $200,000 per year ($300,000 if married). That may seem like a lot, but there are many, many people who fit that definition.

The first thing our Producer has to understand is what investors want to get from an investment. Well, it's first and foremost to make a profit. They want to get their money back and to make more. That's why they have all that money. But we know that investing in a film is a terrible investment almost all the time. So what else does a private investor get? The answer is the excitement of being involved with something different, something that they can talk about at cocktail parties and on the golf course (many of these investors play golf at the country club). Films are sexy to those who don't know how much hard work they are to make.

This kind of, level of, investment is regulated by the SEC, and our Producer has to get a competent lawyer with experience in that type of law to help him prepare the necessary documents to make this investment work. Violating SEC laws can land people in jail, so be sure to get that lawyer. Part of this process will result in the development of an <u>investment prospectus</u>, a legal document, similar in many ways to a proposal, that the investor or their advisors will review – it's call doing their due diligence. Finally, these are investors, and investment means ownership. So our Producer is giving away a big part of the ownership of his films. That's not bad, but it is important to remember.

It is also important for our Producer to remember that even though he doesn't personally know these investors, they are really investing in him, in his track record. And it is very important for him to keep open communications with them – and that includes giving them bad news along with the good news. Don't try to hide things if they are going wrong. Tell them about it and the plan to correct it; and then, hopefully, do it. The nice thing about these people is that they are smart, and while they don't know a focus pull from a three wedge, they know that problems happen in any business. It is the successful Producer who knows how to handle problems, who has done his preproduction, and who is ready.

It is also at this level that our Producer can go to an independent production company with the package and sell it to them. This is called an <u>In-House Deal</u> because the production company buys the entire package and brings it in-house to make it. The Producer ideally negotiates a position for himself as a Producer-for-hire, technically an employee of the company, and continues as the Producer, but now working for the company. He should get a salary and then a Producer's fee once the film is finished. But make no mistake about it, the production company owns the film. So what is the advantage for our Producer? He gets a film made that he developed and produced. It probably gets made at a higher budget than he could have raised on his own. And he gets to work with established people in a successful company, and he may find a home there – it can get lonely out there as an independent Producer – it's not for everyone. These kind of independent production companies pop up all the time, as reported in the trades. They have a pot of money, often an output deal with a studio distributor, and want to make anywhere from two or three and up to a dozen films in a year.

Up and Coming Producer.

The next step for our Producer, assuming she stayed independent, is her fourth or fifth film, now with a budget anywhere from $3 million to $5 million. Serious money. And she is probably casting a TV star for a major role. Earlier films were in festivals and at least one of them won awards. At least one had limited theatrical distribution and decent ancillary success.

At this level the Producer can always keep private investors around. I think it is a good idea to have a continuing relationship with them, even if they are not able to fund the entire budget. I know Producers who shift their investors over to a central company that develops new projects that are then taken out to find the big money for production.

But now we are at a point where our Producer qualifies for a very interesting and very rewarding funding technique called a Negative Pickup Deal. This deal has lots of components and steps. The first step is our Producer goes to several foreign festivals and/or film markets such as Cannes, Berlin and AFM (American Film Market). These are places where foreign distributors come together to meet Producers and license new films. Our Producer pitches her latest film to many foreign distributors and gets genuine interest. They like the material, the talent and the reputation of the Producer for completing her films on-time, on-budget, and on spec - looking like her proposal. They all tell her that they would like to license her film when it is done. They will even sign a contract to do that.

Our Producer needs to understand several things about this deal. One is that it is in the distributor's interest to get a commitment on this film for their country before their competitors do. Second, the Producer will not get any money until she provides the finished film to the distributors. And third, the finished film has to be substantially like the proposed film – story, talent, length, and rating. So our Producer negotiates and signs this kind of distribution contract with different distributors in many foreign countries. And, since these are contracts, our Producer hires a lawyer with experience in this type of work.

Because the foreign distributors are taking some risk by signing this contract – they will have to pay even if the film isn't any good – they want to get a discount off the amount that they would normally expect to pay for a film like this. This discount will be between 10% and 20% of the typical license fee. For example, a distributor in the United Kingdom would pay on average of $250,000 to license this kind of film (similar genre and budget). With a 15% discount, they would only pay $212,500 to license our Producer's film in a negative pick-up deal.

At this point, the Producer has all of these foreign distribution contracts but no money. In fact, she has spent a lot of money on travel and lawyers. Doesn't sound like a good deal so far, but wait, there's more.

Our Producer now goes to what we call an <u>Industry Bank</u>. There are several large multi-national banks that have divisions that specialize in loans to the film industry. They understand the industry and most importantly will accept as collateral the distribution contracts, such as the ones our Producer has. They will do their due diligence on the foreign distributors to make sure that they are financially sound and capable of fulfilling the contract, ie paying the money, once the film is delivered to them. Their due diligence also involves the Producer and her track record for on-time, on-budget, on-spec productions. So the bank loans the money to the Producer with the contracts from the foreign distributors as collateral. The Producer then makes the film, delivers it to the foreign distributors, and they pay what they owe. In all cases, this money doesn't go to the Producer but goes directly to the bank to repay the loan.

So it seems like an easy deal so far, but wait, we've gotten ahead of ourselves. We have to consider who is taking the risk in the deal. It's the industry bank. Right? If the film doesn't get finished, it never goes to the foreign distributors, who never have to pay the bank. The industry bank is left with a loan default, and banks don't like that. They don't like risks of any kind. So the industry bank will not do this deal yet. They need a guarantee that the film will get made. The promises of the Producer won't make the bank feel comfortable enough. They need insurance.

So enters the fourth player in this deal – the <u>Completion Bond Company</u>. A bond is another name for insurance, and this completion bond company is normally a division or subsidiary of one of the large insurance companies. The completion bond guarantees that the film will get made according to the specifications of the distribution contracts and then delivered to the foreign distributors, who will pay the industry bank. As with most insurance policies, the completion bond company looks at the track record of the insured, our Producer. If she doesn't have a good reputation for, you guessed it, finishing films on-time and on-budget and on-specifications, then she won't get a completion bond and the deal will fall apart. But our Producer passed the test, got the money, and now has a representative from the completion bond company on the set and in the production office for the duration. If things were to go wrong, the completion bond company can step in and take over the production. They will even put additional money into the production to get it finished. Any money and expenses will then be recouped from the proceeds of the film – even before the bank is repaid. And what does the completion bond company get? Like all insurance policies there is a fee, which is generally a percentage of the production budget (3% to 5%), and influenced by the track record of the Producer.

So now the deal is done. The Producer was smart enough to put the expenses related to this deal into her budget. The lawyer fees, bank closing fees, foreign travel, and cost of the completion bond will add up and could be as much as 10% to 15% of the actual production budget. But it is worth it to get a film of this size financed and made.

And most importantly, when we look at this deal and the parties involved, has our Producer sold off any of her interest in the ownership of the film? There are distribution contracts, a loan and an insurance policy. None of those involve ownership. So our Producer has financed and completed the film and distributed it internationally without giving up any ownership. And even more importantly, what markets are still open for her to license the film to? Right: domestic theatrical, home video, VOD/SVOD, and broadcast/basic cable. And, of course, miscellaneous. Any deal to these markets would be called an Acquisition (license)/Distribution Deal. Anything earned in those markets is pure profit for our Producer, less royalties, of course. Hopefully you can see that the Negative Pickup can be a great deal.

Established Producer.

Our Producer is now on his sixth or more film, at least two financed with negative pick-up deals. He is now doing films with budgets between $5 million and $20 million. He gets good TV stars plus B-level film talent and even older A-level film talent. His films have had modest but consistent theatrical results, both domestic and international, plus very good home video/VOD/SVOD results. And, of course, he continues to always be on-time, on-budget, and on-spec. He could easily do his next film with negative pickups with the foreign distributors, but he is tired of the hassle of the deal – particularly the bank loan.

He is now in a position to get the Foreign Distributor to agree to a change. Rather than wait for the film to be delivered, he asks for the money up front, when the distribution contract is signed. Then he doesn't have to borrow against it. This new deal is called a Pre-Sale Deal. The foreign distributors like the negative pickup deal because they don't take as much risk. If they give money up front, they are taking a lot more of a risk. And this is compounded by the fact that the average license fee for a film at this budget level is a lot larger. Their bigger concern, however, is that our Producer has been so successful that he could go to their competitors and get this pre-sale deal from one of them. So they agree but ask for a greater discount on the licensing fee. Instead of the 10-20% discount that they got in the negative pickup deal, they now want and get a 35% to a 50% discount. But they will have their money tied up for at least a year or more.

So our Producer goes to all the foreign distributors and gets them all to switch to the pre-sale deal. The problem, however, is that due to the larger discounts he agreed to, he is short of his goal. That means that he has to either bring in private investors or go back to the industry bank. Both require a lot of paperwork, but the bank is the better deal. Hopefully you know why. Right, with a bank loan he doesn't have to give up ownership. So the industry bank gives him what is called a Gap Loan, named because it fills the gap between his budget and the amount he has received from all of the pre-sale deals. The industry bank does not have the collateral of the foreign distributors' license contracts, but they do take a lien or security interest on the film itself.

What about our friends the completion bond company? Our Producer has the money. Who is at risk if the film is not made? The foreign distributors, of course. And the industry bank to a lesser extent. So the completion bond is as essential as it is in the negative pickup deal.

And the upside with the pre-sale is the same as with the negative pickup – our Producer has maintained ownership, and he has all the other markets to exploit for almost pure profit.

And there is another type of deal that our Producer can likely accomplish at this point in his career, particularly as the budgets go up. The Financing/Distribution Deal is a very common deal that is made between experienced Producers and independent production companies and studios. Basically the independent production company or studio gives the Producer money to make the film and in return they get the distribution rights for the film in all markets. In a sense the independent production company or studio acts as a lender, and they charge interest as part of the distribution expenses that they will recoup. But they do not normally take ownership. The exception would be where it is a very expensive film with lots of special effects, and the studio might demand a piece of the ownership as a co-production.

What about a completion bond? The independent production company will probably require it. If it is a studio, they might approach it as self-insured and have the right to step in and take over the production.

This is when our Producer knows that he has arrived in the upper echelon of the producing world, but there is more room to grow. At this point our Producer goes for the big time with films budgeted in the $50 plus million range. He has A-level talent and possibly a big star. Most of his films have had successful theatrical runs and excellent ancillary results. This means that his deals are Finance/Distribution and primarily with the studios, who are the ones with that kind of money.

Star Producer.

Some Producers like to be stars themselves, and our Producer has now made at least one film with a budget in excess of $100 million with a huge star. It gets big, big box office and maybe a few industry awards, but they aren't nearly as important as the box office. She is on a first name basis with all the A-list talent and all the important agents and most of the studio executives in LA.

She is now ready for a <u>Development Deal</u> with one of the major studios. Under this deal, she is given a pot of money – could be $5 million or more a year – for her to use to develop projects. This can include buying underlying property or spec scripts – all in her name and the name of the studio. The studio then gets the right of first refusal to make the film. If it passes, then the project goes into turnaround and the Producer can take it elsewhere. If another studio picks it up, they have to reimburse the original studio for all of its development costs. In reality, the original studio seldom passes outright and instead the project goes into what's called <u>development hell</u> from which there is no hope of return.

Also as a part of this deal, our Producer gets a salary, money for a staff, and her overhead costs are paid including an office on the lot that is cleaned up every night by the studio's housekeeping staff. For this reason, these deals are also called <u>Housekeeping Deals</u>, and the Producer is said to be on-the-lot because they have an office on the studio lot.

Now the studios don't just hand these deals out to any Producer. In the 1990s the studios collectively would typically have 350 or more of these deals at any one time; but that number has fallen to an average of around 150. Today, each of the major studios has between ten and thirty of these deals going at any one time. These contracts are normally for five years, which gives the Producer time to develop projects. Some of these deals are also given to top talent – actors and directors – and as part of the deal they agree to act in or direct one or more films for the studio during the contract period.

Obviously a great deal for our Producer, but why would the studio spend all this money without any guarantee that the Producer will find or develop a good project? The answer is that our Producer has become a magnet for creative people who have ideas, novels, scripts, etc. She is known as someone who gets films made on-time, on-budget, and according to specs. She has worked with a wide variety of talent and has always kept her promises. None of the suits in the studios' development or business offices can say any of that. Creative people don't gravitate to them. So it makes sense for the studio to align itself with our Producer in order to find the best projects.

Of course, not all Producers become stars, not all want to. Many find a comfortable niche with a type of film and a budget level that suits their interests and abilities. So the key for a Producer is to find their passion and figure out how to make it happen.

SUPPLEMENTAL MATERIAL – CHAPTER 14 – FEATURE FILM FUNDING

<u>Review Questions</u>

1. What is the 'standard deal' for funding a film?

2. What are two important elements for success when seeking funding?

3. What makes up a 'good' package to raise money for a film? What is the most important element for a package?

4. What might a Producer have that can attract a big name talent if she doesn't have enough money to pay their normal fee?

5. How important are relationships?

6. What is the most important part of a track-record for a Producer as he tries to move up the ladder of success?

7. Should a Producer take money from just any family member or friend? Why or why not?

8. Are local banks interested in funding feature films? Why or why not?

9. What do Private Investors primarily want from an investment? What else might interest them in a feature film investment?

10. Who are the parties to an In-house Deal and what is their relationship to each other?

11. Who are the parties to a Negative Pickup Deal and what is their relationship to each other? Who takes the most risk in this deal? Why do they take this risk?

12. Who are the parties to a Pre-sale Deal and what is their relationship to each other? Who takes the most risk in this deal? Why do they take this risk?

13. Who are the parties to a Financing/Distribution Deal and what is their relationship to each other? Who takes the most risk in this deal? Why do they take this risk?

14. Who are the parties to a Development Deal and what is their relationship to each other? Who takes the most risk in this deal? Why do they take this risk?

Industry Speak

Accredited Investor – an SEC designation for someone who has a net worth of at least $1 million (not including their primary residence) and makes $200,000 or more a year ($300,000 if married).

Approved elements - significant aspects of a film which have been reviewed and approved by the distributor that has committed to distribute the film once it is produced; often includes major actors and director

Bankable Elements – normally refers to an actor or director whose name and reputation will add credibility to a film package and help it get funding

Barter – an exchange of goods and services in lieu of money

Completion bond - a contractual commitment, similar to an insurance policy, that guarantees that a film will be completed and delivered pursuant to specific requirements that include schedule, budget, the approved script, key talent, and MPAA rating

Completion fund - a sum of money set aside by a film industry organization specifically for the purpose of helping to finance the completion of films, generally the post production

Collateral – an asset that a bank will accept to secure a loan; normally a fixed asset such as a house or automobile or stock

Co-production - a film financed through the cooperation of and with substantial contributions of two or more studios and/or production companies

Crowd funding – a co-operative of people who give money to projects that they like and for which they receive gifts in return

Development deal - an agreement by a studio to provide early funding to a Producer for the development of film projects in exchange for the right of first refusal to acquire, to produce, and to distribute any projects developed by the producer; the studio agrees to pay a salary and the overhead expenses of the Producer

Facilities deal - a film finance transaction in which crews, locations, local cast, studio facilities, cameras or some combination thereof are offered to cover a certain percentage of the cost of a film

Financing - the techniques and/or activities involved in obtaining the monies required to pay the expenses incurred in the various phases of a business; with film this includes the stages of film development, production and post production

Financing/distribution deal - a contractual commitment by a studio or an independent production company to provide production financing to a Producer which mandates that the studio or independent production company will be the distributor of the film; the studio or independent production company may become a partial owner of the film based on the amount of money they provide

Housekeeping deal –see development deal

In-house deal - the funding of the production costs of a film by a major studio, normally using a studio Producer who works for the studio or a Producer-for-hire who may or may not have brought the project to the attention of the studio

Negative pickup deal - a contractual commitment made by a distributor to a Producer to license feature film distribution rights and to pay an agreed upon license fee (pick-up price) when the Producer delivers the completed negative to the distributor; such a deal can be made during development, production or post production of a film; may be used by the Producers as collateral for bank financing

Package - the total presentation of the basic elements needed to do a film; normally includes a script, schedule, budget and commitments by key talent

Pre-sale deal - a contractual commitment made by a distributor to a Producer relating to the licensing of a film which is negotiated and signed prior to the start of principal photography and includes monetary advances that are used for the production of the film

Right of first refusal - gives one party to an agreement the power to exercise its rights to develop a film project under certain circumstances and to the exclusion of all others; found in literary options and studio development deals

Turnaround - a film development situation in which an original studio purchaser of a property has declined to go forward and has provided a turnaround notice to the original Producer. The project is now available to be picked-up by another studio, normally with the reimbursement of development costs to the original studio

SEC – Securities and Exchange Commission – the federal government agency that regulates the stock and bond markets; also regulates private placements investments such film financing deals

Further Activities

Think about how high up the Producer ladder you would want to go. What are the types of films that you would ideally want to make and at what level is it feasible to be able to make them?

Further Reading & Research

Go to variety.com and search for *Facts on Pacts* to find the latest Development deals with the various studios.

Get in the daily habit – read the industry trade papers to know what is going on in the industry. For film and television, I recommend *Variety, Hollywood Reporter, Broadcasting & Cable,* and *Current.* They are all available online. Another good resource for what's happening in television is the *Cynopsis.com* online newsletter. For documentary and nonfiction work, I suggest *Real Screen.*

PART FOUR

PRODUCTION PLANNING AND MANAGEMENT

The old adage "he who fails to plan, plans to fail" is never truer than in film and video production. The only activities that come close are leading an army into battle, building a skyscraper, or herding cats.

The ability to plan and manage a production is not the same as the ability to find underlying property, prepare a proposal or business plan, raise money, negotiate with distributors, and accept awards. Production planning and management is a series of tasks that require carful critical thinking, infinite patience, and an unwavering ability to pay attention to a tremendous amount of detail. A good Producer must recognize within himself or herself whether or not they have the skills to plan and manage a production. If they do, great; it can save time and money in development. If not, also great; all they have to do is hire a line producer or production manager for the project.

Production planning takes place initially during the development stage of a project. Often the Producer does his own work (if he has the ability) to save costs. The goal in development is to get an estimate of schedule and budget. Many things change during development, so many aspects of the original production plan will change. The real planning work is then done in pre-production when there is actually money to spend. The overall process for production planning includes:

Production Strategy

Script Breakdown

Scheduling

Budgeting

Production Management or Line Producing begins in pre-production when there is money to spend and contracts to negotiate. On a feature, the Producer will almost always hire a Production Manager or Line Producer. On a small project or documentary it's an expensive luxury. Production management also extends through production and post production when money has to be accounted for and schedules have to be tracked and analyzed. Critical tasks involved in Production Management that we will examine in this book include:

Working with unions and guilds

Location management

Hiring crews

Obtaining releases

Insurance

Negotiating with suppliers

The chapters in Part Four Production Planning and Management are:

Chapter 15 - Production Strategy

Chapter 16 - Script Breakdown

Chapter 17- Scheduling

Chapter 18 - Budgeting

15

PRODUCTION STRATEGY

Production Strategy is primarily a series of questions and decisions about the nature of the program and its intended uses. These questions have generic similarities for nonfiction and fiction work, but there are also significant practical differences between the two types of programs. It is important to spend time on strategy before beginning any production planning because the strategy that develops will inform many of the assumptions and/or decisions that have to be made during planning. This does not mean, however, that a strategy is ever set in stone. Everything in filmmaking is flexible.

The following are primary questions that Producers should ask themselves and answer in order to guide the creation of an overall production strategy for any project or program – film, television or other.

WHAT IS THE PRIMARY MARKET FOR THE PROGRAM?

Most Producers naturally think big, and that's generally a good trait. Any program will benefit from a hard analysis as to its largest potential market. The critical caveat is to be brutally honest about the program. No one wins when a Producer plots a strategy for a little art-house independent film project as if it were a studio blockbuster. Similarly, all the wishing in the world won't make a prime-time PBS special out of a short nonfiction video.

For a feature length fiction film, the answer to the question comes from the nature of the story. Is it a big action story; or is it a quiet personal relationship story? For most of these films, a theatrical release would be the primary market. But it could be more suited for a pay cable or SVOD movie or even a basic cable network. Whatever the goal, it will impact many areas of the production plan for the film.

For a nonfiction film, the answer also derives from the story. Is it a big story with national or even international interest; or is it a small subject with a narrow educational interest? For many nonfiction films, a broadcast or cable showing is the primary market. For most of them, however, video/digital distribution is the most likely primary market.

WHAT IS THE BUDGET RANGE?

Budgets follow markets as reliably as night follows day. A big action film that has studio distribution potential will not be produced for under $100 million. That small independent personal drama should not be produced for much more than $5 million. An hour nonfiction film for prime-time on a major cable network or PBS will be appropriately in the $250,000 to $500,000 range, while the same film in another day-part should stay under $100,000 or even $50,000.

The good Producer knows these ranges because she keeps up-to-date with the industry by reading the trade press, attending industry gatherings/conferences, and networking with other Producers. She has also identified films that are similar to her project and found some budget/cost information on them.

WHAT ARE THE ANCILLARY MARKETS?

Most films, fiction or nonfiction, do not recoup their investment in the primary markets. It is success in those markets, however, that creates enough activity in the ancillary markets to eventually earn money for the project. The good Producer will naturally consider the potential for these markets and make sure that they are factored into the production strategy. Some things to consider

242

include the content of the story and whether it is appropriate for foreign markets or family television. Are there parts of the story that will offend some audiences? Is the subject one that international audiences will care about or understand? Will the dialogue or narration ever have to be translated and dubbed or subtitled? Is the topic extremely current and will it have any relevance to anyone in 12 months?

UNION OR NON UNION?

This is normally only a concern for fiction films, but a project slated for prime-time on a major network should address it as well. There is no question that a Producer takes on significant financial and other obligations and liabilities when signing a union agreement for a project. It is also clear that unions present the Producer with the most experienced and talented people in the industry. These issues will be addressed fully in chapter 19. In many ways the decision on unions follows the decision as to relative budget. The greater the budget, the more likely it is that at least one union will be involved.

WHO IS ON THE PRODUCTION TEAM?

This question begins with the Producer and works down through the above-the-line personnel. The more experience a Producer has, the more likely she will be able to develop and produce a big budget film. Everyone starts small, even Steven Spielberg. Experience attracts money and money buys experience. A film proposal that contains a Producer, director, writer and actor with name-recognition and a list of credits will attract the money necessary to do a studio type film or a prime-time show for a major network. Lacking that, a project will struggle to get funds and will have a more limited market potential.

ANY UNUSUAL PRODUCTION PROBLEMS?

The Producer should be able to identify elements of the story or the content of the project that will be challenges for the production team and create unusual demands on the budget. Examples of this are: extensive travel, particularly international, required to reach locations or interviewees; an extended time period covered by the story; an evolving nonfiction story that could change rapidly and/or in unexpected ways; hard to manage subjects such as elderly interviewees; working with animals or child actors; and, parts of the story/content that can only be done with expensive special effects, graphics, or animation.

SUMMARY

A Producer may not be able to answer all of these basic questions with any certainty, especially in the early stages of development. It is the thought process and the range of possible answers that will determine the different approaches to planning the project. There is no one "right way" to do it. The only right way is the way that leads to finding the money and getting a production underway.

SUPPLEMENTAL MATERIAL – CHAPTER 15 – PRODUCTION STRATEGY

<u>Review Questions</u>

1. What is production strategy?

2. What are the primary questions that guide the creation of a production strategy?

3. What is the primary market for most fiction feature films?

4. What is the primary market for many nonfiction films?

5. How does a Producer know about budget ranges for type of projects?

6. As a budget increases, is it more or less likely that unions will be involved?

<u>Industry Speak</u>

<u>Further Activities</u>

<u>Further Reading & Research</u>

Get in the daily habit – read the industry trade papers to know what is going on in the industry. For film and television, I recommend *Variety, Hollywood Reporter, Broadcasting & Cable,* and *Current.* They are all available online. Another good resource for what's happening in television is the *Cynopsis.com* online newsletter. For documentary and nonfiction work, I suggest *Real Screen.*

16

SCRIPT BREAKDOWN

S cript breakdown is the identification of the essential production elements of a fiction or non-fiction film or video project. As with many aspects of a Producer's craft, this process takes tremendous patience and the ability to work with lots of details. For those Producers who are not strong in these traits, it's best to hire someone for this task.

Script breakdown cannot be done in a vacuum. A Producer has to have first worked out a production strategy for the project. Make sure you have read and understand chapter 15 on strategy before proceeding with this chapter on breakdown.

SIX STEPS

There are 6 clearly identifiable steps in the script breakdown and scheduling process and they <u>must</u> be followed in the proper sequence. These steps, in their proper sequence, are:

1. preparation of the shooting script or treatment
    1A. shooting script for a fiction film
    1B. treatment for a nonfiction project
2. marking the script or treatment
    2A. fiction script
    2B. nonfiction treatment
3. sorting the production elements to breakdown lists;
4. preparation of the breakdown sheets;
5. preparation of the scheduling or production board; and

6. devising the schedule
    6A. schedule of scenes
    6B. production calendar schedule

This chapter examines steps 1 through 4. Scheduling, steps 5 and 6, is covered in Chapter 17.

STEP 1. Preparation of the Shooting Script or Treatment

A. Shooting script for a fiction film.

For a fiction film, the breakdown and scheduling process does not begin until there is a script. This may not be the final script but it should be one that the Producer is happy with and represents his or her current vision of the film to be made.

There are two basic types of scripts in the fiction world – the master scene script and the shooting script. The master scene script is the writer's vision of the story and is often written without any consideration for the challenges of an actual production. It presents the story and the characters that the writer and the Producer want to bring to life. It should read like good fiction; grab the attention of the reader and carry him along on the characters' journeys from the beginning to the end. The shooting script is a reworking of the master scene script into a format that makes it possible for the project to be broken-down and scheduled.

There are two key elements to the proper formatting of the shooting script: scene structure and scene numbers.

Proper scene structure is achieved by first reading the script for the story. The Producer has already done this, probably many times. But for a production manager, hired to do a breakdown and schedule, this will be her first read. Sit back, relax, and read it straight through without thinking of "how the heck can this be done?" This first read will provide a sense of the characters and the overall story. Whether Producer or production manager, the next read of the script is for production concerns. This is where production experience is critical. They have to be able to read a

THE INDEPENDENT FILM & TV PRODUCER

scene and determine whether or not it is formatted properly for production. For example, read the following scene from a master scene script.

INT – JOE'S APARTMENT – NIGHT

Joe pulls his gun from his coat pocket as he puts his briefcase on the sofa. He looks around the empty room. There are signs of a struggle. He walks into the kitchen. He sees an empty glass with lipstick marks on the rim. A woman's purse is on the table. There is a muffled scream. He races out, back through the living room and out onto the balcony. Flinging open the balcony door, he looks down to see Shirley lying face down in a pool of blood on the ground below. He runs back into the apartment, out the door and into the hallway. Then, seeing a crowd waiting for the elevator, he races down the emergency stairs and out the front door to Shirley.

While not great literature, it's a fairly common style of writing for an action scene. It has some energy and flows quickly. The problems for production, however, should be very evident to anyone with production experience. We have to get a production crew (camera, lights and sound), a director, an assistant director and actors to a location(s) where all of this can be filmed. In our imagination we can follow Joe from living room to kitchen to balcony to stairs to Shirley, but in the reality of production, it's not so easy. A Producer should quickly come up with at least two ways to approach this scene for a shooting script. If the production strategy for the film is that it will be a high-end (read "expensive") production, the Producer might think the scene could be shot with a Steadicam that would follow Joe from room to room, to the hall, the stairs and finally outside. Steadicams are wonderful but expensive. And it requires simultaneous lighting and prepping of all the sets (living room, kitchen, balcony, hallway and stairway). This takes added crew and lighting equipment. And from a director's point-of-view it requires the precision and coordinated work of a Steadicam operator, boom operator and actors to do all of this in one long take.

The more traditional alternative is to break this one scene into several scenes that reflect the realities of filmmaking. There are really six settings in this one scene – living room, kitchen, balcony, hallway, stairs and outside with Shirley. To complicate matters, four of these settings are interiors and two are exteriors. Each set has to be lit for the action, a camera has to be placed in a position to capture the action, and a microphone has to be there to record the sound. And they have to look like the director and the production designer want them to look. It may be that one apartment does not have all these rooms that are suitable for production. The different settings could be in different apartments, and they could be miles apart. For all these reasons, each setting should be its own scene in the shooting script. The reformatted scenes for the shooting script would look like this.

INT – JOE'S LIVING ROOM – NIGHT

JOE pulls his gun from his coat pocket as he puts his briefcase on the sofa. He looks round the empty room. There are signs of a struggle. He walks out toward the kitchen.

INT – JOE'S KITCHEN – CONTINUOUS

Joe enters the kitchen and sees an empty glass with lipstick marks on the rim. A woman's purse is on the table. There is a muffled SCREAM. He races out.

INT – JOE'S LIVING ROOM – CONTINUOUS

Joe comes back through the living room and to the balcony door. Flinging it open, he goes out.

EXT – JOE'S BALCONY – CONTINUOUS

Joe looks down to see SHIRLEY lying face down in a pool of blood on the ground below. He runs back into the apartment.

INT – HALLWAY – CONTINUOUS

Joe comes out the door into the hallway. Seeing a CROWD

waiting for the elevator, he races to the emergency exit door.

INT – STAIRWAY – CONTINUOUS

Joe bolts down the emergency stairs.

EXT – JOE'S APARTMENT BUILDING - CONTINUOUS

Joe races out the front door to Shirley.

Notice that in addition to breaking the one scene into several scenes, the action/description line in each new scene has been revised slightly. This follows the basic rules of script writing which require that the action/description line in each scene identifies by name the character(s) that appear. In addition, if we assume that these are the first scenes of the film, then the character names must be typed in all capitals the first time they appear in an action/description line in the script.

Now it's time for scene numbering. In a shooting script each scene is given a number starting with the first scene and going continuously to the end. Our reformatted scene will now look like this.

1 INT – JOE'S LIVING ROOM – NIGHT   1

JOE pulls his gun from his coat pocket as he puts his briefcase on the sofa. He looks round the empty room. There are signs of a struggle. He walks out toward the kitchen.

2 INT – JOE'S KITCHEN – CONTINUOUS   2

Joe enters the kitchen and sees an empty glass with lipstick marks on the rim. A woman's purse is on the table. There is a muffled scream. He races out.

3 INT – JOE'S LIVING ROOM – CONTINUOUS   3

Joe comes back through the living room and to the balcony

door. Flinging it open, he goes out.

4 EXT – JOE'S BALCONY – CONTINUOUS   4

Joe looks down to see SHIRLEY lying face down in a pool of blood on the ground below. He runs back into the apartment.

5 INT – HALLWAY – CONTINUOUS   5

Joe comes out the door into the hallway. Seeing a CROWD waiting for the elevator, he races to the emergency exit door.

6 INT – STAIRWAY – CONTINUOUS   6

Joe bolts down the emergency stairs.

7 EXT – JOE'S APARTMENT BUILDING   7

Joe races out the front door to Shirley.

These scene numbers are going to be very important to us as we continue through the script breakdown and scheduling process. So important that at this time we "lock" them and make them unchangeable. Locking the script is a convention that means once we have begun the breakdown and scheduling process with a shooting script we will not change the scene numbers, no matter how many scenes we add or delete. This is particularly important with the computer programs for scriptwriting which allow for automatic scene numbering. Fortunately, the better programs all have a function that allows the Producer to lock the script. Once a script is locked, if we add a scene it takes a numerical/alpha designation according to the scene that it follows. Using our sample script, we have, for example, added a scene between scenes 4 and 5.

4 EXT – JOE'S BALCONY – CONTINUOUS   4

Joe looks down to see SHIRLEY lying face down in a pool of blood on the ground below. He runs back into the apartment.

4A INT – JOE'S LIVING ROOM – CONTINUOUS   4A

Joe pauses to grab his briefcase, then runs out the front door.

5 INT – HALLWAY – CONTINUOUS   5

Joe comes out the door into the hallway. Seeing a CROWD waiting for the elevator, he races to the emergency exit door.

We would not make this new scene number 5 and then renumber 5 as 6, 6 as 7 and so on. That would be a disaster for all of our planning efforts. Instead, we number the new scene 4A. If there were another scene after 4A and before 5, it would be 4B and so forth.

If we were to delete scene 6, we would not renumber the remaining scenes. We would simply delete the description and mark the scene as shown below.

5 INT – HALLWAY – CONTINUOUS   5

Joe comes out the door into the hallway. Seeing a CROWD waiting for the elevator, he races to the emergency exit door.

6 DELETED   6

7 EXT – JOE'S APARTMENT BUILDING   7

Joe races out the front door to Shirley.

In addition to the scene numbers, locking the script also refers to the page numbers of the script. As with most word processing based programs, the scriptwriting programs automatically repaginate as material is inserted or deleted. With a shooting script that is being broken-down and scheduled, this is not good. By locking the pages, we make sure that each scene begins on the same page number, no matter how many scenes there are or how much is added or deleted from a scene. If an addition to a scene that originally started on page 2 creates a new page, it is not page 3 but page 2A and the material that originally began on page 3 remains the same as before. Even more material would create page 2B and so on. Again, the importance of this will become more evident as we continue through the process of breakdown and scheduling.

B. Treatment for a nonfiction project.

Most nonfiction projects are based on treatments, and some are based on scripts that have been written in the two-column television format. If a script, the process of reformatting the scripts is similar to the fiction film as discussed above.

For most documentary projects, however, there is no script to follow or to reformat. Instead we have mountains of research on the topic that has been distilled into a treatment. To be useful for scheduling, the treatment should be as detailed as possible including descriptions of the people to be interviewed, where the interviews will take place, and what b-roll we will see during the interviews to avoid the dreaded talking-head syndrome. If there are other elements planned for the documentary other than interviews, these should be described. For example, re-enactments or stylized treatments of historical action, historical or other stock footage and/or photographs, complicated graphic elements, all of these should be detailed in the treatment. Obviously all of these can change as we proceed on the voyage of discovery that is a documentary project, but we have to start with a vision, a detailed vision, so we can prepare a breakdown and a schedule.

STEP 2. Marking the Script or Treatment

A. Marking the Fiction Script

Once the shooting script is reformatted and locked, it's time to begin marking the script. There are two main parts to this process: 1) calculating the scene by 1/8s; and 2) identifying the production elements.

Calculating the 1/8s

Calculating the scene by 1/8s is another of those mechanical yet meaningful exercises that seem to take up lots of time for the Producer or production manager. The goal is to have a means to measure the length of each scene in the script. The need for this will be obvious when we get to scheduling how many pages of script we can shoot in a production day.

According to convention, if we take a normal feature film script of 90 to 110 pages in length, each page will translate into one minute of filmic time. Therefore, the 90-page script will give us a 90-minute film, the 100-page script equates to a film of 100 minutes, and so forth. In practice as well as theory, this generally works. The standard practice developed in the early days of film to calculate each scene by 1/8s. My guess is that it came from taking a standard 11-inch piece of paper, assuming top and bottom margins of 1 inch to 1 ½ inches each, and then dividing the rest (8 inches) into 1 inch sections. The idea is to then count how many of these 1/8s are in each scene. That's all there is to it. After a while a Producer gets pretty good at eyeballing a page and estimating the 1/8s. It's better to be generous with 1/8s even if it means that when the different scene counts are added together there might be a total of more pages than are in the script. The other odd thing about this system of 1/8s is one that would make a grade-school math teacher scream. We never reduce the 1/8s. If a scene is 4/8, we do not reduce this to 1/2 as we were once taught to do. If it is 2/8, it stays 2/8 and is not 1/4. The only exception is for full pages, so if we have 8/8, then that becomes 1 page. So count up the total of 1/8s that comprise an entire scene and write that number at the start of that scene near the slug line. There has to be a total for every scene.

Identifying Production Elements

The next step in marking the script is to identify the production elements. There is really nothing that is more important than this. Production element categories include: characters/cast, extras, stunts, props, set dressing, costumes, vehicles, animals, hair and makeup, sound effects and special effects. The production elements are the critical building blocks of the production and to miss one in a scene is to invite disaster in the form of delays, the waste of lots of money, and getting fired.

The process is to read each scene, now for the third or more time, and underline or otherwise mark each production element. And you only mark each element once per scene. There are several marking schemes in use, and it doesn't matter which one you use as long as you're consistent. The marking scheme that I use to mark each element category uses colors and other markings as follows:

Character/Cast - red

Background extra - yellow

Props - blue

Vehicles - orange

Stunts - purple

Animals - brown

Sound effects - pink

Wardrobe/costume - green

Other markings, using a black pen, are:

Hair/makeup - Circle

Set dressing - box

Special effects - asterisk

Let's be clear about what each of these production elements means and how to identify them.

Character/Cast means a part with lines that the character speaks at some point during the film. It can be only one word in a 90-minute film, but if it speaks at all, it is a "character" and needs to be underlined in red. I need to mention what some people call the 'silent character', which is one that doesn't speak but has some function in the action of the scene or film. A baby is an obvious example if it is part of the family. Another example would be a homeless person who doesn't speak but who aggressively approaches a character causing her to change her path and bump into the man of her dreams. While these characters may not have any lines in the script, they are involved in the action of the scene and may likely be given a line of dialogue, even one word, by the director. At that point, under Screen Actor Guild rules, they become a full "day player" and have to be paid accordingly. It is, therefore, prudent for us to consider them as full cast at this point and to anticipate it in the budget that follows the script breakdown and schedule.

A <u>background extra</u> refers to those nameless, almost faceless patrons in a restaurant, riders on a bus, and people on a crowded sidewalk. Our crowd in scene #5 is probably a background crowd, but they do cause Joe to avoid the elevator and go down the stairs. Sometimes it's a judgment call.

<u>Props</u> are those things that you can move around and often are part of the action. The gun is obviously a prop as is the briefcase and the glass in the kitchen. What we don't need to worry about are those things that are normally found in a setting and don't have any part in the action in any scene. For further discussion of this, see set dressing below.

<u>Set dressing</u> includes all the furniture, rugs, things on the walls, drapes etc. that would be found in a typical setting of the type described. This is often another of those judgment calls. Joe's apartment living room is not described in any detail. We are left to picture the type of apartment that we see this character living in. The production designer and the director will have an idea for the look they want. If this is a production that will be done primarily on location, then the location scout will have to find an apartment that looks right or that can be modified to look right. If this is a sound stage production, then the set has to be built and furnished. This obviously makes a big difference for the breakdown and scheduling. At this point, we concentrate on the set dressing that is specifically mentioned in the script. In this case there is the sofa in the living room that Joe puts the briefcase on and the table in the

kitchen. We should put a box around sofa and table. But we don't have to worry about whether there is a coffee table, a chair, a lamp or paintings on the wall in the living room or any other set dressing in the kitchen. We'll save that worry for the advanced course in Production Design.

In some cases there are some gray areas or concerns when determining whether an item is a prop or set dressing. One illustration I like is a simple wooden chair. If the chair is only used to sit on, then it's set dressing. But if the chair is picked up and used as a weapon, then it becomes a prop. In a similar fashion, a desktop computer is set dressing, but a laptop computer is a prop. Some of these can be distinctions without a difference. The practical impact is to determine which part of the art department will be responsible for the item – having it ready and on set at the proper time. In the instance of the chair as a weapon, it would also involve special effects and stunts because it must be a special chair that can be used safely in this action/stunt.

Stunts are anything that causes an actor to have to fall down, trip, get hit, slapped or punched, jump off something of any substantial height. You get the idea. This marking has to trigger a concern for the actor's safety and whether or not there will be the need for a stunt double or a stunt coordinator on set. As most productions use SAG actors, this area is governed by SAG rules.

Animals are an obvious item and can be a real problem on productions. The presence of an animal should set off alarm bells in the production manager's head. There are issues of safety, care and feeding, control, training, and noise. An animal wrangler is probably needed, as is a quick check with the local ASPCA chapter.

Hair/Makeup and Wardrobe are two categories that are often sources of confusion. If the film is a period piece, then these items take on enormous importance. If it is a contemporary film and the characters are described in terms like "young college student" or "middle aged accountant" then we can make some assumptions that the hair, makeup and wardrobe are not an immediate concern.

258

Any special mention of an item in the script, however, needs to be marked. And using common sense, we should assume that Shirley, having possibly taken a header from the balcony, is going to need some special makeup treatment in addition to the pool of blood.

Special Effects is an item that doesn't refer only to alien spaceships flying overhead. In our little script the gun doesn't go off, but if it had, then that's a special effect that requires time, effort and extra personnel with special training. Special effects also refers to having things on a set that work, especially if the production strategy is to shoot on a sound stage. If we build a set of a kitchen and the character wants to get a drink of water, then the faucet has to work and we need plumbing. If we're shooting on location, we can assume that the sink in the kitchen will work, but the location scout had better check it.

Let's look at how our sample scenes would be marked for production elements. This book is not printed in color, so you have to use your imagination that the underlining is in color. Sorry, but the additional cost to make the book with just a couple of color pages was not worth it. There is, however, a sample script on the companions website (www.theproducerssourcebook.com), which is broken down and marked in color. Details in Further Activities at the end of this chapter.

1 INT – JOE'S LIVING ROOM – NIGHT   1

JOE pulls his gun from his coat pocket as he puts his briefcase on the sofa. He looks round the empty room. There are signs of a struggle. He walks out toward the kitchen.

JOE

Shirley?

2 INT – JOE'S KITCHEN – CONTINUOUS   2

Joe enters the kitchen and sees an empty glass with lipstick marks on the rim. A woman's purse is on the table. There is a muffled scream. He races out.

3 INT – JOE'S LIVING ROOM – CONTINUOUS   3

Joe comes back through the living room and to the balcony door. Flinging it open, he goes out.

4 EXT – JOE'S BALCONY – CONTINUOUS   4

Joe looks down to see SHIRLEY lying face down in a pool of blood * on the ground below. He runs back into the apartment.

Notice that the character element(s) is identified as it appears in the action/description line and not in the dialogue heading which I have added to scene #1. Also note that in scene 4, I marked the 'pool of blood' as a special effect. It could have also been circled as Hair/Makeup and been correct. In fact, it wouldn't be wrong to mark it both ways.

If an element appears in a scene, then it is marked once and only once for that scene. If it appears in the next scene it is marked again. The tricky part is that writers don't think of production management when they write. So they don't clearly identify all the production elements that might be or should be in each scene. If a character is not identified in the action/description lines, but we know that character is there in the scene, then we have to write that character's name in the margin using black ink and underline it in the appropriate color - red. Another example is in scene #1 where Joe takes his gun out of his pocket. In the rest of the scenes the gun isn't mentioned. Is it there? I think it's safe to assume that Joe has continued to carry the gun, and the writer hasn't told us that he put it away, even when he went out into the hall or outside. A big part of this breakdown process is common sense. We can make a decision that he would have the gun in the other scenes. In fact, we would want to err on the side of caution and should assume that he continues to have the gun. We would, therefore, write 'gun' in black ink in the margin next to each scene in which we have determine that he would have the gun, and underline it in blue. Another example is in scene 3 where Joe comes back into the living room – what happened to the briefcase and the sofa? Both are certainly still there and have to be added in the margins.

The reason for all this fuss and extra work is that we need to make sure that all the production elements like the gun are there when each of these scenes is filmed. And they could be filmed days apart and in different locations. If the director decides that Joe would put the gun back in his pocket when he goes into the hallway, that's his or her decision. The job of the production manager is to make sure that the gun is there on the set in case the director wants Joe to continue to hold it. Many of the continuity errors that we see in films are due to the mistakes that were made in the process of identifying the production elements for each scene.

Another essential type of production element is called a production note. These are questions, reminders and items of concern that the Producer or production manager has about the particular scene. There are far, far too many production elements and other details involved with every scene to try to rely on memory. Get in the habit of writing it all down and in this case the best place to write it is in the margins next to the scene that it relates to. For example, in scene #1 there is mention of "signs of a struggle". A production note could simply be: "What does this mean?" For a Production Manager it means a question about damage to set dressing and props. Or can she save money by getting old, damaged stuff in the first place. Do we ever use this set with the place in good shape? Another example is in scene #4 where Joe looks down to see Shirley. Are we going to have a camera on the balcony and just point it down to the ground? We could, however, be in an apartment on the 33rd floor. Did we assume in production strategy that we will have a larger budget, and that would allow for us to have a crane for a shot of Joe on the balcony that will then pull down to Shirley? Or should we plan on getting a shot from the apartment building across the street? The more we think about it, what we probably need is to set up an insert shot of Shirley on the ground and add it as scene 4A. This could also have been done

THE PRODUCER'S SOURCEBOOK

by an alert production manager at the time she was reformatting the script for the shooting script. But no one is perfect, and no one catches everything the first time. That's why we go over the script so many times. Still another example is the mention of a "crowd" in scene #5. We should have marked this as background extras and underlined it in yellow. We also need to ask the question, as a production note – how many is a crowd? We will need to plan for and eventually budget for the assumed number of extras. There is no sex in these scenes, but if there were it would undoubtedly lead to several production notes relating to the need to alert actors during the casting process.

In a script there may be a setting or more where there are a lot of elements that have to be written into the margin in a lot of scenes. This is obviously very tedious and that can lead to errors. A Producer in this case might create what we call sub-lists of elements in a particular category. For example, if our little sample was expanded to 30 or 90 pages, we might have found that there is a long list of prop elements in Joe's Living Room; many more than the gun and briefcase. In that case we can create a sub-list at the bottom of the breakdown list for props. We could call it Joe's Living room props and then indicate that it includes prop items by the numbers assigned to them in the breakdown list. The creation of the prop breakdown list has to happen first in order to give each prop a number and name. Then those numbers are referenced in the sub-list. For an example of this go to www.theproducerssourcebook.com then the Breakdown page and access the file: breakdown lists – The Boomers. A sub-list can be found under set dressing and wardrobe.

It is impossible to spend too much time on identifying the production elements. For a feature length film, a production manager can spend weeks on this task. If they get it right at this stage, then all else begins to fall into place. If they are not correct or are incomplete now, it will just make everything else they do incorrect and incomplete. And probably get them fired.

B. Nonfiction Treatment

The process for marking a non-fiction treatment is similar but different. The concept remains the same – that the Producer needs to identify all the critical pieces of the production such as interviewees, locations for interviews, b-roll, access to special locations, stock photos, stock footage, historical artifacts, graphic elements and so on. Every film might have some unique elements, and production notes play a big part in the process. If there is a need to interview someone at their place of work, it should raise questions regarding permissions, ease of access and all sorts of possible production problems. Will certain b-roll need special equipment? For example, b-roll in a film that profiles a rock climber will require a special crew with special gear. A film with lots of historical photos will need time in the studio for expensive motion control shooting or, on a lower budget film, the use of Adobe After-Effects. Develop a color and marking scheme to identify each of these nonfiction elements. Then create a key of colors/markings so anyone can follow along.

Once a Producer is certain that they've captured all the production elements, then it's time to begin preparing the breakdown lists.

STEP 3. Sorting the Production Elements to Breakdown Lists

After marking the script or treatment, we now have the different production elements identified but still scattered throughout a document of many pages. The purpose of the breakdown list is to consolidate the production elements and sort them by categories. As a result, there will be a breakdown list for every category of production element, and each one will list all of the elements of that category that were found in the script or treatment.

The format for the breakdown list is as seen below.

Breakdown List

Production Element Category _____ page ____

#	Description	Scene(s)

The process is as follows. Prepare a separate breakdown list for every category of production element. Then go through the script, scene by scene, and if there is a production element of that category, it's written on the list along with the scene number.

Let's take props for an example. The first prop we find in the script is Joe's gun, and it's in scene #1. We put that on the Prop list as the first item for that category.

Breakdown List

Production Element Category ____Props_____ page ____

#	Description	Scene(s)
1	Joe's gun	1

Next we see the briefcase, also a prop in scene #1 and we add that as item number 2

Breakdown List

Production Element Category ____Props_____ page ____

#	Description	Scene(s)
1	Joe's gun	1
2	Joe's briefcase	1

Please note that I used a possessive to name the gun and briefcase. This becomes important in cases where there are more than one gun or briefcase or any other generic item. If someone else in this film has a gun, it would be called 'Sam's gun' (assuming, of course, that Sam is the name of the other character). This needs to be done with cellphones, purses, etc.

Not seeing any other props in scene #1, we move on to scene #2 where we have the glass and a woman's purse. We should call it 'Shirley's purse' if we know that it is hers.

Breakdown List

Production Element Category ___Props_____ page ____

#	Description	Scene(s)
1	Joe's gun	1, 2
2	Joe's briefcase	1
3	glass	2
4	woman's purse	2

We have also, if we've been paying attention, written in the gun in the margin as a prop that is not in the action/description line but should definitely be there with Joe in the kitchen. So next to the line item for Joe's gun we add scene number 2 as above.

265

This process progresses through the entire script until we have a list for props that would look like this.

Breakdown List

Production Element Category ___Props_____ page _____

#	Description	Scene(s)
1	Joe's gun	1, 2, 3, 4, 5, 6, 7
2	Joe's briefcase	1, 3
3	glass	2
4	woman's purse	2

Each category of production element is done in the same manner — each with its own list. Some Production Managers go through the script with only one breakdown list at a time. Others prepare a breakdown list for all the categories that they know they use in the script. Then they go scene by scene and mark all the elements from each scene on the appropriate breakdown lists. It's a personal preference, and the only essential is to capture on the breakdown lists all the production elements and all the scenes where they appear.

The numbering system for the items on the breakdown list is that numbers are assigned consecutively as the items are first found in the script. There is no big deal with the numbers at this point. If we forgot an item from scene 3 and have to put it at the very end of the list as number 213, don't worry. This is true of all categories of production elements EXCEPT for the characters/cast. For the characters we write them on the breakdown list as we find them and make note of all the scenes in which they appear, but we don't number them yet. After we have gone through the entire script and have all the scenes noted for each character, then we count how many scenes each character is in. The character that is in the most scenes is then listed as character number 1. The character who is in the next most scenes is character number 2 and so on. If there are

266

characters that are in the same number of scenes, then just arbitrarily select one character for the next number and the other character for the following number. The breakdown list for characters is then redone using this numbering sequence.

Once we are satisfied that we have all the production elements on the correct lists and they all have a good name and number, then we lock the lists the same way we locked the scene numbers. We use these names and number a lot, and we don't want them arbitrarily changed.

STEP 4. Preparation of the Breakdown Sheets

The breakdown lists have sorted all the production elements by category type, so we now know what props, for example, are needed for the production and in what scenes. The breakdown sheets are now created to re-sort the production elements back into the different scenes. Productions are scheduled by scenes and for each scene the breakdown sheet tells us exactly what production elements are needed. There is one breakdown sheet created for each scene.

The following is a typical breakdown sheet.

BREAKDOWN SHEET   PRODUCTION TITLE: _____

PAGE COUNT _____   SCENE # _____
INT / EXT _____   SCRIPT PG. # _____
DAY / NIGHT _____

ACTION: _____
SETTING: _____
LOCATION: _____
SEQUENCE: _____SCRIPT DAY: _____

CHARACTERS/CAST	EXTRAS	STUNTS
	PROPS	SET DRESSING
COSTUME	MAKEUP/HAIR	SPECIAL EFX
SPECIAL EQUIPMENT	VEHICLES	ANIMALS
PRODUCTION NOTES		Other:

PREPARED BY: _____ Date: _____

Let's look at each part of the breakdown sheet and the information it requires. We start in the upper left corner of the page.

PAGE COUNT – this is the total number of 1/8s of a page for that scene, which was calculated earlier and marked on the shooting script. Remember, we use whole numbers and 1/8s and we do not reduce the 1/8s to anything else –2/8 does not become 1/4.

INT/EXT – comes from the slug line of the shooting script.

<u>DAY/NIGHT</u> – also from the slug line of the shooting script.

Now the top right corner of the page.

<u>SCENE #</u> - from the shooting script.

<u>SCRIPT PG #</u> - the page in the shooting script where the scene begins and only that page. Because the script is locked, that page number will not change.

And now the top middle.

<u>ACTION</u> – this is a short phrase that describes the main action of the scene. For example, the action phrase for the first scene in our sample script could be "Joe pulls gun and looks around." The phrase for the second scene could be "Joe sees lipstick, purse and hears scream." It should be just enough to remind anyone what happens in the scene.

<u>SETTING</u> – this is the story setting from the slug line, for example Joe's Living Room. The exact working from the slug line must be used here.

<u>LOCATION</u> – is the actual location for production. This information is often not known when the breakdown sheets are first created. It will be added later in pre-production, after the locations have been scouted, selected and secured.

<u>SEQUENCE</u> – if the scene is part of a sequence then that should be noted, generally by giving the sequence a name. The scenes in our sample script could be called a sequence with a name like "Joe finds Shirley dead." Many, if not most, scenes are not part of a sequence that needs to be noted. If you don't see it clearly, then don't worry about it.

<u>SCRIPT DAY</u> or <u>STORY DAY</u> – results from an analysis of the story in the script and how many different days are represented. It would include any flashbacks or other unusual time shifts like a dream. It is primarily used by the art department, particularly the wardrobe and hair/make-up people to plan different "looks" for

the characters for the different days. It often helps to create an outline of the story days.

Some breakdown sheets, especially those used in pre-production, also have:

SCRIPT TIME – an attempt to estimate the amount of screen time that the scene will take when it is edited. If it is a dialogue scene, then the timing is done by putting a stopwatch on a reading of the scene. If it is a car chase that is described in a couple of sentences, then the timing is just a good, educated guess of how long an edited chase sequence might last.

After the top portion of the breakdown sheet is completed, then the production element boxes are filled in. In the Characters/Cast box you would put the number and name of the characters who appear in the scene. This does not include a character who only "appears" with a Voice Over. The same would be done for props and all the other production elements that were found in that scene. The numbers and names of the items come from the breakdown lists and are very important to use on the breakdown sheets. All production departments will use this number and name scheme to make sure the correct items are on set on the correct day. Most production managers will pull the production elements from both the marked script and the breakdown lists to make sure that all the elements have been captured, numbered and put on the breakdown sheets.

So a breakdown sheet for scene 1 of our sample script would look like this:

BREAKDOWN SHEET   PRODUCTION TITLE: Sample Script

PAGE COUNT: 3/8   SCENE # 1
INT / EXT : INT   SCRIPT PG. # 1
DAY / NIGHT: Day

ACTION: Joe enters and sees signs of struggle
SETTING: Joe's Living Room
LOCATION: TBA
SEQUENCE: _____   SCRIPT DAY: One

CHARACTERS/CAST 1 Joe	EXTRAS	STUNTS
	PROPS 1 Joe's gun 2 Joe's briefcase	SET DRESSING 1 sofa
COSTUME 1 Joe's coat	MAKEUP/HAIR	SPECIAL EFX
SPECIAL EQUIPMENT	VEHICLES	ANIMALS
PRODUCTION NOTES 1 What are "signs of struggle"?		Other:

PREPARED BY: RB   Date Prepared: 5/5/16

The other critical aspect to the breakdown sheets is that they are color coded for the different combinations of interior, exterior, day and night scenes. This color coding starts here and continues into scheduling. There are different color schemes that are used, and most production managers have their own scheme. There is no standard or absolute color scheme. The only critical thing is to be consistent. The color scheme that I use is as follows:

Exterior Day - Green

Exterior Night - Blue

Interior Day - White

Interior Night - Yellow

So, if the scene is an exterior night scene, then I use a breakdown sheet that has been printed on blue paper stock. For interior night, I use yellow paper stock and so forth.

The preparation of the script breakdown and schedule has, of course, been computerized and appears on the laptops of the production managers. The computer programs present their material in a format that mimics the looks of the breakdown list and sheet (even to the use of colors), so it is still important to understand how it looks and works. And it is much easier to learn the software if you're familiar with how it works on paper.

SUPPLEMENTAL MATERIAL – CHAPTER 16 – SCRIPT BREAKDOWN

Review Questions

1. What is a script breakdown?

2. What are the six main identifiable steps in the breakdown and scheduling process? Be sure that you know the proper order of the steps.

3. What are the two basic types of scripts and which one is used for the breakdown?

4. What are the two key elements for the proper formatting of the shooting script?

5. What does 'locking the script' mean and how does it impact changes to the scenes?

6. What value is used to measure the length of each scene? Is this value ever reduced to a different value?

7. What are production elements? What is their importance? How are they marked on the script?

8. What is the difference between a character/cast and a background extra?

9. What is the difference between a prop and set dressing?

10. What happens with a production element that you know should be in the scene but is not in the script?

11. What is a production note?

12. What are the main production elements in a nonfiction project?

13. What does a breakdown list do?

14. How are production elements numbered on a breakdown list? Is it the same for all lists?

15. What are the breakdown sheets used for? Be familiar with the different elements of the breakdown sheets.

Industry Speak

Breakdown list – sorts the production elements by element category such as characters, props, set dressing, etc. Each element is assigned a number on the list that remains with that element for the entire production.

Breakdown sheet – sorts the production elements from the breakdown lists back to a scene by scene order; also includes other information that is used by the production team

Production elements – essential building blocks of a production; people and things that have to be accounted for and scheduled to make the production run smoothly

Script breakdown – the overall process of marking a script to identify all production elements and production notes; normally begins with marking the script with colors assigned to each production element.

Shooting script – a script that has been formatted to work for a production manager; includes a number assigned to each scene

Further Activities

Breakdown a script – the best way to learn this skill is to do it.

ALL these materials can be found at
http://www.theproducerssourcebook.com/

1. Go to the Script Breakdown, chapter 16, page and print and read the script for the short film *The Boomers* (The

Boomers – script for sourcebook). Then mark all the production elements in the script using colored pencils and a black pen for other markings. Once completed, check your work against the sample in the file: marked script - The Boomers.

2. Once the production elements are all identified, including those that are not specifically written in the script, create a breakdown list for each production element category. Be sure to number the lists properly. On the Breakdown Lists, chapter 16, page there is a template for the breakdown list (Breakdown Lists – template). Once completed, check your lists against the completed lists in the excel file: breakdown Lists - The Boomers.

3. Then create a breakdown sheet for the first 19 scenes using the production elements numbers and names from the breakdown lists. A template for the breakdown sheet is on the Breakdown Sheet, chapter 16, page (Breakdown Sheet – template). Once completed, check your sheets against the completed sheets in the excel file: breakdown sheets – The Boomers.

Further Reading & Research

Visit Entertainment Partners at www.ep.com to see their line of software for Producers, including Movie Magic Scheduling and Movie Magic Budgeting. Once a Producer knows the rationales and procedures of the breakdown, scheduling, and budgeting functions, these software programs are the next step into industry professionalism.

Another industry favorite for scheduling and budgeting software can be found at www.junglesoftware.com

Get in the daily habit – read the industry trade papers to know what is going on in the industry. For film and television, I recommend *Variety, Hollywood Reporter, Broadcasting & Cable,* and *Current.* They are all available online. Another good resource for what's happening in television is the *Cynopsis.com* online newsletter. For documentary and nonfiction work, I suggest *Real Screen.*

17

SCHEDULING

This chapter continues the process of script breakdown and scheduling that is essential for the successful planning of any production.

As we learned in Chapter 16, there are 6 clearly identifiable steps in the script breakdown and scheduling process and they must be followed in the proper sequence. These steps, in their proper sequence, are:

1. preparation of the shooting script or treatment
    1A. shooting script for a fiction script
    1B. treatment for a nonfiction project
2. marking the script or treatment
    2A. fiction script
    2B. nonfiction treatment
3. sorting the production elements to breakdown lists;
4. preparation of the breakdown sheets;
5. preparation of the scheduling or production board; and
6. devising the schedule
    6A. schedule of scenes
    6B. production calendar schedule

This chapter examines steps 5 and 6. The script breakdown steps 1 through 4 were covered in Chapter 16.

STEP 5. Preparation of the Scheduling or Production Board

The scheduling or production board is a tool that is used to assist the scheduling of the various scenes. It has been the standard for fiction film work since the beginning of the studio system. The production board has also been computerized, and the format mimics the physical look of the production board, so it is still important to understand how the board looks and works.

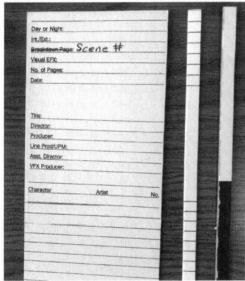

The Production Board consists of several elements:

a. The standard <u>production board</u> is 16 ¼ inches high and 42 to 84 inches wide, depending on the number of panels.

There can be 4, 6 or 8 panels. The 8 panel board is used for feature length films and the other boards are used for shorter films.

b. The <u>header strip</u> is white cardboard, 15 inches by 3 ½ to 4 inches, and fits into the first panel of the board. It is divided into horizontal lines and contains three areas of information. The first section pulls in information from the breakdown sheet including: day/night, INT/EXT, scene number, and number of pages. Below that is information on the production including the title, director, Producer, line producer or production manager, assistant director and visual effects producer. The third area is a list of all the main characters in the film and their breakdown list numbers. The artist or actor names are also added when they are cast.

c. The <u>scene strips</u> are thin, 15 inch by 5/16 inch, cardboard strips that are divided into horizontal lines to match the header strip. There is one strip per scene. They hold all the information from the breakdown sheet that is required for effective scheduling and correspond to the lines on the header board – day/night, INT/EXT, scene number, and number of pages (in 1/8s) in the scene. These scene strips are made on colored card stock using colors that match the color scheme for the breakdown sheets. A blue breakdown sheet begets a blue scene strip. Using the numbers for each production element, the strips contain much of the same information that is found on the breakdown sheets. There is a blank space on the strips to write the setting for the scene. Most people write the short description of action at the bottom of each scene strip.

When preparing the scene strips, it is critical to be careful and double-check for accuracy. When so much information is transposed from one place to another, errors can happen; and important scheduling mistakes can be made using incomplete or incorrect information.

d. <u>Divider strips</u> are used to mark the end of a production day, a production week, or other period. The divider strip for each day gives us the calendar day information and the total number of pages scheduled within that day.

Specialty strips are used to mark holidays, travel days or other events that interrupt production.

I suggest using black ink when preparing the strips, AND neatness is very important. You want to be able to easily read the numbers and other information on these thin strips.

If you're using computer software, you will notice that the template for the screen is designed to mimic the production board. And once the information has been correctly added to the breakdown lists on the program, then it correctly populates the scheduling strips.

STEP 6. Devising the schedule

There are two components to a film schedule: the schedule of scenes; and the production calendar schedule.

A. Schedule of Scenes

It's now time to take all the scene strips and make a schedule of which scenes should be, can be shot together. Whether we use a production board or computer software, the critical thing is to take our time and be flexible. For a feature film with hundreds of scenes, there will be a number of different schedules that could be "correct".

The first step is to make a decision regarding making-a-day. Making-a-day is the determination of how many pages of script you want to shoot on an average day. A normal feature film production (single camera) generally has the goal to shoot 3 to 5 pages a day. But remember, this is an average and there are many factors to consider as we will see in the discussions that follow. TV movies of the week often try to make-a-day with 10 to 12 pages. The largest part of this decision is driven by available financing and budget, and a smaller part of it is in response to the shooting

280

style of the director.

How do we count the number of pages? Good, you were paying attention... by 1/8s. We know how long each scene is in the script and that number is on the breakdown sheets and the scene strips.

Primary and Secondary Factors

There are many factors involved with scheduling scenes and each has a different priority. But we start making our scheduling decisions for any film by considering a primary factor and two important secondary factors.

Primary Factor for Scheduling Scenes - Settings

Secondary Factors – Day/Night; and Characters

The first step in the process is to take all the scene strips and sort them by setting. It might feel a bit like you're back in kindergarten, but it's fun. Take the scene strips and find a large table. Separate the strips according to the different settings. That is our primary scheduling factor. Then add up how many pages are represented by all the scenes in each setting. If using a computer program, use the sort function but start with "sort by settings" only. Don't try a more complex sorting.

We are now ready to take the first stab at making-a-day within these groupings (by setting) of strips. If the number of pages in a setting totals between 4 and 5, and the goal is 4 to 5 pages a day, congratulations, we've made our first production day. Well, almost. Don't get too excited yet, there are plenty of other scheduling factors than can mess up that neat little production day.

One of those factors is the first important secondary factor – day/night. The pile of strips for the setting might have different color strips, which would indicate that some scene are day scenes and some night. When we're doing a schedule in development, it doesn't matter, and we count them all the same. In pre-production, however, we would consider whether the lighting requirements to go from day to night, or vice versa, present any unusual challenges that might delay the production. Normally there are not. But we want to be sure.

We use the other secondary factor, Characters, in pre-production when we are refining things and worried about budgets. For now in development, let's move on to some other factors we need to consider because they can impact whether our 4 or 5-page production day really works.

Other Factors

We need to take a careful look at each scene in the pile for that setting and determine whether there are any other scheduling factors which would affect the goal of making a 4-5-page production day. For example, do any of the scenes involve extras, and if so, how many extras? If there are more than a few extras, that scene will demand more time than the average. Another factor is having a complicated series of stunts and/or special effects. A scene which involves child actors or animals is another case where extra time is normally needed. Is it a scene set in a particular historical period that involves unusual work on sets, costumes and makeup? Will there be special equipment, such as a dolly or a crane or a rain machine, used for the scene that will take time for setup and rehearsal? Musical and dance scenes always take additional time.

We would then reconsider the scenes based on our interpretation of the difficulty of production and may wind up with a setting that has 4 pages, but will need two production days to shoot. It is possible, depending on the scene, to only have one scene in a production day and cover less than a page. Production experience and scheduling experience will obviously help with these judgment calls.

The goal here is to determine how many production days we will need to shoot this film, and we do this setting by setting, scene by scene. The schedule will tell us how many production days we will be in a particular setting, how many production days the different cast members will be needed, how many production days an expensive piece of equipment will be needed, how many production days we will need extras, and so on. All this information is critical for our budget.

B. Production Calendar

After all the scenes are sorted and we've determined how many production days will be needed for each setting, the next task is to arrange the production days on a production calendar. This is normally done during pre-production and is not something that we generally worry about during development.

One of the primary considerations with the production calendar is whether or not we are using any union or guilds in the production. If so, we have to abide by the rules and regulations of the general agreements with those unions or guilds. For example, most of them call for a 5-day work week. This means that we work for 5 days and then have to have two days off. But it does not mean that we have to work Monday to Friday. We can work Saturday through Wednesday and then take Thursday and Friday off. This may be very useful if we have scenes to shoot on some production days that are in an office location, and we only have access to that location during the weekend. There's an exception to the 5-day rule when we are shooting at a location that is a certain distance from our home base and everyone has to spend the night in hotels. With SAG, for example, we can have a 6-day week in that instance.

Most union/guild contracts also require a minimum of a 12-hour turnaround. This means that if we let people go from the set at 8 PM, then we cannot call them back any earlier than 8 AM the next morning. This can affect our schedule if we are trying to go from day shoots to night shoots or vice versa.

One big challenge to creating a good production calendar is how to combine partial production days. For example, we have a setting with two ordinary (meaning lots of dialogue and no special factors involved) pages and would like to combine it with another setting with one or two ordinary pages. This involves what we call a company move, where we have to wrap the one location, pack up and move to another location, set up and shoot. It's a good idea if we can do it, but it's hard to do – remember there are a lot of people and a lot of equipment involved in a production and moving them always takes longer than we anticipate. Some guidelines for combining settings for the production calendar include:

1. don't schedule more than one company move in a day if the settings are interiors;

2. don't schedule more than two company moves in a day if all the settings are exteriors;

3. try to combine settings that have the same or many of the same characters; and

4. remember, in no case should the total page count exceed the goal for making-a-day

One exception to this, during development only, is if we have a number of settings that are in a character's house – a bedroom, bathroom, living room, kitchen, etc. In development, we can assume that we will find a location that has all of these settings in one location. That probably won't really happen, but we allow ourselves some leeway in development. That means that we can make three, or even four, changes in settings within that house in a production day – as long as the total number of pages is okay.

One other thing. If we have a setting that has 8 pages, and we know it will take two production days, we do not have to worry about which scenes will be done on which day. That is something that the director and DP and AD will work out in pre-production.

Another critical factor in the production calendar involves the use of actors. This is in pre-production where we get back to that other secondary factor. There are several SAG rules concerning the scheduling of actors and the ability to have them work for a few days, then let them off a few days, and then call them back. If we do too much of this we can wind up paying them for the days they are not working. A good production manager will try to avoid this by intelligently scheduling actors so their scenes are on consecutive production days. This is often not possible because of other more important scheduling factors, but it's good to keep in mind as it will directly affect our budget.

Locations are another factor in setting the production calendar. Some essential locations are only available on certain days. This will be determined during the location scouting part of pre-production and will often create headaches for the production manager and the production calendar. If alternative locations are not available or acceptable, we just have to work with the restrictions.

Other factors that impact the production calendar are holidays, travel days, special preparation or rehearsal days, and other factors, some of which can be unique to each production.

C. Scheduling of Nonfiction

I've saved the hardest to last. Scheduling non-fiction is difficult because the non-fiction treatment is not like a fiction script. There are no scenes or page counts. There is not a standard technique for covering a scene. This is where experience really counts for a Producer or production manager of nonfiction content.

The more detailed the treatment, the better. We start by reviewing the breakdown list for interviewees and the interview locations. And then we start asking questions. Are they all in the same area or spread around the world? Is the topic for the interview about an event from the past that can be described in one interview? Or does it follow a current process that will be happening in real time over days, weeks or years, and will therefore require a number of interviews over that period?

Then we look at the breakdown list of b-roll and ask questions. How much b-roll will there be, and in what locations, and does it follow a process that happens over time? What b-roll can we anticipate that is not in the treatment? Remember the cardinal rule of b-roll – we can never have too much.

Unlike a fiction production calendar, which is mostly consecutive days, the non-fiction production calendar will likely have periods of production and periods of downtime that are spread out over weeks, months or even years. It's a very different animal. But it's one that can be tamed if approached carefully and with a lot of critical thinking and questioning.

SUPPLEMENTAL MATERIAL – CHAPTER 17 – SCHEDULING

<u>Review Questions</u>

1. What information is typically found on the header strip of a production board?

2. Where does the information for the scene strip come from?

3. What are divider strips used for?

4. What does it mean to make-a-day? Is it the same for all types of projects?

5. What is the primary factor for sorting the scenes to make a schedule?

6. What are the secondary factors?

7. What are the other factors that can impact the schedule?

8. How does the production calendar schedule differ from the scene schedule?

9. What are some of the factors that impact the production calendar?

<u>Industry Speak</u>

12-hour turnaround – a union requirement that insures at least twelve hours of down time between production days

Header strip – the control panel for a production board that contains information on the production and the characters as numbered on the breakdown list

Making-a-day – a target number of pages to shoot on an

average production day

Production board – a device used to hold the header board and scene strips that contained a film schedule; the interface in a computerized scheduling system

Production calendar schedule – puts the days from the scene schedule in a calendar format; based on factors of the physical production

Scene schedule - a sorting of scenes according the the primary and secondary factors; then calculating the number of days that will be needed to shot those scenes

Scene strip – a strip of cardboard, or a computer representation, that contains much of the information from a breakdown sheet for that scene

Wrap – to end the production at a particular location; includes packing up all equipment and restoring the area to its original condition; also the overall end of a production

Further Activities

Create a Schedule – more learning by doing.

1. Go online to www.theproducerssourcebook.com and go to the Scheduling, chapter 17, page.

2. Access the file: Schedule – The Boomers – scene order. Each scene has been entered with the appropriate data. Make a copy of that page, rename it "setting sort", and then sort all the scenes by setting. Then add up the total pages in 1/8s for each setting. After completion, check your work with the file: Schedule – The Boomers – setting sort.

3. Make a copy of your setting sort page, rename it "making days, and them arrange the setting groups into production days with the goal for a maximum of 5 pages per production day (with the exception of the bar setting which is one day

to itself). After completion, check your work with the file: Schedule – The Boomers – making days.

4. Make a copy of your making days page, rename it "calendar schedule", and then arrange the production days into a ten day schedule using two five-day weeks. The weeks don't have to be Monday to Friday; you don't get extra credit by making it less than 10 days if those days are not properly scheduled (for example, too many pages or settings)

If you are in one setting for more than one day, then the average number of pages needs to be 5 or less, but each day doesn't have to work out to exactly 5 pages.

Your calendar must follow these guidelines:

The bar setting is only available on a Sunday;

The Film Department settings, including classroom and conference room, are only available on a weekend;

Clark's Office is available any day;

The Fitness center settings are only available on a Monday.

After completion, check your work with the file: Schedule – The Boomers – calendar schedule.

Further Reading & Research

Visit Entertainment Partners at www.ep.com to see their line of software for Producers, including Movie Magic Scheduling and Movie Magic Budgeting. Once a Producer knows the rationales and procedures of the breakdown, scheduling, and budgeting functions, these software programs are the next step into industry professionalism.

Another industry favorite for scheduling and budgeting software can be found at www.junglesoftware.com

Get in the daily habit – read the industry trade papers to

know what is going on in the industry. For film and television, I recommend *Variety, Hollywood Reporter, Broadcasting & Cable,* and *Current.* They are all available online. Another good resource for what's happening in television is the *Cynopsis.com* online newsletter. For documentary and nonfiction work, I suggest *Real Screen.*

18

BUDGETING

"The lack of money is the root of all evil."
- George Bernard Shaw

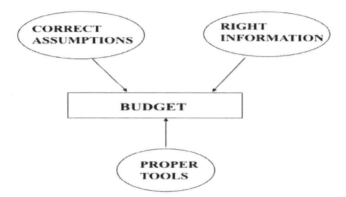

OVERVIEW

B udgeting. The very word strikes fear in the hearts of many otherwise brave creative souls. It's easy to develop a creative treatment, to envision the flow of the edited film. It's tedious but possible to identify all those production elements and make a sensible schedule. But budgeting seems somehow so foreign, so impossible. What is really impossible, however, is to over hype the importance of a budget as a Producer develops a project – fiction or nonfiction. The goal of development after all is to raise money to make a film. And we don't know how much to raise until we do a budget.

In reality, budgeting can be very simple. All it takes are three ingredients as represented in the diagram above:

1. The correct assumptions,

2. The right information, and

3. The proper tools.

We will cover these three ingredients in a moment, but first a few basic concepts need to be discussed.

DIFFERENT APPROACHES AT DIFFERENT STAGES

Budgeting is done at least twice during the course of most film or video projects.

The first budget, the <u>development budget</u>, is done during the development stage when the Producer needs to know how much money she has to raise or secure to produce the project. Ideally, this is more than a "ball-park" estimate because it is based on the breakdown and scheduling work that was done on the shooting script or the documentary treatment. This should be as complete a budget as is possible at this stage. It will rely on assumptions that can change as the Producer is out in the marketplace looking for money for the project. A feature film with low budget assumptions will become a big budget project if a big-name star signs on. A documentary project will take on a new scope as research opens up new possibilities. One of the key differences in developing a budget at this stage, however, is that the Producer does not spend any time or energy negotiating deals or trying to find the lowest rates on the different budgeted items. The smart Producer will use the rate cards that are available from vendors on their web-sites. Don't waste everyone's time negotiating rates when doing a development budget because it may be months, years or forever until there is the money available to actually get into production. A Producer doesn't want get a reputation with the local vendors that she wastes their time asking for bids on projects that aren't funded.

The second budget, the <u>production budget</u>, is done after the Producer has successfully secured funds for the project. At this point we enter the pre-production stage. The amount of money raised will provide the overall context for a final production budget. This production budget will be based on the current assumptions and realities of the project. It will be the basis for future determination of how the production is being managed and whether it is on-budget, over-budget or under-budget. For this budget, the Producer flexes his negotiating muscles and tries to make the best deals possible with all the vendors and crew.

REVENUE AND EXPENSES

Most of the time when we speak about budgets, we refer to expenses. A proper budget, however, contains information about the anticipated sources and amounts of revenue. They are placed first in the budget. The revenue is followed by the expenses and then at the end there is a calculation that hopefully shows either a breakeven or a surplus/profit.

To estimate revenue in the development budget, the Producer operates within a framework based on her production strategy and on her assumptions as to what amount of money she can secure for the project. These assumptions are based on the established marketplace for this kind of project. In the pre-production budget, the sources and estimated amounts of money will be more accurate and could be based on contracts with different distributors.

ABOVE THE LINE and BELOW THE LINE

When we get into the mechanics of the budget, we will see that there are <u>line items</u> for every type of expense including people. More on line items later.

In feature film budgets, certain expenses, or line items, are separated from the others. These are the expenses for the key creative people (Producer, director, writer, big stars) and the underlying property. They are presented first in the budget and then sub-totaled as the <u>above-the-line expenses</u>. Everything else comes after these and are called <u>below-the-line</u>. The people who are above-the-line are those who will most likely be bankable elements in the Producer's package and have some sort of profit

293

participation or points in the project.

Documentary projects do not have this division in their budgets. Probably because there is seldom any profit to participate in.

VENDOR DEALS

When doing the pre-production budget, a Producer will spend the time necessary to get the best possible deal from each vendor or supplier of goods and services.

There are several considerations to making good vendor deals. First of all, vendors are the various suppliers of goods and services for the production. The largest of these are the equipment rental companies, the film labs (if shooting film), the caterers, and the sound stages. In the development budget we used the rate cards from these vendors, but if we are in pre-production, we have money, and we're ready to make some deals.

First of all, try to give yourself as much time as possible to shop around and negotiate. Hopefully, the pre-production period on the project will be long enough to do this. Nothing wastes money faster than trying to get a deal or discount at the last minute.

Second, never accept the price that's on the rate card. Always assume that the rates are negotiable and don't be afraid to ask for a discount. Sure, there may be periods of very high demand for equipment when a rental house will not be willing to make discounts. But that is not the norm. And the smart Producer of a low budget project will try to schedule her production during a time when there is normally not a lot of production activity.

One form of discount that most equipment rental companies give is the weekly rate. This is sometimes published on the rate card and indicates the weekly rate is equal to four times the daily rate or what is called a four-day-week. A Producer should always ask for an additional discount down to a three-day-week. She might not get it, but it never hurts to ask.

The third thing is for a Producer to develop relationships with vendors. A vendor is more likely to give him a bigger discount if he's a steady customer. Some Producers will try to negotiate a very low rate with the promise of more business in the future. This is okay if they keep their word. Many vendors are leery of some Producers because of false promises of this type.

The Three Ingredients.

Now let's focus on those three ingredients for an easy budget.

1. CORRECT ASSUMPTIONS

The good Producer has already begun this process as part of the production strategy. Now that there is a good script breakdown and schedule available, it is time to refine those assumptions and make additional ones.

How much time should be allowed for production?

For a feature film, this assumption is based on the length of the shooting script. The convention is that each page of the fiction script represents a minute of finished film. A 90-page script would give us a 90-minute film. For a documentary film, the assumption is based on the anticipated market. If it's for a television/cable network, then it will normally be either 30-minutes or 60-minutes (or actually less because they need time for commercials). Occasionally, a network will schedule a 90-minute special.

How much time should be allowed for production?

If a Producer is doing a fiction film, then he already knows this. He has a schedule that tells him how many production days he will need. Add in a day or two (or more depending on the nature of the production) for contingencies created by bad weather, sick actors and/or a slow director. There is always going to be something that goes wrong, so plan for it.

If a Producer is doing a documentary, then the answer is not so easy, as we discussed in the previous chapter. It requires some real experience on the part of the Producer to be able to review a treatment and its breakdown and be able to estimate a production schedule. Every project will be different. The positive note here is that most networks and others who fund documentaries know this problem and are flexible with schedules and budgets - to a point.

How much time should be allotted to pre-production and post-production?

This is probably the hardest assumption to make for both fiction and documentaries and requires the most experience on the part of the Producer. It entails doing a very detailed analysis and task list for everything that has to be done in pre and post production. The list, if done properly, should be overwhelming. The oldest adage in filmmaking is that there seldom is enough time for pre-production, and it's the truth. In the development stage, a Producer makes the best educated estimate they can. Then the best approach for a Producer when she is in pre-production is to hire good help and assign them tasks to keep the pre-production timeline manageable.

There are obviously differences in terms of tasks between fiction and nonfiction, but the approach is the same. For example, a fiction Producer would estimate how many days are needed to research head shots and line up actors for casting; while a nonfiction Producer estimates how many days to budget for research on the potential interviewees and what they would add to the documentary?

Post production for a nonfiction project will also generally take longer because it is a process of discovery and often involves hundreds of hours of material. With fiction, the editor is conforming to the script and there are a limited number of shots of coverage and takes for each shot. And, of course, post production is not just editing.

What are the formats to be used?

There are three formats to consider and chose – production

format, editing format and distribution format.

This is the time to decide whether to shoot the project on film, digital tape or digital non-tape media (hard drive, P2 card, or memory card), and standard definition or high definition. There are a number of creative and financial factors to consider. The debate on the creative advantages / disadvantages or the various "looks" of film versus digital is not part of the discussion for this book. What we know is that this assumption of a production format will impact the budget in significant ways.

Let's say that, in general, it costs more to shoot on film rather than digital tape or a digital media. 35mm film will cost significantly more than 16mm or super 16mm film. However, the costs of shooting a feature film in 4K HD with the best cameras will approach the costs of shooting on 35mm film.

One way to approach this assumption is to focus on the primary market and what that demands in terms of distribution format. A feature film that is planned for theatrical release is no longer required to be available in a release print on film. Digital projection is approaching 100% of all screens, but there are still some theaters that require a film print. For smaller budget independent films, the reality is that a film print is still necessary. And 35mm film is very much preferred over 16mm or super 16mm film. In fact, if theaters have a film projector at all, it will be 35mm.

To get the best release print on film it is advisable to shoot on film. It is possible to transfer a digital production to film and make a release print. However, most people still believe that it doesn't look as good as a print struck from a film negative. If it doesn't look good, it had better have an incredible story and brilliant acting to have any chance of success. This is a creative decision as well as a financial one.

Documentary projects, on the other hand, are most often shot on digital tape or media. Generally the budgets for these projects don't allow for film production, and they will not be projected in theaters. Distribution to television/cable is on digital masters or data files. HD has become the standard acquisition format for television. Network fiction dramas and some sitcoms are the only exceptions, as many of these are still being shot on 35mm film.

No matter what are the production and distribution formats, the editing format will be some digitized, non-linear, hard-drive stored system. Everything today is edited on an Avid, Lightworks, Final Cut Pro, Premier or other NLE program. Material shot on film is transferred to digital files and then loaded onto editing hard-drives. The film to digital transfer is an additional and not insignificant cost. Material shot on digital tape or media saves a step and cost in the process, while material can also be shot and stored initially on hard drives. With film, once the edit decision list (EDL) of the off-line edit is ready, a negative cutter prepares the film negative for subsequent processing and printing in the lab. With digital projects, the data files from the edit systems are seldom ready for "prime-time" and generally require some additional sound and/or picture work in a post-production facility.

What will be the shooting ratio?

The shooting ratio is the ratio of the amount of material shot as it relates to the length of the finished project. For example, if 50 hours of material are shot and eventually edited into a one-hour documentary, the shooting ratio is 50 to 1. If the shooting ratio for a 90-minute feature film is budgeted to be 10 to 1, then 900 minutes of film will be shot. The ratios in these examples are the norm except that documentaries are much harder to estimate. Fiction films generally have a shooting ratio that ranges from 8 to 1 up to 15 to 1. The lower ratios are found on low budget projects that use a lot of master shots and very little coverage. TV movies-of-the-week are often shot using a very low ratio because they schedule a lot of pages per day. Studio films can be profligate wasters of film stock. The late Stanley Kubrick worked with ratios that rivaled documentaries.

This assumption of shooting ratio plus the decision on production format, gives the Producer the ability to budget for film, digital

298

tape stock, hard drives, memory cards, film processing, work prints and film-to-tape transfers. In a film production, these are very important numbers as seen below. These assumptions will also impact the budget in the assumption of the number of crew needed for the project. 35mm and 4K HD shoots require more crew than 16mm shoots which require more crew than digital video shoots.

Let's look at a feature film of 90 minutes with a 10 to 1 ratio. That equals 900 minutes of material being shot. If we're shooting 35mm, each roll of 1,000 feet of film stock gives us approximately 10 minutes of material (it's actually slightly more than 11 minutes, but 10 is much easier for budgeting purposes). If we're shooting 16mm or super 16mm, each roll of 400 feet of film stock gives us approximately 10 minutes of material (it's also actually slightly more than 11 minutes). Given that information, a 35mm budget for film stock, processing, transfers will be more than $70,000. For a super 16mm production, the budget drops to just over $22,000.

In comparison to these film budget numbers, let's consider shooting this feature on HD digital, which is now the television standard format. HDCAM or DVCPRO tapes for field production come in 30 or 40-minute cassettes. Longer tapes are available but use a slightly thinner and less robust tape stock. These tapes cost around $30 each. Using our 10 to 1 ratio, we would need 30 tapes for a cost of $900. There are no costs for processing or work prints but there is a cost for the transfer of the footage to hard drives for storage and use with the editing systems. You want duplicate hard drives for all the footage so that adds up to several thousand dollars. Therefore, our materials cost is approximately $2,900 compared to $70,000 for 35mm and $22,000 for 16mm film. A fairly dramatic difference isn't it.

When we consider that documentaries are often shot with a 50 to 1 ratio or greater, the budgetary impact of the format decision becomes even more apparent. A one –hour documentary project shot with a 50 to 1 ratio on 35mm would have a film stock, processing, work print and film-to-tape budget of close to

$350,000; while the same project on super 16mm would be in the range of $110,000; and, on digital HD the project would cost less than $8,500. This clearly illustrates why documentaries are not shot on film.

Will any union or guild agreements be signed?

Please refer to chapter 19 for a discussion of the financial ramifications of this decision.

How will the crew be paid?

Please refer to chapter 20 for a discussion of the budget ramifications of this decision.

Will the project be shot on locations or on a sound stage or a combination?

There is a complete discussion of production on location and sound stage in chapter 22.

Are there any special production needs and/or problems?

A properly done breakdown of a script or documentary treatment will present the Producer with a list of the special production needs and/or problems that should be anticipated with the production. These could involve a lot of computer graphics or special equipment such as dollys, cranes, car-rigs. Maybe there are big stunts that call for additional personnel as well as equipment. Big scenes with lots of extras create a number of budgeting issues including cast/extras, personnel (more 2nd ADs), and more catering. Period scenes with costumes increase a budget in many ways including wardrobe, props, set dressing and production time for set up and wrap.

What music will be used?

Music has its own special rules and problems which are discussed in chapter 25.

Documentary and non-fiction project budgets will often cover the same assumptions as above. In addition, there are some additional assumptions that are unique to a documentary or nonfiction project. These include the following, all of which should have been considered during the breakdown and scheduling process. How many interviewees will there be? What are the locations for the interviews? How much b-roll will be needed for each interviewee? What other b-roll needs will there be?

Here are some additional assumptions that would get considered in nonfiction production planning. Will stock footage be required? And if so, how much is anticipated? Will there be extensive use of art work, graphics and/or photographs? Who on the production crew will travel to distant locations? The answers to these questions will directly impact the budget.

2. RIGHT INFORMATION

This simply means that a Producer has to have up-to-date information on what things cost. She should also have some experience with negotiating vendor deals and know what she can expect from that negotiation. This information initially comes from the rate cards and price lists that we consult for the development budget. And in that development budget we go no further. If we can't find rates then we need to contact the vendor and get a price, but remember that in development we don't waste anyone's time by negotiating.

A simple internet google search will find vendors in almost any market. Most film commissions publish production guides that list the vendors in their area who work with Producers. The vendors want Producers to find them and talk to them and obviously use them. Act like a professional and good results will follow.

3. THE PROPER TOOLS

Thank goodness that the days of having to use a paper spreadsheet, a pencil and a calculator to prepare a budget are long gone. Today we have the extensive abilities of computer spreadsheets such as Excel to prepare, calculate and check our budgets. We also have software that has been developed specifically for our industry that helps us prepare budgets.

Flexibility

Whether a Producer uses Excel or budgeting software, the goal is to have the ability to make changes to the assumptions and have them automatically impact the budget. For example, if we change the assumption on number of production days from 25 to 30, the spreadsheet or software should automatically change all the line items that use the number of production days as a part of their calculation. And there are normally many of them, including crew, equipment rental, catering, etc. The budgeting software is designed to do this while the Excel sheet must be set up to do it with formulas (an advance/beginner skill level on Excel).

Format

Most budgets have a standard look and structure. Except for the header line, each line in the budget is what we call a line item when it refers to a specific expense. Other lines can be used to name departments or section headings or for totals.

Here is a sample of part of a budget with a variety of lines and line items.

ACCT. #	DESCRIPTION	AMOUNT	UNITS	X	RATE	SUBTOTAL	TOTAL
1400	Talent / SAG						
	Name of Character 1	8	days		$100	$800	
	Name of Character 2	6	days		$100	$600	
1430	Day Players	1	days	18	$100	$1,800	
1480	PHW	14.8	percent		$3,200	$474	
1490	payroll taxes	15	percent		$3,200	$480	
							$4,154
2100	Film Stock & Processing						
2101	16mm film	15	rolls		$120.00	$1,800	
2102	processing	6000	feet		$0.14	$840	
2110	Work print	600	feet		$0.19	$114	
2120	transfers	11.25	hours		$375.00	$4,219	
							$6,973
3100	Camera Department						
3101	Director of Photography						
	preproduction	5	days		$700.00	$3,500	
	production	2	weeks		$2,800.00	$5,600	
	post production	2	days		$700.00	$1,400	
3105	Camera Operator	2	weeks		$2,000.00	$4,000	
3110	1st AC	2	weeks		$1,000.00	$2,000	
3112	2nd AC	2	weeks	2	$800.00	$3,200	
3120	camera rental	2	weeks				
3190	payroll taxes	15	percent		$19,700.00	$2,955	
							$22,655

First, let's examine the header line from left to right.

ACCT. # Account Numbers are created by the accounting department to keep track of expenses and be able to compare them

303

to the budget. Each studio and production company has its own set of account numbers. In a development budget, if you haven't already developed a chart of accounts, you can just make them up, or better yet, you can ignore them.

The Description of the line item is important and should be short and concise and describe the line item thing. In most cases it refers to a generic thing such as a camera operator. In the case of talent/cast, there is a specific line item for each of the principal characters because their details, number of days worked and amount paid, will differ. Then there is normally a line item for "day players", which totals the number of days for the balance of the speaking characters (all of whom are paid the same amount), and a line item for "extras", which is again a total of extras anticipated for the whole film (all paid the same amount).

The Amount refers to the quantity of the Units, which are often "days" or "weeks" for many of the line items. There are, however, other unit measures such as "flat", which is used to designate a negotiated amount; "estimate", which is just that, a good guess; and "percent", which alerts us to a specific calculation. Some line item units are the thing that is bought such as "rolls" for rolls of film, "feet" for how much film is processed, "tapes" for number of tapes, or "meals" for catering.

Skipping the X for a moment, the Rate is how much you will pay for each unit. Then a simple multiplication of the Amount times the Rate gives us a Subtotal. At the end of each section or department there is a Total which is an addition of all the subtotals for that section or department.

The X factor is a way to indicate that there are more than one of a particular person or thing as described in the line item. So if there are 18 Day Players, 45 extras, and two 2nd ACs; and each will work for the same number of units and get paid the same rate, then the addition of the X factor means the subtotal is increased by that factor. If, however, that second 2nd AC was to work a different number of units or get paid a different rate, then they would have to be put in the budget as a separate line item.

In some cases, such as the "payroll taxes" in the above example, the amount and unit is a percentage of a number in the <u>Rate</u> column that is itself a sum of a range of subtotals. For example, the PHW line item under Talent/SAG shows that 17.5 percent is calculated against a figure in Rate that is a formula for the sum of the subtotals for the four line items – Character 1, Character 2, Day Players, and Extras. That is because the SAG pension-health-welfare payment is calculated as a percentage of the total of the payroll for the actors. The same applies for the calculation of the payroll taxes in each department. The percentage is calculated against the total of all the personnel costs in that department.

This and other formulas have to be set up carefully to be accurate and to be flexible. This is particularly important in the event a new line item is added to a group of line items that is being subtotaled. All of this requires that the Producer has to have a solid understanding of Excel or the budgeting software he is using. Formulas are wonderful but can be tricky, and mistakes can sometimes be hard to catch and can cause significant problems.

PROCESS

There are a lot of elements or steps in the budgeting process that need or are helped by having production experience. A new Producer without production experience should hire someone with that experience who will assist them with the budget.

One of the best ways to start is to carefully walk through pre-production, production and post production, and think carefully. Jot down all the tasks that need to be done and the people needed to do them. Think of all of the production departments and crew and pieces of equipment and other expenses that are needed. Go through all the breakdown lists to estimate costs. Review the production notes for clues on expenses. Don't skimp. This is not the time to try to think of cutting costs. It is far more important to account for everyone and everything, to not forget something critical and expensive. A good budget takes time, don't rush.

Supplemental Material – Chapter 18 – Budgeting

<u>Review Questions</u>

1. What are the three ingredients for budgeting?

2. What are the differences between a development budget and a production budget?

3. What people are normally above-the-line on a budget?

4. What factors are involved when making a vendor deal?

5. On what basis does the Producer assume the length of a fiction production? A nonfiction production?

6. How does a Producer estimate the time needed for preproduction and post production?

7. What is a shooting ratio and how does it impact the budget?

8. What are the assumptions that are unique to a documentary or other nonfiction project?

9. What does it mean for a budget to be flexible?

10. Be sure you know what each column of a line item contains and how they relate to each other.

<u>Industry Speak</u>

Above-the-line – the section of a film industry budget that contains line items for Producer, director, writer, and cast

Below-the-line – the portion of a film industry budget that contains the line items for all personnel and expenses that are not in the above-the-line section

Bid - a written proposal stating the terms and price for goods and/or services

EDL - Edit Decision List- details on every edit point in a production used by an online editor to complete the final film

Line item – part of a budget that contains the detail on a specific expense

Off-line edit – the initial edit done by the editor, director and Producer; created the final EDL

Points – a reference to percentage points that are calculated in a budget; also refers to the profit participation of certain people in the project

Rate card – the official pricing for goods and services from a vendor

Shooting ratio – the amount of material that is shot in order to produce a segment of finished film; normally calculated by minutes

Vendor – the provider of a good or a service to a production

Further Activities

1. Internet Assignment:

To practice working with vendor websites, please access and review these web-sites on the Internet and try to find the prices for the items in **bold**.

www.thewashingtonsource.com The Washington Source for Lighting – lighting and grip equipment rental. Find the daily rate for: **an HMI lighting package; a 3-ton with small grip package; and a Fisher Model Ten dolly.**

www.studiodepot.com Studio Depot – camera and other supplies. Find the price for **a dolly track kit; a roll of Gaffers tape 2" black; and a Canvas Sandbag 15 lbs.**

2. Create a Budget

Go to the website www.theproducerssourcebook.com, access the Budgeting, chapter18, page. Using the excel template (budget template for Sourcebook), create assumptions and a budget for the fiction script *The Boomers*. This should be a detailed "real-world" production budget with no deferrals and no "freebies".

Review the feature film template from EP Budgeting file on the website to assist in determining what crew and expenses might be needed. Obviously not all the same expenses would be incurred for a short film.

There is a file, rates for budget exercise, that you can use for non-union crew pay rates and other information. For other rates search for vendors' published rates for equipment rental and other services.

Develop your budget assumptions including:

The number of production days comes from the breakdown and schedule done in previous chapters.

Use the SAG Ultra Low or Modified Low Budget Agreement, which can be found at www.sagindie.com/resources; be sure to pay attention to the maximum budget amount allowed by the agreements. The number of days for the actors comes from the schedule.

Decide whether to use the other unions/guilds, but everyone gets paid some form of industry rate, including Producer, who has to be paid for all her time – from the beginning of pre-production through the end of post-production.

There should be pre-production, production, and post-production periods. A production office would be needed for this entire time.

Decide on production format – film or video/digital; and

shooting ratio, which must be within industry norms.

Make sure that the budget includes an adequate crew to make this kind of film; everyone should be paid their full daily or weekly rate. Read chapter 20 for more information. Review the Pro-forma for crew ideas.

Locations cannot be free – assume some average fee plus other costs if necessary; several settings can be assumed to be in one location; daily rate is normal; read chapter 22 for more information

Assume some work in a professional post-production house for at least 3 hours each of sound sweetening and color correction

There has to be basic production insurance coverage; read chapter 21 for more information

This is a production budget, and there is no need to include marketing costs or distribution costs; but don't forget a photographer to take publicity stills on at least one day of production

After developing a budget, check it against the file: sample budget - The Boomers.

Further Reading & Research

Film and Video Budgets, 6th Edition, Maureen A. Ryan, Wiese Productions. ISBN: 978-1-61593-221-4

This is a very good resource for anyone who has to do a film budget.

Visit Entertainment Partners at www.ep.com to see their line of software for Producers, including Movie Magic Scheduling and Movie Magic Budgeting. Once a Producer knows the rationales and procedures of the breakdown, scheduling, and budgeting functions, these software programs are the next step into industry professionalism.

Another industry favorite for scheduling and budgeting software can be found at www.junglesoftware.com

Get in the daily habit – read the industry trade papers to know what is going on in the industry. For film and television, I recommend *Variety, Hollywood Reporter, Broadcasting & Cable,* and *Current.* They are all available online. Another good resource for what's happening in television is the *Cynopsis.com* online newsletter. For documentary and nonfiction work, I s uggest *Real Screen.*

19

UNIONS AND GUILDS

T he rationale for unions in the United States is clear. The powerful force of collective bargaining was as needed and as effective in the film industry in the 1930s as it was in the coal, steel, railroad and many other industries. The large studios were not above squeezing the last bit of blood, sweat and tears from their workers, even the key creative people.

The primary unions and guilds in the film and television industry are:

Screen Actors Guild / American Federation of Television and Radio Artists
Directors Guild of America
Writers Guild of America

Other unions and guilds in the industry include:

American Society of Cinematographers
IATSE – International Alliance of Theatrical and Stage Employees
The Teamsters
Motion Picture Editors Guild
Set Decorators Society of America

Most Producers will be faced with the decision of whether or not to sign with a union or guild at some point in their career. Those working with feature films will have to make that decision almost immediately, primarily because they will want to work with SAG actors. Documentary Producers are not as frequently concerned with the unions and guilds. There are occasions, however, especially when producing programs for the broadcast or cable networks, when this decision might come up. In order to make a rational decision it is important to understand what the unions and guilds do and what benefits they provide to their members.

INDUSTRY CONTRACTS

Each union and guild has negotiated a basic agreement with the different organizations that represent the studios and the television and cable networks. These agreements are contracts that contain hundreds of pages of detail on rates, royalties, and work rules. One of the main provisions of all the basic agreements is that all union members who are hired to work on a production are considered employees of the Producer. More on that in chapter 20.

Copies and summaries of these agreements are found on the various websites. A good Producer will be familiar with the main provisions of the contracts. A good production manager, line Producer, or AD will be very familiar with all of the terms in the basic contracts – and there are a lot of them.

Contract information can be found as follows:

Writers Guild www.wga.org

Home / Employers & Agents / What Producers
Needs to Know
Home / Contracts & Enforcement / Schedule of
Minimums

Directors Guild www.dga.org

Home / Contracts / Agreements
Home / Contracts/Rate Card

Screen Actors Guild www.sagaftra.org

Home/ Contracts / Theatrical Film

BENEFITS TO MEMBERS

The role of collective bargaining should be obvious from the history of unions and guilds. A solitary employee has no bargaining leverage with an employer, especially one as large as the studios and TV networks. As a group, however, the employees have a lot of leverage and can substantially improve their conditions. This concept works almost as well with the independent artists who make up a guild. They are most often not full-time employees of the studios/networks, but they are essential to the success of the business of the studios/networks.

The basic agreements that have resulted from this collective bargaining process all provide the members with a number of important benefits including:

- Set pay rates – eliminates the need for each individual to negotiate with the studio or production company; assures that everyone is treated equally and fairly

- Consistent work rules – spelled out in great detail in the contracts; address safety and other issues that can arise during a production; some rules have monetary penalties if the studio or production company breaks them

- Pension, Health and Welfare (PHW) – critical in an industry where most people are freelance workers and don't have access to employer group health care or pension plans; the studios pay between 17% and 19% of wages into the union fund on behalf of the workers. The union/guild then has group plans that the members can take advantage of.

- Residual collection – a complex system that provides additional income if a film or TV show is exploited in a market other than the original market covered by the basic payment; see examples from the WGA in Supplemental

315

Material for this chapter

- Legal assistance – financial assistance for a member who has to sue a studio or production company or someone else in the industry

- Artistic rights – all union work is "work for hire" but some would like more control of the end product, as they have in other countries

MEMBERSHIP REQUIREMENTS

Membership in the various unions and guilds is restricted, and the restrictions are primarily based on experience and/or employment in that area of the industry. They all have initial costs to join and then either monthly or annual dues, which include a percentage of the income the member makes in the industry. For further information, access the following.

Directors Guild www.dga.org

Home / The Guild / Departments /Membership

Screen Actors Guild www.sagaftra.org

Home / Union Info / Membership

Writers Guild www.wga.org

Home / Members / New Members

LOW BUDGET AGREEMENTS

In recent years, most of the unions and guilds have made concessions to the Producers of low budget independent films. This has been part of an effort to make it easier for these independent Producers to work with the union and guild members. Beginning in the 1970s as the independent film movement blossomed, the guild actors, directors and crew were unable to participate because the independent Producers would not sign a basic agreement and pay the standard rates. But these Producers were doing exciting work and people wanted to work on these projects. So first SAG, and then the others, developed special agreements for low budget productions.

The range of concessions varies by the different unions and guilds, as does the definition as to what makes a low budget film. For new Producers and Producers of low budget films, the SAG agreements are the most interesting because it is more likely that an agreement will be made with SAG than with the other unions and guilds. SAG/AFTRA has a special website, sagindie.com, that is designed to help the independent filmmaker with information on low budget agreements and casting.

You can access the following to learn the differences between the different low budget and short film agreements.

Screen Actors Guild www.sagindie.org

Home / Contracts / Theatrical Film

Directors Guild www.dga.org

Home/ Contracts / Agreements/ Low Budget

Writers Guild www.wga.org

Home/ Contracts & Enforcement / Other Contracts

THE PRODUCER'S DECISION

The major studios, production companies and networks are all signatories to the basic agreements of the various unions and guilds. As such, any project that they produce falls under the terms of those agreements. Independent Producers generally do not become signatories to the basic agreement as a company but instead make a decision separately for every project. Each project is normally set up in its own distinct company, and a decision to sign a union contract for one company will not affect the union status of the other companies controlled by the Producer.

The essential thing for a Producer to know is that the unions and guilds have absolutely no power over a project <u>unless</u> the Producer signs an agreement with them. And if he signs with one union or guild, it does not mean that he has to sign with any or all of the others.

If a Producer is doing a non-union project, and he hires an actor who is SAG, the guild can't do anything to him. Nothing! The guild can fine and even expel the actor from the guild, but it has no right to do anything to the Producer because he did not sign an agreement with it. If, however, he signs with SAG or any of the others, then he has to abide by the rules and regulations of the agreement. There can be severe monetary penalties for violating the agreement, and they are enforceable in court.

The Producer has to look at each project and weigh the pros and cons of whether to sign with any of the unions and guilds.

Pros:

- Access to a pool of experienced talent or crew

- There are set rates and work rules so a Producer can avoid the hassle that comes from dealing with each person individually. This does not mean, however, that some talent or crew will not negotiate for a rate that is greater than the minimum guild rate.

- There is a reliability factor that comes with hiring a professional union talent or crew. They are more likely to show up on time and to know their lines or their jobs. Plus, the union will assist the Producer if a member is not performing professionally

Cons:

- There is a higher cost involved – higher day rates plus Pension/Health/Welfare. For example, in many areas a very good non-union actor will be happy with $200 to 300 per day, flat rate. The same actor under the current SAG Basic Agreement (rates effective through 6/30/2019) will get a minimum of $980 per day or $3,403 per week plus 17.5% for PHW. The cost difference is an easy comparison for most Producers, but can be a false savings depending on the quality of the talent pools.

• There are residual payments due on any use of the project other than the primary use covered by the contract. For a theatrical film made under the basic agreement with SAG, an exhibition on television will cost the Producer a percentage of the distributor's gross receipts from the television license. This money is then distributed to all the SAG actors on the film.

• The basic agreements require special considerations for members that can also increase the costs for Producers. For example, the SAG Basic Agreement requires that all "transportation supplied by the Producer must be business class."

• A higher level of insurance coverage, including worker's compensation, is required; this also increases costs

• A Producer who doesn't follow the regulations of the Basic Agreement can face a monetary penalty. For example, a violation of the SAG credit provisions carries a $5,000 fine; and a delay of ½ hour in the required mealtime will cost $25 for every person on the cast.

• An increase in paperwork with the guild forms. On a feature film this can necessitate the addition of at least one person on the production management staff

• There is a security agreement that gives the guild the right to grab control of the film if the Producer has

violated the agreement. The guild files a UCC
statement to establish a lien on the film

- Most unions and guilds require the Producer to post a
deposit with them to cover penalties and fees incurred
during production

The bottom line for the Producer is that, as film budgets go up, it
is more likely that he will sign with one or more of the unions and
guilds. In some areas of the country it is also very hard to find
qualified talent and crew who are non-union. Signing with the
unions and guilds is not inherently good or bad. It's just one of the
major business decisions that a Producer makes with every project.

SUPPLEMENTAL MATERIAL – CHAPTER 19 – UNIONS AND GUILDS

<u>Review Questions</u>

1. What are the primary unions and guilds in the film industry?

2. What is the role of collective bargaining in the relationship between a union or guild and the industry?

3. What are the benefits to a person to belong to a union or guild?

4. What is the primary restriction for membership in a union or guild?

5. Do all Producers have to work with unions and guilds on all projects?

6. For a Producer, what are the pros and cons of working with a union or guild.

<u>Industry Speak</u>

Artistic rights – similar to copyright in that it gives the creator of a film some control over it, even if they do not legally own the copyright

Basic agreement – the agreement negotiated between the unions and the studios / networks that set the standard rates and work rules for the industry

Collective bargaining – individuals organized as a union negotiate as a group with employers

PHW – pension, health and welfare – a critical benefit for union members; includes their health insurance and their retirement fund

Residual – the money owed to union members when a film is released in any market that is in addition to the original market of the film

UCC Security agreement – Uniform Commercial Code; a legal hold on a property that insures the payment of a debt by the owner of that property; crates a lien on the property

Further Activities

Find more information on the history of the major unions and guilds in the film industry by going to the following:

The Directors Guild of American

www.dga.org

The Guild / History

The Screen Actors Guild / American Federation of Television and Radio Artists

www.sagaftra.org

About / History

The Writers Guild of America

www.wga.org

The Guild / About Us / History

IATSE – International Alliance of Theatrical and Stage Employees

www.iatse.net

American Society of Cinematographers

www.theasc.com

Motion Picture Editors Guild

www.editorsguild.com

Set Decorators Society of America

www.setdecorators.org

Teamsters

www.teamster.org/divisions/motion-picture-theatrical-trade

Further Reading & Research

WGA Residuals Guide (from WGA website)

EXAMPLE 1 - RESIDUALS ON A MADE-FOR-THEATRICAL MOTION PICTURE

Writer A is hired by a signatory Company on May 3, 2011 to write an original story and screenplay for a high budget theatrical motion picture. He is paid at least the WGA minimum of $119,954 for his writing services. (An overscale payment would not change this example.) When credits are finally determined, he receives sole "Written by" credit on the film. Within 30 days of the final determination of credits, the $5,000 DVD Script Publication Fee is due to Writer A.

In October 2011, the film is released theatrically. In January 2012, it is released to in-flight markets. Writer A will receive no residual compensation for either the theatrical or in-flight release because both were covered by his initial compensation.

In May 2012, the film is released on DVD and Blu-ray. In the quarter ending June 30, 2012, the Company received $1,000,000 in receipts from the distribution of DVD and Blu-ray sales. A residual payment of $15,000, 1.5% of the revenues, is due to Writer A. Writer A should receive payment within 60 days of the end of the quarter in which the Company received payment, or no later than August 31, 2012. Writer A will continue to receive residuals, calculated at 1.8% of any receipts over $1,000,000, payable within 60 days of the end of the quarter in which the Company receives additional receipts.

In September 2012, the Company licenses the film to pay television for a license fee of $3,900,000. Pursuant to the payment schedule, the Company will receive payment in three installments of $1,300,000 each. The first payment is received by the Company on October 1, 2012. A residual payment of $15,600, 1.2% of the installment received, is due to Writer A within 60 days of the end of the quarter in which the Company received payment. Because the quarter ends December 31, 2012, payment is due to Writer A on or before March 1, 2013. Future residual payments of 1.2% of the remaining installments are due to Writer A within 60 days of the end of the quarter in which the Company receives the payment.

In November 2012, the film aired on network television, for which the license fee was $2,000,000. The Company receives full payment of the license fee from the network on November 1, 2012. A residual payment of $24,000, 1.2% of the license fee, is due to Writer A within 30 days of the Company's receipt of payment, or by December 1, 2012.

EXAMPLE 2 - RESIDUALS ON A MADE-FOR-FREE TELEVISION PROJECT

On June 1, 2013, Writer A is hired by a signatory Company to write an episode of a half-hour network prime time series. Writer A receives sole "Written by" credit on her episode.

In November 2013, the episode has its first broadcast. The writer will not receive residuals for this telecast because the initial broadcast was covered by her initial compensation.

On March 1, 2014, Writer A's episode is rerun during network prime time. For this rerun, Writer A will receive $12,857, 100% of the residual base, which is the Other Than Network Prime Time 30-minute story and teleplay minimum. (Note that in the 2011 MBA, the rates for Network Prime Time residuals are frozen from the last period of the 2008 MBA). Payment for the network second run is due by March 31, 2014, 30 days from the telecast date.

On May 1, 2014, the series is sold to foreign free television where Writer A's episode airs on May 5, 2014. For this use, Writer A is entitled to a residual of $4,751.95 (35% of the 2013 residual base). The initial payment of $2,036.55 (15% of the residual base) is due 30 days after the Company's knowledge of the May 5 telecast, and no later than November 5, 2014, 6 months from the date of telecast. In addition, Writer A will receive 1.2% of foreign free television and basic cable gross receipts once foreign gross exceeds $365,000.

Subsequently, the series is sold into syndication where the episode has its third, fourth, and fifth runs on June 1, July 1, and August 1, 2015, respectively. Writer A will receive residuals for these runs as follows: 3rd run - $4,073.10 (30% of the residual base), 4th and 5th runs - $3,394.25 each (25% of the residual base). Payments are due four months from the telecast date as follows: 3rd run - October 1, 2015, 4th run - November 1, 2015, 5th run - December 1, 2015.

In September 2015, the series is sold to basic cable for a license fee of $25,000 per episode. The Company receives the entire license fee on September 30, 2015. A residual of $500, 2% of the license fee, is due to Writer A within 60 days of the end of the quarter in which the Company receives payment. Since the quarter ends September 30, 2015, payment is due to Writer A on or before November 30, 2015.

Finally, the various episodes of the series, including Writer A's episode, are licensed for in-flight at $15,000 per episode. The Company receives payment on November 30, 2015. A residual of $180, 1.2% of the license fee, is due to Writer A within 60 days of the end of the quarter in which the Company receives payment.

Since the quarter ends December 31, 2015, payment is due to Writer A on or before March 1, 2016.

Get in the daily habit – read the industry trade papers to know what is going on in the industry. For film and television, I recommend *Variety, Hollywood Reporter, Broadcasting & Cable,* and *Current.* They are all available online. Another good resource for what's happening in television is the *Cynopsis.com* online newsletter. For documentary and nonfiction work, I suggest *Real Screen.*

20

HIRING A CREW

H iring the right crew can make the difference between months of torture or pleasure for a Producer. In most major metropolitan areas of the world, and especially in North America and Europe, there are plenty of potential crewmembers to choose from. Some will be union, some not. Some will have years of experience, while others are starting their careers. Some will have experience in all types of film and video projects, while others might specialize in documentaries or in features. The trick for the Producer is to hire a crew based on several objective criteria.

- The overall budget level for the project

- The type of deal that is contemplated for the crew

- The type and complexity of the project, and

- the experience level required from the crew

There is also a subjective criteria involved in this decision. The crew of a film or video project works long hours, under intense pressure. If the crewmembers do not work well together and have a good attitude about the job and each other, then it's not only an unpleasant experience for everyone, but the quality of the work will suffer. Obviously this criterion is hard to judge about someone based on a quick interview. Most Producers will ask for references from a person that they haven't previously worked with. And then they will check them. Not all Producers are candid when giving references, but listen carefully and read between-the-lines of what they are saying about someone they have hired in the past. One question that is helpful to ask is, "Would you hire that person again?" If there isn't a quick and positive answer, move on to another person.

The Producer has the overall responsibility for hiring the crew. In a big feature film, the director may determine whom she wants for the DP and the 1st AD; and the DP may have his favorite crew that he wants to bring along. But, it is the Producer who actually negotiates with all of them and makes the final decision. In addition, the Producer has the responsibility to fire a crewmember who is not performing as expected. If it is a union member, there are strict rules regarding this process that must be followed. For non-union crew, the rules of decency, fair play, and non-discrimination apply. There might be local laws regarding hiring and firing employees that must be recognized and observed. It is an unpleasant task that is made more so by the legal complexities of employee rights.

EMPLOYEES VS. INDEPENDENT CONTRACTORS

When a Producer works with a union or guild, it is clearly stated in the agreement that the talent or crewmembers are employees of the Producer. As such, the Producer has to withhold taxes from the employees' pay and make the employer contributions to social security and state and federal unemployment benefits. These employer contributions will add an additional 15%-20% to the payroll costs of the project. Keeping records and filing the required tax forms will require lots of additional time and cost. In addition, the Producer will have personal liability for these taxes, even if she is producing the project in a corporate structure like a Limited Liability Corporation (LLC).

In a nonunion situation, the Producer might be tempted to treat all the talent and crew as independent contractors and not employees. This would seem to save money, paperwork and potential personal liability. Most talent and crew would prefer to have a larger paycheck with no taxes deducted. Unfortunately, this is not legal for more than 95% of the people who work on a film or video project.

According to the rules of the Internal Revenue Service, all the talent and most of the crew on a media project are employees of the Producer. The only exceptions to this might be the director, the DP, and possibly the editor who could be considered independent contractors. For a larger feature, other department heads such as production designer and casting director might be independent contractors as well. The "test" for the IRS has to do with control and independence of action in the production, the workplace. In the hierarchical structure of a film production, there are very few at the top who would meet the test. For more current information on the IRS's treatment of the independent contractor versus employee question, see the following site:

http://www.irs.gov/Businesses/Small-Businesses-&-Self-Employed/Independent-Contractor-Self-Employed-or-Employee

Many Producers, especially those doing small non-fiction projects, ignore these rules and treat everyone as independent contractors. They sign deal agreements or memos with the talent and crew members that state that they are independent contractors. But those agreements and all the wishful thinking in the world won't sway the IRS if the Producer is audited. If the IRS determines that the Producer failed to properly treat certain talent and crewmembers as employees, the Producer is liable for all the taxes that should have been paid plus interest plus big penalties. Such an audit can be a financial nightmare for the Producer. The talent and crewmembers involved will be okay as long as they properly declared all the income they received on their tax returns.

PAYROLL SERVICE

One industry resource that is available to the Producer who dreads the added paperwork of having employees is the payroll service company. These companies become the official employer of the talent and crew. They pay them; they keep the records; and file the tax returns. For this service the Producer pays a fee that is a percentage of the overall payroll. This fee can range from 5% to 8% of the payroll amount. Examples of such a company can be found at www.payreel.com and www.maslowmedia.com.

DEALS WITH THE CREW

The Producer should have a firm deal in place with all crew members before the production begins. This deal should be written in a deal memo or agreement. A sample of such an agreement for an employee (which is most people on the crew) follows.

CREW DEAL AGREEMENT (employee)

This Agreement contains the understanding between Sample Productions LLC, with its office at address ("Producer") and _____ (name and address), Social Security # _____ ("Employee") in regards to the services to be performed by Employee as a crewmember for Producer in conjunction with _____ (the "Program").

Employee is hired for the position of _____ , during the production dates of _____ .

The compensation paid to Employee shall be $_____ per day or $_____ per week, with the weekly rate in effect for a _____-day workweek. In addition, the Employee shall be paid $_____ per day for Box or Kit Rental, payable upon receipt of invoice. No increased or additional compensation shall accrue or be payable for the rendering of services at night or on weekends or holidays, or after the expiration of any particular number of hours of service in any period.

Wages shall be paid to all Employees no later than Friday following the week in which services were performed. Pay date may be delayed by reason of an intervening federal or state holiday. Employee is responsible for providing the requisite documents required by the U.S. Internal Revenue Service and the

Immigration Reform and Control Act of 1986 (IRCA), and any local tax authority documents. This includes completing and signing the required IRS W-4 Form and the Form I-9 pursuant to IRCA Section 274a.2. Employee shall comply with the immigration verification employment eligibility provisions required by law. Employee represents that he/she is at least eighteen years of age and legally able to enter into this Agreement.

Box or Kit Rentals are subject to W2 or 1099 reporting. No mileage payments or car allowances will be paid unless expressly stated below. Invoices for Box or Kit Rentals must be submitted to the Producer in a timely manner in order to be included in the Employee's regular payment.

Employees are responsible for liability and collision insurance and deductibles on her/his personal equipment and/or vehicle used in conjunction with their employment. Box or Kit is sole responsibility of Employee and Producer assumes no responsibility for same. Producer shall not be responsible for any loss of or damage to Employee's personal property or any personal injury to Employee subject, however, to Producer's obligation to obtain the insurance policies covering workman's compensation, accident, and third party damages. Copies of such insurance shall be on file and available at Producer's office.

Producer shall be the owner of all of the results and proceeds of Employee's services and may use and otherwise alter at the sole discretion of the Producer the results of the Employee's services for all purposes in any manner the Producer may determine. Producer shall have the right to use Employee's name, voice, picture and likeness in connection with the Program, the advertising and publication thereof and any promotional films or clips respecting the Program without additional compensation therefore. All rights in any work performed by Employee hereunder shall be freely assignable to any third party by Producer and may be exploited in any and all media whether now known or hereafter created in any manner in perpetuity without further compensation due Employee.

Producer reserves the right to discharge Employee at any time for any reason. Producer shall attempt to notify Employee a minimum of 24 hours in advance of layoff. Use of alcohol or drugs during hours of employment will result in Employee's immediate termination. This Agreement is subject to immediate suspension and/or termination, at Producer's election, without further obligation on the part of Producer in the event of any incapacity or default of Employee or in the case of any suspension, postponement or interference with the production of the Program by reason of labor controversy, strike, earthquake, act of God, governmental action, regulation, or decree or for any other customary *force majeure* reason.

Unless otherwise specified in this Agreement, screen credit is at Producer's discretion subject to Employee's performing all services required.

This Agreement represents the entire understanding between Producer and Employee. The terms and conditions of this Agreement are binding on Producer and Employee and shall not be waived or altered by any method other than by written agreement signed by both parties.

AGREED TO AND ACCEPTED:

EMPLOYEE (signature)

_____

Date: _____

PRODUCER (signature)

_____

Name: _____

Title: _____

Date: _____

The following is a sample of a deal memo for an independent contractor.

CREW DEAL AGREEMENT (independent contractor)

This Agreement contains the understanding between Sample Producer LLC, with its office at address ("Producer") and _____ (name and address), Social Security # _____ Fed. I.D. # _____ ("Contractor") in regards to the services to be performed by Contractor as crewmember for Producer in conjunction with _____ (the "Program").

Contractor is engaged for the position of _____, during the production dates of _____.

The compensation paid to Contractor shall be $_____ per day or $_____ per week, with the weekly rate in effect for a _____-day workweek. In addition, the Contractor shall be paid $_____ per day for Box or Kit Rental. No increased or additional compensation shall accrue or be payable for the rendering of services at night or on weekends or holidays or after the expiration of any particular number of hours of service in any period.

Compensation shall be paid to all Contractors no later than ten business days following the submission of the Contractor's invoice for services that have been performed. Pay date may be delayed by reason of an intervening federal or state holiday. No mileage payments or car allowances will be paid unless expressly authorized in writing by the Producer. Invoices for Box or Kit Rentals must be submitted to the Producer in a timely manner in order to be included in the Contractor's regular payment.

The Contractor warrants that he/she is an independent contractor under the current guidelines of the Internal Revenue Service ("IRS") and is not an employee of the Producer. As an independent contractor, the Contractor is solely responsible and liable for any income tax, unemployment insurance, FICA, or any other payment normally associated with an employer/employee relationship. Any and all payments to Contractor, including Box or Kit Rentals, shall be reported to the IRS as Contractor's income.

Contractors are responsible for liability and collision insurance and deductibles on her/his personal equipment and/or vehicle used in conjunction with their work. Box or Kit is the sole responsibility of Contractor, and Producer assumes no responsibility for same. Producer shall not be responsible for any loss of or damage to Contractor's personal property or any personal injury to Contractor subject, however, to Producer's obligation to obtain insurance policies covering accident and third party damages. Copies of such insurance shall be on file and available at Producer's office.

Contractor agrees that this is work-for-hire and has no claim to benefits that the Producer may derive from the Program. Producer shall be the owner of all materials related to or produced by the Contractor in the course of performing services under this Agreement. Producer may use and otherwise alter at the sole discretion of the Producer the results of the Contractor's services for all purposes in any manner the Producer may determine. Producer shall have the right to use Contractor's name, voice, picture and likeness in connection with the Program, the advertising and publication thereof and any promotional films or clips respecting the Program without additional compensation therefore. All rights in any work performed by Contractor hereunder shall be freely assignable to any third party by Producer and may be exploited in any and all media whether now known or hereafter created in any manner in perpetuity without further compensation due Contractor.

Producer reserves the right to discharge Contractor at any time for any reason. Producer shall attempt to notify Contractor a minimum of 24 hours in advance of layoff. Use of alcohol or drugs during hours of work will result in Contractor's immediate termination. This Agreement is subject to immediate suspension and/or termination, at Producer's election, without further obligation on the part of Producer in the event of any incapacity or default of Contractor or in the case of any suspension, postponement or interference with the production of the Program by reason of labor controversy, strike, earthquake, act of God, governmental action, regulation, or decree or for any other customary *force majeure* reason.

Unless otherwise specified in this Agreement, screen credit is at Producer's discretion subject to Contractor's performing all services required.

This Agreement represents the entire understanding between Producer and Contractor. Contractor warrants that he/she has the right to enter into the Agreement and that the representations made herein do not conflict with any other person or entity. The terms and conditions of this Agreement are binding on Producer and Contractor and shall not be waived or altered by any method other than by written agreement signed by both parties.

AGREED TO AND ACCEPTED:

CONTRACTOR   (signature)

_____

Date: _____

PRODUCER   (signature)

_____

Name: _____

Title: _____

Date: _____

A downloadable version of both deal memos can be found on the companion website www.theproducerssourcebook.com

The key elements to both these agreements are:

1. a clear statement of the position of the crew member and

the amount they will be paid;

2. a statement regarding overtime pay, evening and weekend work;

3. all work is work-for-hire, and the Producer owns all material produced by the crew member; and

4. the Producer has the right to fire or terminate the services of the crew member.

It is very important for the Producer to be consistent with the talent and the crew in terms of deals. Always assume that there are no secrets on a film set and that a preferential deal with one person will quickly be known to all. If a Producer believes that it is necessary to make a special deal with someone on the crew, that's her prerogative. But be prepared for a bit of grumbling from other crew members if they don't see those special qualities in that person.

TYPES OF DEALS

For a union or guild employee the deal is set by the guild agreement. For all others, there are a variety of ways to structure deals with the talent and the crew.

Daily, Weekly or Flat Rate

Most non-union talent or crew is paid either on a <u>daily rate</u> or a weekly rate. The <u>weekly rate</u> is negotiated and normally amounts to payment of four times the daily rate for five consecutive days of work – has to be consecutive but doesn't have to be Monday-Friday. The days are eight to ten hours, and there is an overtime rate. An alternative is to negotiate a <u>flat rate</u> or a <u>run-of-the-show</u> rate for the entire project. This is often done with the key talent and crew members who will be needed every day. This arrangement often involves a pay-or-play clause, which means that the person will be paid whether or not they are used for any or all of this time.

Deferral payment

Whether the rate is daily, weekly or run of the show, a Producer might negotiate a deferral with non-union talent and/or crew. The concept is that both the Producer and employee agree that they are due to get a certain rate. They also agree that only a portion of this rate will actually be paid at the time of production. The balance will be due when the project is completed, gets distributed and some money finds its way back to the Producer. A 50% deferment means that the person is paid 50% of their rate and 50% is deferred. A 30% deferment means that 70% is paid and 30% is deferred. There is no set percentage for a deferment deal. It is normally an amount that the Producer has calculated from the budget that she needs to have deferred to make the project work financially.

There are obvious advantages for the Producer with deferment payments. It is a potentially large savings in cash flow when cash is tight. The problem is that some talent and crew members will not accept such a deal because of their own cash needs. These are often the best, most experience people. Another important consideration for the Producer is that the deferments are legal obligations based on written agreements. When the Producer gets money from the distribution of the project she is obligated to pay the deferments. The problem for the talent and crew, besides the lack of cash flow, is that there is no guarantee that there will ever be any money available to pay the deferments. And it is difficult for these individuals to keep track of what happens to a project over a period of years.

Credit & tape/DVD

There are times when the Producer has no money for the non-union talent or crew but is able to convince them to work for free and in return have their name appear on the credits for the film and receive a DVD or a digital download of the project. The advantage to the Producer is obvious in terms of cash flow. Another advantage is that, unlike a deferment, there is no liability for payments – not ever.

Why would talent and/or crew work for credit & tape/DVD or even a substantial deferment? Some will do it for the experience when they are starting out. Some will do it because they really love the project and want to be a part of it. This is particularly true with documentaries. Others, those with experience, will do it because it is a different kind of project than what they are used to doing. For example, a camera operator who does corporate training videos for a living might be willing to work for free or a large deferment on a feature film. Actors with years of experience on the stage will often work for free or deferred pay on a feature film just to get the experience.

SOURCES FOR FINDING CREW

Union crews are easy to find through their respective websites. Nonunion crew can be found from a number of sources: other Producer referrals; film commission lists; local industry associations; job sites such as mandy.com and craigslist; and from film schools.

There are also companies that work with Producers to find crewmembers in locations all over the world. They are also potential sources of work for freelance crew. For more information, access the following: www.crewconnection.com; www.crewscontrol.com

SUPPLEMENTAL MATERIAL – CHAPTER 20 – HIRING A CREW

<u>Review Questions</u>

1. What are the objective criteria that a Producer can use when hiring a crew? What is a subjective criterion?

2. According to the IRS, who is an employee on a project? Who can potentially be an independent contractor?

3. Does it help a Producer to have a written deal memo with a crew person that states that they are an independent contractor? What is the IRS position?

4. What does a payroll service do and what do they charge?

5. What are the key elements to the crew memos for both employee and independent contractor?

6. How many days of pay make up a weekly rate?

7. What is a run-of-the-show deal and who is it used for?

8. What are the advantages and disadvantages of a deferral deal?

9. What is the primary difference between a credit & tape/DVD deal and a 100% deferral deal?

<u>Industry Speak</u>

Daily rate – full pay for a day's work based on negotiate daily rate for crew member

Deferral deal – payment of a portion of the crew member's daily rate at the time of the work and payment of the remainder of the money when certain conditions happen

Employee – a crew person the IRS considers an employee and the Producer must treat as such in terms of taxes

Flat rate – a negotiate rate that applies to the whole production, no matter how many days are actually worked

Independent contractor – a crew member who is not considered an employee by the IRS

Pay or play – an agreement that obligates a Producer to pay a crew person whether or not they actually work

Payroll service – a third party company that is paid by the Producer to be the employer of record for the crew; they handle all tax payments and filings

Weekly rate – normally equal to four times the daily rate as negotiated between the Producer and the crew when an employee works for five consecutive days

Work for hire – a legal agreement that transfers to the Producer any copyright that may be attributed to a crew person based on the nature of their work on an production

Further Activities

Further Reading & Research

Get in the daily habit – read the industry trade papers to know what is going on in the industry. For film and television, I recommend *Variety, Hollywood Reporter, Broadcasting & Cable,* and *Current.* They are all available online. Another good resource for what's happening in television is the *Cynopsis.com* online newsletter. For documentary and nonfiction work, I suggest *Real Screen.*

21

INSURANCE

We all know about insurance, right? If we have a car, we have insurance (required by law in most places). We have health insurance (hopefully). Anything we have of value, we try to insure. In business, it's the same, and all businesses have their unique kinds of insurance coverage that reflect the unique aspects of that business. Film and video is no different. Accidents, injuries, thefts and/or damage are surprisingly frequent on a film or video production, particularly a large feature film operation. And unfortunately every year or so someone dies on a film set. And don't think that the small documentary production is exempt from problems.

Normally, a Producer who owns a production company will have an overall business policy that covers the different projects that it does during a policy period, which is generally a year. The insurance company will look at the history of the Producer and his company, the types of projects it has done and any problems it has had, including claims on other insurance policies. The rate for the insurance will depend the claim history and on the level of business that the production company has done and expects to do during the policy period. In addition, for larger projects that may come up during the policy period, a supplemental policy would be taken out for that project alone. This is often required by a commissioning organization such as a cable network. For feature films, the project is always set up in a separate legal entity and that entity will get its own insurance policy for that film.

GENERAL CONCEPTS OF INSURANCE

First, we should review some general concepts that apply to all types of insurance coverage.

Certificate of Insurance

This is a document that states the types of coverage and the limits that have been issued by the insurance company. It is often required by locations and by vendors such as camera or equipment rental houses or prop/costume rental companies.

Additional Insured and Loss Payee

Often a vendor will be leery of having to wait for a Producer to file an insurance claim, follow-up on it, and then forward the proceeds to the vendor. Sometimes a Producer will be hesitant to file a claim, fearful that the renewal rate on the insurance will increase. If a vendor is named as an additional insured, they can make a claim directly to the insurance company to pay for a loss. If the vendor is also listed as a loss payee, they can be paid directly by the insurance company.

Deductibles and Limits

A big concern to a vendor is that if the deductible on the Producer's coverage is too high, they still might have to look to the production company for payment of a lost item. A deductible of $500 or even $1,000 is not uncommon in business policies. For many items that would be rented for a film or video production, the cost of the item would be within the range of the deductible. The vendor would then have to be paid by the Producer, and they don't want to rely on this. Many vendors may require a deposit to cover the deductible.

Also, the overall limit of coverage must match the potential liability. A limit of $50,000 for third party property might be okay for a small documentary project but would be totally unacceptable for a 35mm feature film project that was going to rent cameras, lenses and other very expensive equipment.

GENERAL BUSINESS COVERAGE

There is a level of basic coverage that most businesses have, no matter what industry they are in. These are some of the normal elements of such a package.

Comprehensive General Liability

This protects the Producer against third-party claims of bodily injury and/or property damage arising out of the filming of the project. Third-parties are people who are not connected to or employed by the production. The coverage does not include automobiles, which require a separate policy. This coverage is required for filming on most state and federal sites and most commercial locations. The minimum coverage is normally $1 million.

Workers Compensation and Employers Liability

Federal and state laws require that if an employee is injured on the job, for any reason whatsoever, the employer must pay all of the doctor and hospital bills incurred by the injured person. The employer must also pay a salary (disability income) to the employee for as long as that employee is not able to work as a result of the injury, even if it is the rest of the employee's life. This coverage protects the company from these claims. This coverage is required by all the unions and guilds when entering into an agreement with them, even the low budget or student agreements. Proof of coverage must be supplied by a Certificate of Insurance before anyone will show up for work.

Office contents and equipment

Coverage for the value of office property, including furniture, equipment and supplies, plus any tenant's improvements that are lost, damaged or destroyed. This coverage often includes protection against employee theft or embezzlement.

THE PRODUCER'S PACKAGE

In the film and video industry there are special types of coverage that meet the needs of our business. Not all of these are needed for all projects, and a Producer should work with his insurance agent to make sure he has adequate coverage for each project.

Cast Insurance

Reimburses expenditures incurred in completing principal photography as a result of an insured artist's inability to commence, continue, or complete their duties in a production due to death, injury or sickness. This coverage is essential for feature films especially where a talent is seen as vital to the success of the project. Smart investors and lenders will require it. Most actors don't have any problem with this coverage. But there are a few who have a troubling history of illness or drug use, and they can become uninsurable.

Negative film & videotape

Reimburses expenditures incurred to re-photograph, in substantially the same manner, any necessary portion of the insured production due to loss of or damage to film, video elements, or hard drives by perils other than faulty stock (film or tape), faulty camera or faulty processing. This is essential for all projects to protect the most valuable commodity we have.

Faulty Stock, Camera & Processing – "Faulties"

Reimburses expenditures incurred to re-photograph, in substantially the same manner, any necessary portion of the insured production due to loss of or breakage to exposed film, video tapes and audio tapes caused by fogging or the use of faulty materials (including film or tape stock), faulty equipment (including hard drives), faulty processing or developing. If film is fogged or scratched, if videotape is damaged or hasn't recorded properly, there are any number of causes or culprits. The lab blames the camera-operator; the operator blames the stock and so on. It's an endless loop of a debate and impossible to prove who is at fault. This coverage says that it doesn't matter who is at fault. If something is wrong, it will pay to re-shoot.

Props, Set & Wardrobe

Coverage for the value of scenery, costumes and theatrical property, which is lost, damaged or destroyed.

Miscellaneous Equipment

Coverage for the value of lost or damaged or destroyed equipment including cameras, camera equipment, sound and lighting equipment, electrical and mechanical/special effects equipment. This is coverage for equipment that is owned by the production company.

Third-Party Property Damage

Pays because of damage to or destruction of property of others while such property is in the care, custody or control of the insured and is used or to be used in connection with the production. This is always required in order to be able to rent equipment.

Errors and Omissions (E&O)

This coverage is essential if the project is ever to be distributed by any third party including theatrical distributors. It is also required before any television or cable network or most home video or educational video distributors will license a program. It will be required in any commission or co-production agreement. In other words, it's very important for a Producer.

E & O coverage protects the production company (and its assigns) from lawsuits alleging the following:

- invasion of the right of privacy or interference with the right of privacy

- plagiarism, piracy or unfair competition

- infringement of copyright or trademark

- libel, slander or other forms of defamation

- unauthorized use of names, trade names, trademarks, service marks, titles, formats, ideas, characters, plots, musical compositions, performances, slogans, program material or any similar matter

Please note that the E&O coverage will not cover an issue if the Producer is found to be acting fraudulently or trying to cheat the insurance company or her financial backers.

After reviewing the nature of the potential problems as outlined above, it should be obvious why this coverage is so important to the distributors and networks. If there is a claim of damages and a lawsuit, it will be the distributor and the network that stands to lose the most. They have the money to pay damages while the Producer is likely a small company or an individual.

The E&O coverage is purchased for a specific project. And a Producer who has a poor track record, meaning claims on previous E&O coverage, will find it hard to get coverage for new projects. A Producer who becomes uninsurable for E&O is almost out of business.

This coverage is generally expensive to get because the potential liabilities are high. It can cost up to 10% of the overall production budget. The cost is determined by the markets that are anticipated for the project and the nature of the project, particularly the underlying property.

For a feature film and for network commissions or co-productions, most Producers are required to get his E&O coverage before production starts. Smart lenders, investors, networks and distributors (if involved in a pre-sale deal) will demand this. For documentary projects that are not commissioned or co-productions, the Producer will often wait to get E&O coverage until she finds a network or distributor that wants to license the project. But then the warnings in chapter 23 are critical. Make sure to get all agreements, deal memos, releases, etc. signed in advance and not after the production is over.

SUPPLEMENTAL MATERIAL – CHAPTER 21 - INSURANCE

Review Questions

1. What is a certificate of insurance?

2. What are the advantages for a vendor to be named an additional insured and a loss payee?

3. Why would a vendor be concerned about the amount of the deductible on a Producer's policy?

4. What does comprehensive general liability insurance cover?

5. What is worker's compensation insurance?

6. Be familiar with the different types of coverage in the Producer's Package.

7. What specifically does E&O insurance cover? What does it not cover?

Industry Speak

Additional insured – a vendor who is listed on a policy as a direct beneficiary; can make a claim directly to the insurance company

Deductible – the amount of an insured loss that the Producer would have to pay

Loss payee - a vendor who can be paid directly by the insurance company

Worker's compensation – insurance that covers the Producer's liability to pay expenses for an employee who is injured on the job

Further Activities

Further Reading & Research

For further information on insurance, you can go to:

C&S Insurance www.csins.com

The Film Emporium www.filmemporium.com

Get in the daily habit – read the industry trade papers to know what is going on in the industry. For film and television, I recommend *Variety, Hollywood Reporter, Broadcasting & Cable,* and *Current.* They are all available online. Another good resource for what's happening in television is the *Cynopsis.com* online newsletter. For documentary and nonfiction work, I suggest *Real Screen.*

22

LOCATIONS

In this chapter we will look at the advantages and disadvantages of film production on location and compare it to the use of a sound stage.

In the "good old days" of film production (and truly "film" because this is before video), almost all films were shot on location. That's where life was happening, and it was inexpensive. Few even thought of using a studio-like environment. Film making moved to the southern California area because of the weather and the ability to be outside filming more days of the year. Back lot locations grew up as the early film companies grew and turned into "factories" churning out films at a very fast pace. All of this changed dramatically (pun intended) with the advent of sound. The heavy and cumbersome sound recording equipment was very hard to take on location, and the location noise, that had not bothered filmmakers before, was now a real problem. So the sound stage era was born, and everyone moved indoors, built sets and didn't see the sun for weeks at a time.

It was the 1960s when things began to change again. The invention of the portable Nagra (means "will record" in Polish – the inventor was Polish) tape recorder in the mid 1950s was the first step. The development of the lightweight Arriflex 16mm and 35mm film cameras in the early 1960s was the next step. With this new and very portable equipment, a new breed of independent filmmakers found a way to escape the confines (physical and financial) of the studios and use real locations for their films. Sound stages did not disappear and continue to have a very important role in filmmaking, but location production created a whole new "industry" that many cities, states, and countries eagerly compete for.

THE BEST LOCATION?

What is the best location for a film shoot? If you think about it there might be or should be an answer but…

It is really one of those rhetorical questions because the correct answer is - it depends. It depends on the viewpoints of a lot of people and on a lot of variables.

Some of the important people who have a vested interest in the selection of a location include: the director, director of photography (DP), art director, sound mixer, gaffer, and, of course, the Producer. It should be obvious as to what they each look for and/or need in a location, and I'm sure that it comes as no surprise that they might not, probably won't, agree. I've found that the director, DP, and art director often have the most leverage and the sound mixer and gaffer have to make do with what they get. They might not like it, but they are professionals and will find a way. Since our focus in this book is on the Producer, we will continue to look at locations through her eyes and pocketbook.

DEVELOPMENT

As with most things we do in development, our Producer's location activities during development are minimal and generalized. We make a strategic assumption in budgeting as to whether or not we are shooting on location. Generally, we are, so we look at all the settings (as found on the breakdown list for settings) and think of the kind of locations we will need. We can make some initial assumptions here. For example, if we have settings in a bedroom, living room and kitchen in the hero's house, we can assume that we will find all of them at the same house location. This may not actually be the case when we get into pre-production, but we'll burn that bridge when we get to it. For now, we just want a sense of how many locations and what types. From that we will estimate a location budget including fees and a standard guestimate that will include things like parking, special access costs and security. That is as far as we go unless there is some really unusual location that jumps out at us and demands extra research and budget consideration. Finding a medieval castle location in the mid-western part of the country might be one such problem. Locations involving travel beyond the local area, especially international, are another issue and trigger additional research on costs such as transportation and lodging.

PRE-PRODUCTION

Once we have our money and a more established shooting script and schedule, we really begin the hard work of locations. A Producer is fortunate to have a great resource available to help him – the film commission. Virtually all states and most foreign countries have a film commission whose goal is to help filmmakers work in their area. Many major cities such as New York, Los Angeles, Toronto, and Washington DC also have film commissions or film offices. At any level, these commissions are normally part of a department of business or commerce, which makes sense because their goal is to bring filmmaking to the area because it generates revenue for its local businesses and citizens. Large feature films can spend many millions of dollars in a local area. And the various film commissions work hard and compete with each other to capture these projects for their cities/states/countries.

Film commission services include: help with location scouting through a data base of specific locations; identify potential crew and vendors; and help with the different types of permits required by local governmental units. And the best news of all is that they don't charge the filmmaker for their services. In fact, many of the states and countries offer tax breaks and other financial incentives to attract filmmakers.

LOCATION SCOUTING AND SELECTION

During pre-production, the Producer or his production manager will prepare a list of settings/locations that are needed for the production. It will contain a general description that begins with the script and is augmented by the director and art director. The idea here is to be as open as possible. Good writers use the minimum description necessary for a setting in a script in order to give the production team as much leeway as possible.

A location scout will be hired who is familiar with the local area and has experience working with film productions. Film commissions are good sources to find location scouts, and they are a great resource to assist the scout's search. A Producer could search the film commission's data base of information and photographs from anywhere, but the experience of a good local location scout can prove well worth the money, particularly for those unusual locations. The objectives for the location scout are: to find a number of locations that meet the general criteria provided by the Producer; to ascertain their availability during the production period (as set by the Producer); and to identify the owner or decision maker connected to the location. Good scouts will also provide a review sheet that lists any positive and negative features of the location from a production standpoint; for example, is it located near a busy intersection or the local airport. Most good location scouts have a production background, often including film school. Their report may also include any input from the local film commission regarding the locations, including history of working with filmmakers, general costs, etc. The scout's report will then be reviewed by the Producer, director, DP, art director and the other department heads.

TECHNICAL SITE VISIT

After a review of the location scout's report, the Producer will arrange a technical site visit.

The goal for this visit is to select and confirm the final location(s). The team that goes on the technical visit normally includes the

Producer, director, DP, art director, and occasionally the sound mixer. Sound mixers always complain that they are not included on most technical visits because of a lack of respect for the sound department. I think all good filmmakers appreciate the sound department, but the fact is that they have often not been hired at the time of this technical visit. Sometimes it may be a financial consideration, and I know Producers, including myself, who argue that the director and DP will look out for the sound department's interests.

The technical team will review the locations through the various lenses of their crafts and make a recommendation. The director is concerned with the overall look as it fits her vision; the DP is concerned with space, light (source, amount and control), power and noise (for the sound department if they are not there); and the art director looks at existing set dressing, colors and possible alterations (particularly if the film is a period piece). The Producer has his own set of items to consider. What is the accessibility to the location? This means both the physical location and how easy it is to travel there, but also the access to the location if it is inside a building. For example, is there a freight elevator for the equipment or is it a 3rd floor walk-up? Is there enough space for the production? Film crews take up an enormous amount of space in addition to the part of the location that will be the actual setting. Camera, lighting and sound departments need space for equipment. The various art departments (props, set dressing, wardrobe) all need space to set up and work. There needs to be someplace for the actors to hang out and not be underfoot. Craft services and catering need room to feed the crew. Consideration of a private residence to use only one bedroom for a setting can easily involve taking over the entire house. An office setting can require use of an entire floor of an office building. This obviously creates complications and costs money.

Based on the input and recommendations from the entire team, the Producer will make a preliminary decision and begin the process of negotiating a fee with the property owner.

NEGOTIATING FEES

The owners of locations most often want to be paid, and why shouldn't they. The right location adds value to a film production, plus the film crew's presence will inflict a good bit of wear-and-tear on the property. The Producer will try to negotiate the best deal she can, and there are several factors that come into play.

The primary factor is the uniqueness of the location. A corollary to this factor is if the location has some glamour to it, whether by its history or occupancy or interesting architectural style. If there is no other location like this anywhere else, then the price will probably be astronomical. There are a lot of places that you can fake with film magic, and the increasing sophistication of digital manipulation is helping filmmakers in this area. Is a unique location really worth the money? It depends. There may be a creative alternative, and there may not. Each case will be different.

Another critical factor is the amount of time that the production will need the location. The fee for a location for a day is going to be much different than for a week or month. At some point it begins to make more economic sense to build a set on a sound stage. A related factor is the amount of space needed, and remember that's a lot.

I've never met an art director who loved everything about a location. There was always some paint that he hated or curtains she despised or furnishing that just didn't fit the character. So even at a minimum there might be some alteration proposed, maybe just to paint a wall. The production obviously pays for the painting, but it must also pay to paint it back to the original color. Sometimes you get lucky and the owner likes the new color, but don't count on it. However, if the location is a private residence with current furnishings, décor etc and the story needs a 1940s look, then there is a lot of work to do. Not only is the work going to cost, but it will take time to change it and then change it back. And many owners will get nervous with this much going on and need a higher fee to make them comfortable. The same obviously holds true with commercial locations – a retail story looked much different in the

1940s or 60s than it does now.

And speaking of commercial locations, the next factor is the loss of income that an establishment might suffer as a result of its use as a location for a film. If a restaurant is normally closed on a Sunday, and we only need it for a day, then there is no loss of income. If, however, we need them to close for a few days, then we will have to reimburse them for their loss of income.

The final factor is that film making has become so much a part of the popular zeitgeist that everyone sees dollar signs when a film production comes calling. The studios are to blame because they throw money around and buy their way out of problems rather than think their way out. So a Producer of a low-budget film spends a lot of time trying to explain to people that they are not from Paramount Pictures and can't pay $5,000 a day for the location. Some will listen and some won't.

RELEASES AND PERMITS

Once a fee is established and the rest of the details set, and before the production starts, it's time to get the location owner to sign a location agreement. This agreement will set out all the details as agreed upon. It will also be a location release that gives the Producer the right to use the pictures of the location in the film. Another important clause is the one that will allow the Producer to return if something happens to the film or HD tape or hard drive and the scenes have to be reshot. It will cost again, but the Producer is not at the owner's mercy if they want to take advantage of the situation and increase the fee. Or the production crew might have worn out its welcome, and the owner wouldn't let anyone back if there wasn't this agreement. A copy of a location agreement can be found at the end of this chapter, and a downloadable version is on the companion website www.theproducerssourcebook.com.

An important warning here is to make sure that the owner of the property signs the agreement. Be sure that it is not someone who is renting the house or a building manager or an engaging employee.

The signature of anyone other than the owner, or someone legally able to sign for the owner, is worthless. And, in fact, it is more than worthless because a Producer might spend a lot of time and money and not be able to use the footage.

Permits are obtained from the local governmental jurisdiction and give the Producer the right to work in that area. A permit is not needed to film on private property, but will be needed to park the production trucks, vans and cars on the city streets. Permits are not hard to get and our friends at the film commission will do most/all of the work. There can be a fee, but it is not onerous and often can be waived (again with the help of the film commission). The permit for filming will allow the Producer to reserve parking on the street for their vehicles. The police will put up signs, and they will enforce the restrictions. That's cool, especially in high density urban areas where parking is a real problem. If it is necessary to block traffic from a city street so it can become an active set, that will involve a lot more work and cost, but it's done all the time and isn't a big deal. One additional cost in these situations is the need to hire security to keep people off the set. Off-duty police are good for this and can be arranged by… right – the film commission.

One of the most important things a Producer should do when filming at a location, whether commercial or residential or other, is to alert the neighbors. This will avoid a lot of headaches and wasted time. I have one case where I was filming in my own house. We had a permit and reserved parking on a busy street. We were doing an exterior night scene and had just begun to put up lights shining on the house and some grips were on ladders putting gels on the windows. It wasn't 10 minutes before the police arrived because a neighborhood-watch-type neighbor had called them to report suspicious activity. Well, I had my permit and all was fine, but I spent almost an hour dealing with that and the resulting questions from the crew. I had assigned a production assistant to pass out notices to the neighbors, but that hadn't been done. It was an unpaid PA, and you get what you pay for.

With commercial locations the issue can be tricky. A Producer has a deal with the owner of the location for his lost revenue, but what if the production hinders customers from going to the retail stores next to the location? They would be upset and rightly so. Sometimes they have to be paid also if the disruption can't be helped. At a minimum we want to alert them to the filming and maybe even buy something from them. I once had a situation where the store next door was a coffee shop, and we just bought all of our coffee and craft service snacks from them. Everyone was happy.

PRODUCTION

An important member of the production staff is the location manager who can assist the Producer with many of the details during pre-production and becomes the key point-person during production. It is critical to have all of the location agreements, releases, and permits done before production starts. If there are a lot of locations and a lot of moving around, the location manager might have several assistants, each one assigned to different locations. They are responsible for all the logistics of dealing with the owners, neighbors, police, etc. They will have a list of additional services that might be needed such as trash disposal, private security, fire department, and hospital. They will be responsible for parking if it is not solved by the local permit. If it is a big production, city street parking will never suffice. Church parking lots are often used during the week as a parking and equipment staging area. If there is transportation needed for cast and crew, the location manager will coordinate that.

If a problem arises, the location manager should be able to solve it without involving the Producer. Obviously some problems might need to involve the Producer, but a good location manager tries to restrict them to those life-or-death kinds of things. Normally the location manager will be from the local area and have a great knowledge of how and where to get things done – from last minute copies of script pages, to finding a hardware or drug store, to knowing a local assistant cameraperson who can take the place of a sick crew member.

The location manager will also carry a supply of petty cash for contingency matters. This pays for a PA to go to the store for batteries; it pays for the pizza that the lighting crew needs while wrapping after an unusually long day; it pays for the neighbor to stop cutting his grass and go inside, drink a beer and watch a football game during filming. This is particularly important when filming in many foreign countries where cash gets things to happen. This does not condone doing anything that is illegal, but simply acknowledges that money talks loudly in many situations.

If a production is going to be filming in an area for a period of time, a local production office is normally set up where the location people and others can work.

THE SOUND STAGE

Despite the lure of filming on location, there are some real advantages to working on a sound stage. It is often more expensive, but not always, and sometimes money isn't the most important factor.

As mentioned earlier, sound stages have been a big part of filmmaking since the beginning of sound pictures. The majority of sound stages are in Los Angeles and are owned by the major studios. There are a number of sound stages in New York City and there are others in different parts of the country. Internationally there are good sound stages in many countries. England in particular has excellent facilities.

Let's review the advantages and disadvantages of sound stages for a Producer. It often takes a "fine pencil" to calculate the differences between shooting on location and on a sound stage. A good Producer with some flexibility of schedule can often work great deals with a sound stage that might have a slow time period in their bookings.

Advantages

A. Well, they are quiet and the sound department is happy.

B. The art department is very happy because they can design a set from the floor up.

C. There is no problem with bad weather which can cause very expensive delays when filming on exterior locations.

D. The sets are built to accommodate film production with movable walls and overhead lighting grids. No more squeezing a camera, operator and AC into a tight corner. No more worry about light stands in the shot.

E. A sound stage set combined with green screen can allow for almost anything to happen in the film. Dragons, flying wizards, exploding cities –imagine it, and it can happen.

F. It can eliminate some or all of the costs of travel and lodging required for distant locations. This, of course, assumes that the sound stage is local. To take advantage of a great deal on the rental of a sound stage, some Producers book a sound stage in another state or country and take the cast and key crew to live there during the production. In this case, the bulk of the crew is local to the sound stage.

G. It also eliminates many of the other costs and hassles of location production including: parking; permits; space requirements; accessibility; etc.

Disadvantages

1. Well, they're not free. The process is much different, and it all costs money. Rather than arrive at a location that is basically done and ready to shoot, the sets must be created from scratch. This requires the art department to design the sets to everyone's satisfaction (remember our stakeholders in selecting locations). Then a crew has to build the sets and these construction people normally work for the sound stage and are often union. Then the sets have to be decorated and furnished by the art department. Some sound stages, particularly those owned by the major studios have large prop and set dressing warehouses that can be utilized.

Otherwise the Producer has to rent or, worse case, buy a lot of stuff that they don't need after the production is over. All of this takes time that would not have been spent if shooting on location.

2. Some sound stages require Producers to use the sound stage's crew for basic operations – grip and electric. Again, they are often union. But they are always very experienced.

The bottom line for sound stages is that they can be very sensible solutions to some problems for some productions. They should not be discounted just because of the fear of expenses. One fairly typical situation is where a Producer has a setting that is used a lot during the production and the costs for access to a real location are very high. Building that setting on a sound stage will often be less expensive. And it can provide a cover set for use when bad weather cancels an exterior shoot.

So, review the challenges of the production, run the numbers, and see what happens.

LOCATION AGREEMENT and RELEASE

(sample)

Date: _____

Name: _____

("Owner") Phone: _____

Address:

_____

_____

City/State: _____ Zip code: _____

Owner hereby grants to _____ ("Producer") its respective parents, subsidiaries and affiliates, licensees, successors and assigns, for good and valuable consideration, receipt of which is hereby acknowledged, permission to enter upon and use the property and the contents thereof and the appurtenances thereto located at _(address)_____ (the "Property") for the purpose of photographing and recording certain scenes in connection with a program titled _____ (the "Program") during production thereof, and as necessary during any extension, re-shooting or preparation of publicity or promotion thereof. All physical embodiments of filming, recording and photography on the Property shall hereinafter be known as the "Materials".

Producer may place all necessary facilities and equipment on the Property and agree to remove same after completion of work and leave the Property in as good of condition as when received.

Producer will use reasonable care to prevent damage to said Property, and will indemnify the Owner, and all other parties lawfully in possession, of said Property, and hold each of them harmless from any claims and demands of any person or persons arising out of or based upon personal injuries, death or property damage suffered by such person or persons resulting directly from any act of negligence on Producer's part in connection with Producer's use of the Property.

Owner grants to Producer all rights of every kind in and to the Materials including without limitation the right to exploit the Materials throughout the world, an unlimited number of times, in perpetuity in any and all media, now known or hereafter invented, and in connection with the Program or otherwise and for advertising and promotional purposes in connection therewith and all rights, including copyright in the Materials shall be and remain vested in Producer, and neither the Owner, nor any tenant, nor other party now or hereafter having an interest in the Property, shall have any right of action against Producer or any other party arising out of any use of said Materials whether or not such use is, or may be claimed to be, defamatory, untrue or censorable in nature.

The undersigned acknowledges that Producer is photographing and recording such scenes in express reliance upon the foregoing. The undersigned represents and warrants that the undersigned has all rights and authority to enter into this agreement and to grant the rights granted hereunder.

LOCATION FEE: _____ dollars ($_____) per shooting day. The Location Fee shall be payable as follows: _____ . Producer and/or Client shall have the right to reenter the Property for further work as needed for the above fee or a pro rata portion thereof.

(A description of any other parts of an agreement would be described here. Sometimes a lawyer is needed.)

Producer is not obligated to actually use the Property or produce the Program or include the Materials in the Program for which it was shot or otherwise. Producer may at any time elect not to use the Property by giving the Owner written notice of such election, in which case, neither party shall have any obligation hereunder.

This is the entire agreement. No other authorization is necessary to enable Producer to use the Property for the purpose herein contemplated.

AGREED AND ACCEPTED

<u>For Owner</u>, by:

_____

(signature)

Date: _____

Name:

_____

Title:

_____

<u>For Producer</u>, by:

_____

(signature)

Date: _____

Name:

_____

Title:

_____

Instructions:

Print this agreement on two-sided on company letterhead.

Multiple part forms are also helpful to give to each party to the agreement.

SUPPLEMENTAL MATERIAL – CHAPTER 22 - LOCATIONS

<u>Review Questions</u>

1. What is the best location for a film? Who is involved in that decision?

2. What services does a typical film commission provide? What do they charge?

3. What are the objectives of the location scout?

4. Who normally goes on the technical site visit?

5. Who makes the decision on the location and negotiates with the owner?

6. What are the factors that impact the negotiation for a location and its cost?

7. Who does the Producer need to make sure signs the location agreement?

8. Who issues permits and what are they needed for?

9. What does a location manager do during the production?

10. What are the advantages to working on a sound stage? The disadvantages?

<u>Industry Speak</u>

Film commission – a government department, normally commerce related, that attracts and assists filmmaking in its jurisdiction

Green screen – a green color background that can be digitally changed to any image

Location manager – assists the Producer during production in all matters related to the locations for filming; should be able to solve most problems that occur on location

Location release – a legal agreement that allows a Producer to film on a location and use the material in the film

Location scout – takes a wish list from the Producer and finds suitable sites for her to consider

Sound stage – soundproof space that is used for filmmaking; normally a large open space with a high ceiling that includes a lighting grid

Further Activities

1. Check your local area to see if there are any sound stages. If so, get information and ask to visit.

2. Find the film commission that covers your area –state and/or local; investigate the services they offer. Check out their resources for location scouting.

Further Reading & Research

Get in the daily habit – read the industry trade papers to know what is going on in the industry. For film and television, I recommend *Variety, Hollywood Reporter, Broadcasting & Cable,* and *Current.* They are all available online. Another good resource for what's happening in television is the *Cynopsis.com* online newsletter. For documentary and nonfiction work, I suggest *Real Screen.*

23

DELIVERABLES

T he term "deliverables" derives from the delivery schedule that is a part of all acquisition/license agreements and distribution agreements in the industry. It lists the legal, technical, accounting, marketing documents, and other materials that have to be presented to the studio, network, or distributor before they will consider the contract valid. Which means before a project gets distributed or aired and before a Producer gets paid.

The delivery schedules for feature film distributors, cable networks, PBS, and other distributors, have their unique items, but they all contain many of the same requirements. Preplanning is essential to make sure that a Producer has these items available to complete the licensing of their film. It is very difficult to go back after the fact and get many of these agreements. And a Producer runs the risk that some agreements will be much more expensive.

These are some of the things that would be found on the typical delivery schedule, which can be more than twenty pages long.

Technical Requirements: depends upon the nature of the project and how it is to be distributed. For a feature film on film there must be an original negative, an inter-positive, an inter-negative and an answer print. If digital, there is the final edited digital file.

A unique item for feature films is coverage material which is used with an R-rated film so that it can be re-edited to be acceptable for television viewing (U.S. and foreign), or so it can meet the censorship rules of some foreign territories.

If the project is completed and delivered for television, the requirement will be for an NTSC master in a specific tape and/or digital format.

Records and Documentation: the following are normally required for most projects as applicable. It is of the utmost importance that a Producer compile these as she goes and doesn't have to go back to secure them. These are the main things, but it's not an exhaustive list.

- Underlying property agreements - chain of title

- Copyright registration

- Synopsis

- Shooting script

- Final script, timed, for subtitles and closed captioning

- Transcripts of all interviews

- Cast list, agreements and releases

- Depiction releases

- Crew list and deal memos

- Location permits and releases

- Product & logo usage agreements and releases

- Acquired stock footage or photo agreements and releases

- Acquired public domain material documentation

- Graphic elements agreements and release

- All contracts related to residual requirements

- All union and guild agreements

- Music licenses

- Copy of main and final credits

- Access letter to all original footage and elements

Insurance: evidence of coverage of the following during and after the production.

- Errors and omissions

- general liability

- workman's compensation

- third party damage

- cast coverage

- negative film and video

Legal and Accounting: this material will be required if the distributor or network is providing funding for the production. If a distributor has not provided any financial assistance, then they do not have the right to these records. This material is also required by most grants, especially the government ones.

- all bank records- including statements and reconciliations

- canceled checks

- payroll records

- tax filings and payment records

- equipment list and whether owned, leased, rented

- petty cash records

- insurance claims

• final budget-to-actual analysis

<u>Publicity Materials</u>: normally required for any type of project. Make arrangements to have the publicity stills taken during the production.

• production photos

• bios of creative personnel and principal cast

• press clippings

SUPPLEMENTAL MATERIAL – CHAPTER 23 - DELIVERABLES

Review Questions

1. What is a delivery schedule and why is it important to be aware of it at the start of a production?

2. Are all Producers required to provide their accounting records in a delivery schedule?

Industry Speak

Coverage material – extra footage that is shot to allow for different versions of a scene, particularly one that involves violence or sex

Delivery schedule – an addendum to a distribution contract that lists the material that the Producer must provide in order to complete the contract.

Further Activities

Further Reading & Research

Get in the daily habit – read the industry trade papers to know what is going on in the industry. For film and television, I recommend *Variety, Hollywood Reporter, Broadcasting & Cable,* and *Current.* They are all available online. Another good resource for what's happening in television is the *Cynopsis.com* online newsletter. For documentary and nonfiction work, I suggest *Real Screen.*

24

RELEASES

Most films, fiction or nonfiction, contain some material or elements that belong to someone else, whether it is their own image, a home they own, or a photograph they took. All of these things require releases for the Producer to legally be able to use them.

The types of elements that we will examine in this chapter are:

Personal appearances

Locations

Copyrighted material

Trademarks

THE ISSUES OF RELEASES

One. A Producer must always assume that he needs a signed written release or license for every visual and audio element in his film. There may be times and circumstances where the failure to have a release or license will not kill a project, but he can't count on that. Get a release or license or find a different element.

Two. The gatekeepers set the rules. The distribution companies, network programming executives and nervous clients are all gatekeepers, and if they are concerned about a release then the Producer has to be concerned. It doesn't matter if he can point to a legal precedent or argue the fairness of fair use, if the gatekeeper demands a release then the Producer has to have it.

Three. Releases are <u>ALWAYS</u> easier to get during pre-production or at the time production, then they are after the fact. And if a Producer finds beforehand that she is not going to be able to get a release from someone, then she has time to move on and work with someone who will give her the release. Imagine the "lucky" Producer who has licensed her film at Sundance for $10 million and now tries to negotiate releases with the talent and crew who worked on the film for credit & tape/DVD. Good luck with that.

Four. There is a big difference between documentaries and fiction films in how important releases can be. Documentary Producers have now and are getting more leeway in the matter of releases. We will discuss this in more detail later in this chapter under copyrighted material.

Five. For documentary films there is a big difference between a visual or audio element that happens to be in the background of a shot and one that is used purposefully as b-roll or a transitional element.

Six. It does not matter how a fiction film is distributed or whether it makes a profit. The expectation is that a Producer makes a fiction film to have it seen by the public and to make a profit.

Now let's look at the various visual and audio elements.

PERSONAL APPEARANCE

In fiction films the concept is easy – everyone who appears in the film has to have signed an Appearance Release. A standard Appearance Release is found at the end of this chapter and a downloadable version is on the companion website at www.theproducerssourcebook.com. The good Producer follows this rule at all times and avoids future heartache. If he has signed an agreement with SAG, then the paperwork that he completes with each SAG actor incorporates the necessary appearance release, and he doesn't need a separate document. If an actor is non-union, then have them sign a release. All extras have to sign releases, even if they are so far in the background that no one can see them. And, please have them all sign before the shooting starts.

For documentaries the concept is not as clear. Much of it revolves around the legal concept of the <u>reasonable person</u> and whether the filming is in a private or public place.

Let's start with someone being interviewed for the film. If they are in their home, they have a very clear expectation of privacy, and the Producer has to have a release from them. That same person being interviewed on the street-corner will have much less expectation of privacy, but the fact that they are being interviewed means that the Producer should have a release. Bottom line is that if someone is being interviewed, even man-on-the-street style, get a signed release. Have a PA stand there with the releases; and consider printing them on 2-part forms that provides the interviewee with a copy after they sign.

Don't rely on having the interviewee give a verbal release on camera. Yes, it is better than nothing, but it is far, far, from satisfactory. Plus, there is additional data on the release form such as the correct spelling of their name, their address and telephone number, and even social security number, which is needed if they are going to be paid for their time.

Now, what about people who appear in the background while the interview is being filmed or who appear in the b-roll? We go back to place and reasonable person. In a private place a reasonable person has some level of expectation that what they do is private and will not be filmed. There is a continuum of such places from a private home to a private office, to a restaurant or nightclub or sports arena, to a sidewalk. The more private the setting, the more important it is to get a release for everyone. As we move along the continuum to the more public end, we can get a <u>presumptive release</u> by posting a sign at every entrance to alert everyone that they might be filmed in this place. The signs have to be very clear, easy to read, probably in English and Spanish in many places, and give a contact person and phone number. It is advisable to film the sign at the head of each tape or film roll or at least the first one of the shoot. A still photo is a good backup and make sure to keep a sample of the actual sign in the production notebook.

If filming in a public area, then the privacy expectation of our reasonable person is very small, and a Producer generally does not need a release from people in the area where she is filming. This does not mean, however, that she should feel safe filming someone doing something that would be potentially embarrassing to them if shown in a film. We are talking about normal people doing normal things in that particular area.

LOCATIONS

Property owners have certain rights which a Producer has to respect. He needs to get permission to be on their property to film, and he needs a location release to use the image of their property in his film. A sample Location Release is at the end of chapter 22 and on the website of supplemental resources.

As with appearances of people, this standard is different for fiction and documentary films. In a fiction film, a private location is a visual element and there has to be a signed location release, which includes permission to film and the right to use the image. In a public location, there is often no need for a release but there may likely be a requirement to have a permit. This is particularly true for parks and monuments. Also, do not confuse public access with free access for filming. Airports, train stations, and subway systems are run by government agencies but that does not make them public in the sense that any of us can film there without permission. In our post 9/11 world, there are very strict rules about filming public infrastructure. Be sure to research this carefully.

For a documentary, there is the same issue of permission for both private and public locations. A Producer should get a release to film the interior of a private location. Notice that I said interior because most exteriors are okay to film, even fancy places with special architectural elements. But this is just for documentaries.

An important consideration for all location releases and permits is that you need to make sure that the person signing the release is the owner of the property and has the legal authority to sign a binding agreement. If it is a private home, make sure it is the owner and not a tenant. If filming in the lobby of a private building, make sure to get either the owner to sign or make sure that the building manager has the authority to sign such an agreement.

COPYRIGHTED MATERIAL

I'm sure that you remember the basics of copyright from chapter 1. If not, please review. In this section we consider copyrighted material other than music, which we will look at in the next chapter.

What if a Producer film wants to use someone's photograph or artwork or film footage in her film? Her first move is to find out if the material is in the public domain, probably because of either its age or the fact that it was produced by someone as a part of their government job. If it is, then she's pretty much home free; but she would still be advised to have a piece of paper that verifies this status. This could come from the copyright office or a law firm that specializes in copyright searches. If it's not in the public domain then she has to review it through the lens of whether she is doing a fiction film or a documentary.

As with most things in this area, if a Producer doing a fiction film then she has to have a license to use any of this material; and the license would include a release. There are no exceptions to this. The key parts of this license agreement would include the nature and extent of the use of the material, the nature of the project, the markets for the film, the territories for distribution, and the term or length of the license. Each of these parts will factor into the cost of the license. Obviously, the broader the terms of the use, the more it will cost. Exclusive and hard to duplicate footage or photos, such as that of wildlife or important historical events, can be incredibly expensive. The standard in film is to charge for the use of <u>stock material</u> by the second of screen time it will have. This can be from a few dollars per second to thousands of dollars per second. Sometimes it is cheaper for a Producer to go shoot this material himself; or at least he should do the math to see if that's feasible. If he does shoot it himself, then he will have stock footage that he can then license to others to help defray his costs.

For documentary films the matter is a good deal more complicated. There is certainly some copyrighted material such as stock footage or photos that have to be licensed, and the license has the same parts and considerations as it would for a fiction film. This is particularly true if the material is part of the b-roll of the film. If, however, the material is only in the background of a shot because it happens to be there, then it is generally okay to use it without a license.

For documentaries, there is also the legal concept of <u>fair use</u>, which allows for the use of copyrighted material in limited circumstances even if it is used as b-roll. To repeat what we learned in chapter 1, the legal test follows the <u>rule of reason</u> and looks at four factors.

1. What is the purpose and character/nature of the use? News, criticism, teaching, and research are the main allowable uses.

2. What is the amount used? This is often misinterpreted. There are the false rumors that only using a few seconds of a work is okay. It's not that simple.

3. What is the nature of the original work? Some types of work are more protected than others; this is particularly true in the fine arts. And,

4. What is the effect of the use on the potential market or value of the material? If there is no effect or a minimal effect, it will really help.

For many years the documentary film and nonfiction television gatekeepers virtually disregarded the fair use argument because they didn't want to have to take the time and effort to prove it in court. Then in 2005, The Center for Media and Social Impact in the School of Communication at American University prepared a *Best Practices in Fair Use* statement that has been adopted by PBS and many cable networks. This statement argues that in some cases the social and/or cultural benefits of some documentary films are greater than the costs to the owner of the copyright. The statement focuses on four situations including social, political or cultural critique, illustration of an argument and historical sequences. There is an inherent dilemma here, however, as many copyright holders need the economic benefits and protections of copyright for their survival. While they may be all for social and cultural good, they also need the money from license fees to continue their work. This statement potentially undermines their rights and has to be used carefully.

TRADEMARKS

Trademarks are the things that make things recognizable – like the Coca Cola logo or the MGM lion or thousands of other images, logos and designs that companies have spent billions of dollars creating and branding onto our brains. The assumption of many filmmakers is that we have to stay away from these things. Actually, that's not the case. It is okay to use any of these products in a film as long as they are used in the proper way, the way they are intended to be used. If a Producer wants an actor to drink a bottle of Coke or Pepsi, then do it. But don't have them take that bottle and use it as a weapon. Misusing the product will cause trouble – it's called defamation.

The other important thing to be careful of is that, while it is okay to use the product in the film, it is NOT okay to use it in the advertising for the film. Just keep it out of the trailer or a still shot for the poster.

If use of a trademarked product is okay, then why don't more people do it and why do some filmmakers go to such lengths to keep them out? There are a couple of reasons. One is that they were hoping to get some product placement money right up to the end but did not, so they stayed with the generic brand. The other and more important reason is that, if they haven't received any product placement money, they don't want to use one product and risk alienating the competition. This is particularly true for films destined for television, where the presence of Coke in the film might keep Pepsi from signing up as an advertiser.

APPEARANCE RELEASE

For good and valuable consideration, receipt of which is hereby acknowledged, I authorize _____*name and address* _____("Producer") and _____ (" ") and their respective parents, affiliates, subsidiaries, licensees, successors and assigns to make use of my appearance for the following: ___*name of project*_____ ("Program").

I agree that you may film, tape and photograph me, and record my voice, conversation and sounds, including any performance of any musical composition(s), during and in connection with my appearance and that you shall be the exclusive owner of the results and proceeds of such filming, taping, photography and recording with the right, throughout the world, an unlimited number of times in perpetuity, to copyright, to use and to license others to use, in any manner, all or any portion thereof or of a reproduction thereof in connection with the Program or otherwise.

I further agree that you may use and license others to use my name, voice, likeness and any biographical material concerning me which I may provide, in any and all media and in the promotion, advertising, sale, publicizing and exploitation of the Program and/or otherwise (and ancillary products in connection with the Program) and in connection with Producer, and/or "_____ " or "_____ "'s affiliate services, throughout the world in all media, an unlimited number of times in perpetuity. I further represent that any statements made by me during my appearance are true, to the best of my knowledge, and that neither they nor my appearance will violate or infringe upon the rights of any third party.

I hereby waive any right of inspection or approval of my appearance or the uses to which such appearance may be put. I acknowledge that you will rely on this permission potentially, at substantial cost to you and hereby agree not to assert any claim of any nature whatsoever against anyone relating to the exercise of the permissions granted hereunder.

(Please print) Name: _____

_____

Signature

Address: _____

_____

Date _____

City/State: _____

Zip: _____

Telephone: _____

Social Security Number: _____

Date of Birth _____

Note: SS number is used for accounting if the person is to be paid.

I am a parent (or guardian) of the minor who has signed this release and consent and I hereby agree that all the provisions contained herein will bind the said minor and me.

(Please print) Name: _____

_____

Signature

Address: _____

_____

Date _____

City/State: _____

Zip: _____

Telephone: _____

Social Security Number: _____

Producer Name

(Please print) Name: _____

Signature _____ Date _____

Complete the form to fit your circumstances and then copy on your letterhead. Having multiple part copies is advisable so you can give a copy to those who sign.

SUPPLEMENTAL MATERIAL – CHAPTER 24 - RELEASES

Review Questions

1. What are the six issues of releases?

2. Who has to sign a personal release in a fiction film?

3. Who has to sign a personal release in a documentary? Who should sign one?

4. What are the key parts to a license agreement for the use of a copyrighted element in a fiction film?

5. What are the four factors that impact the rule of reason for fair use?

6. What are trademarks and can they be used in a film without a license? In what way can they not be used?

7. Why do Producers sometimes avoid using trademarks?

Industry Speak

Appearance release – a legal agreement that allows the Producer to use the image of the actor, interviewee or other person in the film

Defamation – misusing a trademarked product in a film in a way that will cause harm to the value of the trademarked product or service

Gatekeeper – a distributor, network, or anyone who controls the flow of films from Producer to audience

Presumptive release – using a sign at a filming site to warn people that filming is taking place and that by entering the area they give the Producer the right to use their image

Product placement – a Producer gets money from a company to use their product in a film

Reasonable person – a legal concept that is used by the courts to make judgements in areas where it is hard to have a firm and measurable standard

Further Activities

Further Reading & Research

Review the material Best Practices in Fair Use from the Center for Media and Social Impact at http://cmsimpact.org/

Get in the daily habit – read the industry trade papers to know what is going on in the industry. For film and television, I recommend *Variety, Hollywood Reporter, Broadcasting & Cable,* and *Current.* They are all available online. Another good resource for what's happening in television is the *Cynopsis.com* online newsletter. For documentary and nonfiction work, I suggest *Real Screen.*

25

MUSIC RIGHTS

W e all know that music is a critical element for most films – fiction or nonfiction. And we find music used in two general ways in a film – incidental and music bed.

Incidental use occurs in the documentary film when we are shooting b-roll in a factory and there is music playing in the background. Or we're shooting an interview and there is music playing in the room. We will probably want to turn it off, but that's for the sake of getting good sound for the interview and not because we will run into an issue of music rights. We generally do not need a license for this incidental use in a documentary film.

But in a fiction film there is no such thing as incidental use of music because everything is found or placed in a setting for a reason.

A music bed on the other hand is music that we place in the film for a specific reason. Most distributors require a music cue sheet for a film, which identifies each piece of music, the length used and the placement in the film (normally by time code). All of this music must be licensed whether it is a documentary or a fiction film.

We will examine three general sources of music for a film:

1. Pre-recorded music

2. Music library

3. Original composition

PRE-RECORDED MUSIC

Pre-recorded music is what most of us have on CDs or in our iTunes file or on Spotify or Pandora. It's what we're familiar with and the music that many of us have in our heads as we write a script and/or edit a film. We occasionally even have a film created around such a piece of music or its title. It's very easy to dump this music into our edit system and it creates a very compelling scene, sequence, end credits, etc. The problems are that we have to license this music, and that process is time consuming, and the license fees can be very high.

There is more than one license required for pre-recorded music. Think of the levels of copyright that are involved with its creation. Someone wrote the music itself, the composer, and that's copyrighted. Someone wrote the lyrics, the lyricist, and that's copyrighted. Someone, the record label, made the recording using work-for-hire musicians, and that's copyrighted. The composer and the lyricist might be the same person, which makes the negotiation easier but doesn't change the levels of copyright.

The license that a Producer gets from the composer/lyricist is called a synchronization license, which refers to the fact that a film synchronizes the music to the visual images. This license comes from the publisher of the song, which is either the composer/lyricist or a company representing them such as ASCAP or BMI. The publisher of most songs can be found through ASCAP at http://www.ascap.org/ or the National Music Publishers' Association at http://www.nmpa.org/.

The other license is the master use license that comes from the record label. This allows a Producer to use that specific recording of the song in her film.

390

If using the pre-recorded music as a music bed, no matter how much or how little is used, a Producer needs BOTH licenses. This is true for both fiction and nonfiction films. If the music is heard as incidental in a nonfiction work, then it is allowed without a license. This is a special exception, similar to fair use, which has been granted to nonfiction filmmakers. In fiction films there is no such thing as incidental use and that exception does not apply.

The key terms for these licenses are similar to those discussed in chapter 24 with the use of other copyrighted material – amount of use; nature of use; markets; territories; and term. It is possible to develop a license with predetermined steps that pertain to levels and types of use. For example, it might start out with film festival use, then move up to a theatrical or television distribution, then onto other ancillary markets and/or international territories. Each step would require an additional payment. It is advisable to determine these steps at the beginning if a Producer thinks that the film might have some potential beyond festivals. Like most kinds of negotiation, it is easier to get a reasonable deal before becoming famous and/or successful. Not all publishers and/or record labels will work out a step deal with an independent filmmaker. And even those that do might still charge a lot of money for the first step.

The process can be very time consuming and frustrating. Not all publishers are interested in dealing with any filmmakers other than the studios. The same is true with the record labels. Also, consolidation in the music industry has caused many record labels to be absorbed by larger companies, and often these large companies don't know what rights they own. Many hours can be spent on the phone (emails often go unanswered) trying to get to the person who can give some answers, and then the answer can often be "no".

An alternative approach is to get a synchronization license for the song from a publisher and then hire musicians to make an original recording for the film. The important thing is to make sure that all the musicians sign an agreement that gives the Producer all of the rights to their performance on the recording. They are performing a work-for-hire service.

There is some pre-recorded music that is now in the public domain and free for anyone to use. Make sure that both the song and the recording are in the public domain, and they don't always follow the same rules and time pattern.

MUSIC LIBRARY

Another general source for music is a music library. This is recorded music, primarily instrumental, that someone has written and recorded as a business. They then sell blanket licenses for a reasonable, one-time license fee that allows the Producer to use the music whenever, however, and as many times as she wants. The libraries are distributed on CDs or as digital files. Even small production companies have a couple of them for use in their projects. Post production houses have extensive music libraries that they can use in the productions they are editing for clients.

On the internet it is possible to find many sites that offer either music libraries or single songs to license for a film. Some of these are available for a fee and some are free. Generally, you get what you pay for, but a diligent search can unearth some real gems. Be sure to read the fine print and keep a copy of the terms and conditions that appear on the site for the deliverables file.

ORIGINAL COMPOSITION

The last general source for music is an original composition. There are many talented composers/lyricists out there who are eager to write music for films. They might be a solo performer or even a band. There are several advantages to working with a composer on a film. The Producer will have a collaborator who will bring their musical talent to the film and raise the overall level of quality. Their composition will be be timed to follow the pacing of the story and the beats of the editing pattern. And the financial arrangements are often flexible and suitable for an independent low or no budget production. That doesn't mean that all composers work for free; John Williams certainly doesn't. But a combination of a new filmmaker and a new composer can be beneficial to both. It is also possible to find an experienced composer who is bored with a routine of commercial jingles or nonfiction films and would love to work on a fiction film for little, if any, money.

One advantage of today's technology is that most composers are also able to perform their music and have it sound like a large band or even an orchestra. If there are other actual musicians involved, it is important for the Producer to get them to sign a work-for-hire agreement. The digital music file can then be easily merged with the digital editing file.

The normal deal with a composer revolves around who has the copyright to the music. If the Producer pays the composer an agreed upon fee, then the Producer will own the copyright and become the publisher of the music. If the Producer does not pay or if it is a below market rate, then the composer will normally keep the copyright and be the publisher. The advantage to the composer in this case is that, if the film ever gets distributed, they will receive royalties as the publisher. These royalties don't come from the Producer but from the exhibitor or television/cable network that shows or airs the film.

SUPPLEMENTAL MATERIAL – CHAPTER 25 – MUSIC RIGHTS

<u>Review Questions</u>

1. What are the two general ways that music is used in a film?

2. Do we need a license for incidental music in a documentary? How about in a fiction film?

3. What does a music cue sheet do and who uses it?

4. What are the three general sources of music for a film?

5. What are the different levels of copyright in a pre-recorded music selection?

6. What are the two licenses that are needed in order to use pre-recorded music as a music bed? Who issues these licenses?

7. What are the key terms to these licenses?

8. What is an alternative to getting the master use license?

9. How often can a Producer use the music in a music library that they have purchased?

10. What are the advantages to using a composer to create music specifically for a film?

<u>Industry Speak</u>

Composer – the creator of music

Lyricist – the person who writes the lyrics for a song

Master use license – permission from a record label to use a pre-recorded version of a song in a film

Music bed – music that is added to a film as a production element

Music cue sheet – tracks all uses of music in a film with detail that include starting point and duration.

Publisher – a company that represents the composer and lyricist of a song; can issue a synchronization license to the Producer

Record label – a company that records and distributes a song

Synchronization license – permission from the composer and lyricist to use the music and lyrics to a song in a film

Further Activities

Further Reading & Research

Check out the American Society of Composers, Authors and Publishers at ascap.org and/ or Broadcast Music Inc. at http://www.bmi.com/ to see what they do for their members

Check out the National Music Publishers' Association (NMPA) at http://www.nmpa.org/

Get in the daily habit – read the industry trade papers to know what is going on in the industry. For film and television, I recommend *Variety, Hollywood Reporter, Broadcasting & Cable,* and *Current.* They are all available online. Another good resource for what's happening in television is the *Cynopsis.com* online newsletter. For documentary and nonfiction work, I suggest *Real Screen.*

PART FIVE

PROPOSALS

As we learned in chapter 14, the package that a Producer prepares to sell or finance a fiction feature film can be as simple as a great script. However, for Producers of documentaries and other nonfiction content, it is hard to over emphasize the importance of a great proposal. And the process of creating the proposal is as important as the final product.

CREATING THE PROPOSAL

We will examine the basic elements of a nonfiction proposal in a minute, but first let's consider the benefits that accrue from the proposal process itself. Each of the sections of a proposal serve a specific function and the process of researching and writing each section forces the Producer to develop her idea and hold it up to her own intense scrutiny and to some of the standards and practices of the industry. The creation of the proposal forces the Producer to consider whether the idea is good enough to find money and a home in the media industry. There are plenty of ideas that seem great as ideas, but unfortunately they lack enough substance to be able to be developed into a full proposal, let alone a fully developed film. And it is far better to find that out in the proposal creation stage than in the post production stage, after a lot of time and money has been spent.

WHY DO A PROPOSAL?

In addition to the process of discover about the substance of the idea, there are two other benefits from a proposal. The first is that the nonfiction industry runs on them. Pitching and scripts are the way into the fiction world, but proposals are the way into nonfiction. Sometimes a nonfiction Producer gets to pitch an idea, but even then they are expected to have a written proposal to leave behind. This is true whether the Producer is dealing with a network or a funding source.

The other reason to develop a proposal is that it is a great way to protect an idea. Remember from Chapter 1 and the discussion on copyright, ideas are not copyrighted. But if a Producer develops that idea into a proposal, then it has a tangible format, which is copyrighted.

COMMON SECTIONS OF A PROPOSAL

Many networks and foundations have preferred structures or formats for a proposal. Some make it very clear what they want, and the Producer should obviously follow that format. Others just expect the standard sections from a professional Producer. Here are those standard sections.

Project Summary or Executive Summary

This is the first thing people read, but it is the last thing that is written by the Producer. It summarizes the key points of the proposal and entices the reader to continue into the detail. It is primarily a selling hook, a tease, and if successful will get the entire proposal read, and if unsuccessful will get the proposal tossed, unread, into the trash. But the Producer doesn't really know enough to write effectively about the fully developed project until it is fully developed, and that is after the rest of the proposal is written.

Having said that, it is very common for a Producer to draft an Executive Summary at the very start of the process as a way to get her initial ideas on paper.

Synopsis and Treatment

The proposal is for a piece of visual content so the first thing people want to know is what it will look like, what the viewer will see. The synopsis is a summary, in 2 to 3 pages, of what the audience will see; and the treatment is a detailed description that can be 15 to 20 pages for an hour or feature length project. Both of these are written after all the research is done and the film has taken a solid shape in the Producer's imagination. I normally suggest that a Producer develop the treatment first with all the detail and a very clear structure for the project. In third person, present tense, it takes the reader step-by-step through the film. What we see and what we hear. No theory, no justifications, nothing intangible. The reader should be able to clearly, easily, visualize the film as she reads. Then the synopsis is written as a summary of the treatment.

The reason for both is that the synopsis goes at the front of the proposal to give the reader a clear sense of what the film will look like but without the many extra pages of detail that are in the treatment. The synopsis allows the reader to keep some momentum as they go through the proposal, and not get bogged down in the treatment, which would go at the end of the proposal as an addendum. If the synopsis is successful, the reader will eagerly continue into the proposal.

Statement of Need

Most nonfiction projects are created to fulfill or meet a need. The need to tell a story to bring awareness to a problem. The need to educate people to make an informed decision or have a rational opinion. The need for viewers to know something important. You get the idea. So this section tells the reader why this project is important. Why is it necessary to make? This section often relates to the mission of a foundation and is critical for the funding function of the proposal.

Competition

It is a fact of media life that there are very few new and original ideas. Most things have been done at least once. Now that doesn't automatically mean that there isn't room for another film, but the

THE PRODUCER'S SOURCEBOOK

Producer has to know what has been done before, so their proposal, their approach, their treatment is done accordingly. So this section outlines all the other film projects that are similar to the proposed project. This should be a broad search, not a narrow one. For example, if the Producer's project is about saving the bonobos (as done very nicely by a former student of mine), then it should also consider any project about saving the gorillas, the orangutans, the chimpanzees, etc. It should even look at projects that focus on saving any kind of African wildlife. Know the landscape of all projects and then dig down to what is closest to the project being proposed. So this section should have a summary that describes the overall landscape – both narrow and broad focused. Then it presents the details for the films that are the most similar to the idea. It should include specifics for each of those projects including: brief synopsis; Producer; date of production; network airing if any; ratings if aired; and specifics of any other distribution. For the projects that are close in content, a Producer must also include a brief statement that analyzes how his project will be different, better.

Not only is this information necessary for your proposal, but the search will help inform the development of the idea. It may tell the Producer that there are just too many projects and that she shouldn't waste her time. It may tell her that there has never been anything like it, and she should rush ahead.

Be careful, however, when analyzing the landscape. An empty landscape could mean a great opportunity to be first; or it could mean that many have tried and no one has succeeded. A full landscape can mean that it is saturated and doesn't need another film; or it could mean that there is such a large interest in this topic, that it can absorb one more film, especially one with a new and different approach or story hook.

One of the most important results of this research comes when a Producer pitches to a network and the programming executive mentions a similar show on their network or on a competing network. The Producer has to know about it and be able to talk about it and explain why his project will be better, different. If he doesn't know about it, he might get thrown out of the office.

Audience

Every project has to be designed for a specific audience, using the standard demographic groups as covered in chapter 4. A project that a Producer designs for "everyone" is normally a boring mess.

A Producer should select a primary audience and be able to justify why this group of people will be interested in the film. The more thoughtful and specific this rationale, the more effective the proposal. This often takes research, possibly doing focus groups or maybe more informal market surveys. The worst mistake for a Producer is to assume that others will like something that she likes. Or to assume that all 18 to 34-year-old females are the same.

After researching and confirming a primary audience, then the Producer decides on a secondary audience. This audience, also identified by a standard demographic set, will offset the primary audience and give the project a greater reach. But the difference cannot be too great. A secondary audience of 12 to 16 is generally not a logical fit for a primary audience of 35+. What they each want to see, and what is appropriate for them to see, is very different and can't co-exist in one program – at least not in a good program. The secondary audience can have some overlap with the primary. For example, if the primary is adults 25 to 54, which is the traditional network television "sweet spot", then the secondary can be adults 18 to 34, or maybe women 18 to 34. But the secondary can never be a group that is already a part of the primary. For example, if the primary is adults 25 to 54, the secondary cannot be women 25 to 54 because they are already included in the primary. The secondary audience also needs the rationale of the Producer – why will they be interested?

Markets

Similar to the audience section, the markets section describes a primary and a secondary market.

The primary market should be the largest market that the Producer believes is reasonable for the project. For most documentaries and nonfiction work, television/cable is the largest market as we discussed in chapter 12. But not all projects are strong enough or suitable for television. So maybe home video or the educational market is the largest. My advice is always to think big but be realistic. A show developed for television/cable can always, and fairly easily, be scaled down for home video, VOD/SVOD, or educational use. But a show developed for educational video has a hard, if not impossible, time getting ramped up for television/cable.

The Producer should summarize this market and describe how the project fits. If it is a specific network, then the Producer has to analyze the schedule and the programming strategy of the network to make a case for how his show fits. This is hard and won't be perfect, but that's okay. The programming executive just wants to know that the Producer has done his homework and really knows what the network develops and airs. As you can hopefully see, the work done for the competition section will often help in this market research.

Once the primary market is set, then the Producer decides on a secondary market, where the project will go after the primary market. For films that have been on television, the secondary market is almost always home video or educational video. Occasionally, depending on the subject matter, it is international television or video.

This section should also describe the revenue potential from both the primary and the secondary markets. More research.

A Producer has to prepare this element but it is not always included in a proposal. If the Producer is presenting to a network, then the proposal might not have this information. There are two reasons for this. One is that the network knows itself far better than the Producer can know it. And two, the network will often want to control the project into the secondary markets. This is particularly true if they are considering a full commission or a co-production deal.

However, if the Producer is presenting the proposal to a foundation for funding, then the market section must be there to show how the Producer intends to get the project seen by the audience. This is a vital part of how a Producer convinces the foundation that the project will help meet the foundation's mission.

Outreach and Dissemination

This section builds on the Market section if the proposal is being presented to a foundation for funding. Most nonfiction films are not screened in theaters or even aired on a broadcast or cable network. Most have to find other ways to reach their audience, and the Producer has to have a realistic plan for this. Outreach primarily refers to how the Producer will go about letting people know about the film. It could be advertising in magazines or journals that relate to the topic of the film. It could be through mailing lists or social media outlets. And the good plan will have a number of ways to reach out to the potential audience.

Dissemination normally refers to the distribution of the physical format that will reach the audience – DVD is one important way; digital streaming or download are others. Are there distributors who work in this area and who would be interested in distributing the film? A list of those distributors and a short summary of their work/success is important.

Another aspect of dissemination that applies to many projects is a bundle of extra materials that the Producer creates to accompany the film. One prime example of this is a teachers' guide that will go with the film to help its effective use in the classroom. Or there could be a booklet of facts and figures, which do not make good video, but is important information for the viewer to know. Here again, the Producer needs to be creative in his approach to make sure the film has the greatest impact on the audience.

Funding Sources

As discussed in chapters 5, 6 and 8, a Producer very seldom gets a full commission for a nonfiction project. They have to find additional sources of funds. And the people they approach want to know who else the Producer plans to approach. So this section contains the results of research to find all the potential funders for the project. Review chapter 8 for more details.

As a Producer finds potential funders, they should investigate what films the funder has previously supported. A look at the credits for those films will reveal other funders and also information on who distributed it.

Project Background and Production Plan

Often a Producer does some work on a project before ever creating a proposal. It could be preliminary interviews or shooting some b-roll (particularly of an event that will not happen again). Some of this could be on a sizzle reel to help sell the proposal, but most will be a narrative description of what has been done.

This is then followed by a plan to complete the film. It incorporates schedules and a discussion of the challenges to be faced. It must be thorough because it has to feed into the budget and insure that enough money is being raised to be able to complete the film. Producers with very little production experience should consult with or partner with an experienced production manager to work on this section.

Research

This section discusses the resources available to the Producer to create a film that is accurate and thorough. Most Producers are not experts in all or any of the fields or subject matter areas that they film. Most Producers are generalist with intense curiosity and large areas of interest. But they have to prove to the network or the foundation funder that there is enough research material available for them to create a film. So this includes a list of primary sources available and a list of the organizations that work in the area. It also refers to the section that has outlined the competition – what other films are out there that deal with this topic/subject.

Budget

As discussed in chapter 18, a Producer can't raise money unless she knows how much she needs. This is true for fiction films and nonfiction films. The biggest challenge, however, is that it is often a lot harder with nonfiction films. Nonfiction films, particularly documentaries, are an exercise in discovery and that can lead to all sorts of changes and occasionally dead ends. The filming may have to be done sporadically over a long period of time. B-roll can be planned based on research, but it often changes because of what is learned in actual interviews.

A new Producer should always consult an experienced Producer or production manager for help. There is nothing that will kill a new Producer's career faster than a reputation for not being able to finish a project or having to constantly raise more money.

In the body of the proposal, the Producer only includes a summary of the budget and the major categories of expenses. A detailed budget would be attached as an addendum.

Business Plan

This section tells the foundation funders and the networks how the Producer is organized and what protections he has in place for liabilities, fiscal controls, etc. Most Producers operate as, or set up, a Limited Liability Corporation (LLC) for a project. People or organizations, who are asked to give a Producer money, want it to go to something other than the Producer's personal checking account. The Producer should have a lawyer and an accountant on call for assistance.

Advisors

Most nonfiction projects need to have experts in the field or content area who have agreed to lend their expertise to the film. Hopefully, they are leading people in the field or content area. Short bios are provided here and detailed resumes are attached as another addendum. If a Producer is trying to get money from a government foundation, this list is much more critical than the list of credits that the Producer has.

Key Personnel

Starting with the Producer, this is a series of short bios that highlight the contributions of each of the key members of the production team – writer, director, editor. If they have awards, make sure that is included. More detailed resumes and lists of credits go in the addendums. We don't list the crew.

Addendums

Depending on the nature of the project, there could be only a few or many things to add as addendums. These provide additional information and details that would potentially bog down the reader as he goes through the main body of the proposal. Some standard addendum items for most proposals would be:

Treatment

Detailed budget

Resumes – advisors and key personnel

SUPPLEMENTAL MATERIAL – PART FIVE – PROPOSALS

<u>Review Questions</u>

1. What are the benefits to the Producer from preparing a proposal?

2. Is the project summary done at the beginning or the end of the proposal process?

3. Is the existence of a lot of similar films necessarily a bad thing?

4. How does dissemination relate to distribution?

5. Is budgeting generally easier or harder for nonfiction than for fiction?

<u>Industry Speak</u>

Hook - something unique that will set a project apart, attract the attention or gain the interest of a target audience; this can be a story element or an individual involved in the project

<u>Further Activities</u>

Craft a proposal based on an idea that you would want to develop into a nonfiction film or video. Prepare each of the five following proposal elements for your idea. It is best to do them in order because information that you learn from your research on one proposal element will help with a subsequent proposal element.

1. Project or Executive Summary.

This is the first thing a reader of your proposal will see and is arguably the most important part of the proposal. It has to grab the reader's attention with a solid story hook and relate to their organization's target audience and markets. Because it is a summary of your proposal, it is normally the last element or section that is completed. However, it is also useful to prepare a draft statement of your idea at the very beginning of the process.

A. Select a documentary or nonfiction ideas for development and prepare a draft of your Project Summary. It can be for a series of shows that revolve around one topic or theme.

B. Decide on a Working Title for the show. This may change as you develop the idea and the proposal.

C. Then, write a short (one or two paragraph) summary of your idea for the project. Make sure it has a great story hook, which normally involves people.

D. Include an additional paragraph on what is your anticipated primary audience and network.

2. Research Element.

An important part of any project is the availability of information on the subject. Will it be easy to research for and obtain the information necessary to develop a good treatment? This information can come from primary resources including interviews and from secondary resources.

Another important element is the nature of the competition. Has this idea been done before? It is neither good nor bad to find either no programs or a lot of programs. Competition is not bad in a business where success breeds success and programmers like to copy a winner. If nothing has ever been done, it's either a great opportunity or maybe a flawed idea.

The Research Element should include the following:

A. original sources of information on the topic or subject

of your idea. These sources can be books, magazine articles, newspaper articles or other primary sources. Do not include interview subjects as sources for the purposes of this assignment. The Research Element should include a citation for the source and a brief abstract of the information it presents. For this assignment, you don't need to read all this material, just know where to find it and what it contains.

B. web sites that apply to your topic or subject. These shouldn't be sites that are just source content i.e. articles. They should be organizations that are involved in the subject area. List the web sites and give a brief abstract of what the site contains.

C. Do a broad search and list the film or video programs or projects that are similar to the project that you are developing. If there are many similar projects, then list the ones that are the closest to your idea. The places to look depend upon the nature of the idea and program you are working on. If it is an idea for the Travel Channel, then that is probably the first place to look. It would be the same thing for an idea that is targeted for PBS. For other videos, try the Internet. Be sure you know how to retrieve this information again.

The things you find probably won't be exactly like your idea, so use your common sense as to what could be either competition or a source of additional subject information. If there are general observations about the other programs, you can prepare a summary paragraph that describes them.

The Research Element should include the following additional information on the films you find: title; production (or air) date; and production company and/or distributor.

You should also briefly describe the program and discuss how it relates to your idea.

It is possible that for some topics you will not find any videos. If this is the case, prepare a detailed description of your search process and the results.

3. Target Audiences and Target Markets.

There is nothing more important to a programming executive that whether or not the show being pitched will attract their target audience. The first step is to determine the probably audience for your idea, then see if it matches the market or network you would like to pitch. This element should cover the following material.

Audience – you need to determine who will watch the program and why.

Primary Audience

> A. Describe the primary audience for your project. You must use the standard demographic sets that are in chapter 4.

> B. Give your rationale for targeting this primary audience and why this project would appeal to this audience.

Secondary Audience

C. Describe the secondary audience also in standard demographic terms. This audience will normally be smaller and possibly less commercially attractive than the primary audience. Part of the secondary audience might overlap with the primary audience but it cannot be a sub-set that is totally within the primary audience set.

> D. Why would the project appeal to this audience?

Markets - where the project will be seen or available to the primary and secondary audiences.

Primary Market

The Primary Market should be the largest possible market for your film. Try to find a television network (broadcast or cable) that would be appropriate.

E. Describe the market or network that you see as the primary market for your project and explain why. Make sure that this market has compatible audience demographic targets.

F. Describe how your project fits into the current schedule structure of the market or network, for example, PBS or a cable network's current schedule of programs.

G. What are the submission/acquisition policies and procedures for this network?

Secondary Market

The Secondary Market will be at a distribution level below the Primary Market. For example, if your primary market is a cable network, then your secondary market probably is home video, VOD or SVOD, educational, or international.

H. Describe the secondary markets that you see for your project after its use in the Primary Market. Make sure that this market has compatible audience demographic targets. You need to describe why you think this market will be successful – why people will be interested in watching and/or buying.

I. Describe some ways that your project might be marketed to the audience in this market. How would you make them aware of the project? You cannot just rely on the show appearing in a catalogue or list of videos available on a SVOD site. You must have ideas to make them interested and then, once they are interested, they can go to a site to watch and/or buy.

4. Distribution.

Despite the growth of the internet for distribution, there is still the need for organized companies who take films and videos to the various markets. There are distributors who can help you with all markets except for the major broadcast or cable networks. This element should cover the following material.

A. Identify and describe potential distributors for your project. If your Primary market is PBS or a cable network, then don't use the video division of that network as a distributor for this assignment. Your distributors should be independent companies that work at the secondary market level, which is probably home video, educational, or international. These must also be real distributors and not internet sales sites like Netflix, iTunes or Amazon.com.

B. Proper identification and description for all distributors would include: distributor name, address, telephone number, web site and the name of an acquisitions executive. And it should have a description of the types of films they distribute and to what markets.

C. Describe their acquisitions policies.

D. Research their web site and/or catalogues to ascertain what programs they currently distribute which are similar to yours. List and describe these programs. You must try to compare and distinguish each title from your idea.

5. Funding.

Now that you know the target audiences and markets for your project, it's time to focus on where the money will come from. Assume that the primary market will provide some but not all of the funds needed for the production. As Producer, you have to raise the rest of the money from other sources. Because these are nonfiction projects, the most likely sources are foundations and corporate sponsors.

For this element, identify and describe potential funding sources for your project. Proper identification and description for all funding sources would include:

A. The name, address, telephone and web site. If you talk to them, please note the name and position of the person you talked to.

B. A discussion of their funding guidelines. The discussion should include the following:

1. their mission and the types of projects they fund;

2. how your project fits that mission;

3. what types of entities (individuals or non-profits; geographical limits) they will work with; and

4. the typical range of grant amounts.

C. For each source, try to find shows that are similar to yours that the source has funded in the past. For each show include the following:

1. Describe the shows and how they relate to yours.

2. Where and when were these shows aired and/or distributed?

Individual investors and crowd sourcing sites such as

Kickstarter can be one funding source for this section.

Other points to consider. Some ideas might have more commercial appeal than others and corporate underwriting might be a possibility. The corporate department that would most likely handle this would be marketing. Also check to see if a corporation has a foundation

Further Reading & Research

Foundation center proposal writing section – go to: http://grantspace.org/training/self-paced-training/proposal-writing-short-course

PBS – go to: http://www.pbs.org/about/producing-pbs/ and look at Submission Guidelines and Proposal Process

Get in the daily habit – read the industry trade papers to know what is going on in the industry. For film and television, I recommend *Variety, Hollywood Reporter, Broadcasting & Cable,* and *Current.* They are all available online. Another good resource for what's happening in television is the *Cynopsis.com* online newsletter. For documentary and nonfiction work, I suggest *Real Screen.*

APPENDIX

INDUSTRY HISTORICAL TIMELINE

	Technology & Regulation	Television / Studios	Cable & Satellite	Home Video / DVD / Internet
1820	British develop the telegraph			
1826	First photograph; taken by J. Niepce			
1876	Alexander Bell patents the telephone			
1885	Eastman's first film camera			
1889	Edison's first motion picture camera			
1895		Screening of Lumiere's short films		
1896	Marconi patents first wireless radio			

1910s					
	1912	Federal Trade Commission created: charged with overseeing content and methods of advertising	Universal Pictures and Paramount Pictures begin		
	1914-18	WW1 is instrumental in the developlment of wireless radio; at end of war the military tried to control radio			
1920s			film studios grow into major cultural institutions		
	1923		first ads heard on radio (NYC) Disney Pictures and Warner Brothers Pictures begin		
	1926		NBC formed as first national radio network by GE and Westinghouse		

	1927	The Radio Act began to regulate the airwaves with the licensing of radio frequencies and transmission power	CBS radio network formed		
1930s		development of the technologies for television			
	1934	Communications Act of 1934: has remained the basis of communications law ever since; created the FCC	20th Century Fox studio begins		
	1936		first live coverage of a sports event - Berlin Olympics		
	1939	concept for TV demonstrated at NY World's Fair	first major league baseball game telecast: Brooklyn Dodgers vs. Cincinnati Reds		

1940s		development of the technologies for television are delayed by the war but ultimately energized by the spending on defense related projects		cable systems begin developing in areas underserved by broadcast stations	
	1941	NTSC approved TV standard still in use today FCC issues first commercial TV license to WNBT in New York (NBC)	the first commercial airs on NBC for Bulova watches (10 seconds)		
	1943	NBC ordered to divest one of its networks, which becomes ABC			
	1947		first baseball World Series telecast: Yankees vs. Dodgers		

1948		NBC, CBS and ABC begin broadcasting 4 hours of progamming each night first regularly scheduled evening news program (CBS) Film studios begin boycott of television which will last until early 1960s	first cable antenna community system established (PA)	
1950s		situation comedies begin to appear		
1951	East and West coasts linked with coaxial cable for national connection	first live sports event telecast nationally: college football game, Duke vs. Univ. of Pittsburgh		
1952	the first AFTRA Network Television Code FCC rules set 12 VHF channels and 70 UHF channels	The Today Show begins on NBC		

1953		first color broadcast (NBC) first public TV station goes on air (KUHT Houston)		
1954	RCA sells first color TV sets			
1955	1st practical wireless remote control (Zenith Space Commander; uses an ultrasonic signal)	CBS becomes #1 in ratings and continues so for 21 years		
1956	videotape recorder developed by Ampex and first used by CBS			
1960s	launching of first commercial satellites public internet conceived as global network of computers			
1960		1st televised presidential debate (Kennedy-Nixon)		

1962	FCC requires all new TV sets have to have UHF tuner			
1963			Comcast started as MSO	
1965			Cablevision started as MSO	
1967	first battery powered color video tape recorder	Corporation for Public Broadcasting created		
1968	research begins on high definition television			
1969	first handheld video camera slow motion and stop action available	Public Broadcasting Service created Sesame Street debuts		
1970s	modern communications satellites allow for easier and cheaper distribution of programming to local stations and cable operators	portable video equipment allows for more inexpensive and on-location productions		video games begin with Pong

1970		**number of US households with:** TV = 60 million Monday Night Football begins on ABC	**number of US households with:** Basic cable less than 10% of US households	
1972			HBO goes on air	
1973		PBS reorganized as a coop of member stations		
1975	HBO begins broadcast by satellite	Saturday Night Live launches	Ted Turner buys WTCG which will become TBS Superstation	
1976	beginning of consumer satellite distribution		Showtime begins	Betamax and VHS introduced
1979			ESPN begins Nickelodeon begins	
1980s		FCC makes new licenses available for UHF stations and encourages minority ownership	syndication of old TV shows grows into a major revenue stream	

1980		number of US households with: TV = 78 million	number of US households with: Basic cable = 17.6 million CNN, USA and Bravo begin	number of US households with: VCR = 23.5 million
1981		News Corp buys 20th Century Fox studio	MTV debuts	
1983	Supreme Court allows recording of films for home viewing as allowable "fair use"		Disney Channel begins	
1984	Cable Communications Act: gave FCC authority to regulate the operation of cable systems	ABC acquires ESPN	A&E and Lifetime begin	
1985		Home Shopping Network goes national	Discovery channel begins	first Blockbuster store opens
1986		FOX network begins GE buys NBC (part of RCA) Turner buys MGM library		

1988		ITVS formed by CPB		
1989	Japan begins first HD TV transmissions from satellite	Time Inc and Warner combine		AOL is launched
1990s	birth of internet as consumer medium implementation of the People Meter	introduction and acceptance of digital production tools		
1990	Childrens Television Act: limits amount of advertising	**number of US households with:** television = 93.1 million Time/Warner formed in $14 B merger	**number of US households with:** basic cable = 50.5 million pay cable = 39.9 million 60 cable networks	**number of US households with:** VCR = 65.4 million number of US households with: PCs = 21.9 million internet - 1.6 million
1991	1st www. pages or sites put online using HTML			
1992			Cartoon Network begins	

1994		Viacom buys Paramount Pictures - $10 B Viacom buys Blockbuster for $8.4 B (sold in 2011 for $228 million)	Hughes Direct TV starts Direct Broadcast Satellite	Amazon founded
1995	repeal of the Financial Interest and Syndication Rules	Disney buys ABC - $19 B Dreamworks Studios formed UPN and WB networks created	KU-band (18" dish) satellite receivers enter market	Streaming audio/video delivery begins on internet
1996	1996 Telecommunications Act: relaxed ownership restrictions and allows for group ownership	Turner sold to Time Warner for $7.6 B	Fox News starts	
1997				introduction of DVD
1998	MiniDV digital video tape format introduced			
1999	consumer DVRs hit market (TiVo)	Viacom buys CBS -$37 B		

2000s		high definition comes of age			DVD quickly dominates home video market
2000			**number of US households with:** television = 102.2 million AOL and Time Warner combine in a $135 B merge	**number of US households with:** basic cable = 66.6 million pay cable = 49.2 million satellite = 11.6 million digital cable = 10 million 281 cable networks	**number of US households with:** VCR = 88.1 million DVD player = 13 million number of US households with: PCs = 51.5 million internet = 42.8 million
2001				Comcast launches VOD service	
2002				Comcast buys AT&T cable	
2003			NBC buys Universal and becomes NBC Universal		first Blu-ray consumer device released
2004		Facebook launches	Sony buys MGM for $5 B		Blockbuster stores reach peak of 4,500 in U.S.

427

2005		number of US households with: television = 110.2 million Paramount buys Dreamworks for $1.6B	number of US households with: basic cable = 65.4 million pay cable = 51.2 million satellite = 22.3 million digital cable = 29.9 million 531 cable networks	number of US households with: VCR = 97.7 million DVD player = 84 million number of US households with: PCs = 73.7 million internet = 70.7 million broadband = 36.3 million Apple makes TV shows available for download/ purchase Netflix has 4 million subscribers News Corp buys MySpace for $580M
2006		UPN and WB networks merge to become CW Viacom splits up CBS and Paramount/cable nets Disney buys Pixar $7.4B		Google buys YouTube for $1.65B
2007	Apple introduces the iPhone		NBC buys Oxygen for $925 M	Hulu formed

2008		Dreamworks splits from Paramount/Universal; winds up at Disney	NBC buys Weather Channel for $3.5B	
2009	US broradcast television converts from analog to digital	Disney buys Marvel $4B GE and Comcast form joint venture with NBC/Universal; worth $37B		
2010s	digital delivery/distribution of content presents major challenges and opportunities for film and television			
2010	Apple introduces the iPad	**number of US households with television =** 115.9 million	**% of US TV households with:** basic cable = 61% pay cable = 45% satellite = 29% digital cable = 55% 625+ cable networks	**% of US TV households with:** VCR or DVD player = 86% DVR = 45% % of US households with: PCs = 76 internet access = 72 Netflix has 20 million subscribers Blockbuster files for bankruptcy

2011		number of US households with television = 114.7 million: first year-to-year decline		
2012		Disney buys Lucasfilms; $4 B		
2013				Jeff Bezos, founder of Amazon, buys Washington Post Company for $250 million Netflix begins original productions
2014		Disney buys Marker Studios - $950M Facebook buys Oculus - $2 B		

2015	FCC establishes "net neutrality" rule	**number of US households with television = 116.4 million**	**% of US TV households with:** basic cable = 60% pay cable = 45% satellite = 30% digital cable = 63% 700+ cable networks AT&T buys Direct TV - $49 B	**% of US TV households with:** VCR or DVD player = 86% DVR = 55% % of US households with: PCs = 76 Netflix has 75 million subscriber Verizon buys AOL - $4.4 B
2016		NBC Universal buys DreamWorks Animation- $3.8 B AT&T buys Time Warner- $85.4 B Lions Gate buys Starz - $4.4 B		65% of TV HH have at least one streaming device
2017		Disney buys 20th Century Fox studio - $66 B	Discovery buys Scripps cable networks - $14.6 B	
2018	FCC repeals "net neutrality" rule			

ACKNOWLEDGEMENTS

I want to thank all the students in my classes who have used the first edition of this book and given me such wonderful and constructive feedback. This second edition is so much better because of them. I would also like to thank my colleagues in the School of Communication at American University. They are a fantastic group of filmmakers and teachers, and a constant source of inspiration to me.

Special thanks to my wife and daughter who encourage me to write and put up with my odd hours for doing so.

ABOUT THE AUTHOR

Randall Blair is a filmmaker and a professor of film and media arts in the School of Communication at American University (Washington, DC). He is also the founder and Director of the graduate program Producing Film, Television and Video. At American University, he teaches courses in producing, media entrepreneurship, film and video production, directing, and scriptwriting.

In addition to *The Producer's Sourcebook*, Mr. Blair has also written two novels, *Lovely Rita* and *Curse of the Nice Guy*. All of his books are available in print and eBook on Amazon.com and as eBooks at Smashwords.com and all book retailer internet sites.

He has created award-winning documentaries, short dramatic films and educational/corporate videos. These films have been shown on PBS stations and on television networks in Germany, the Czech Republic, Hungary and other countries. His films have been screened in film festivals and film markets including Berlin, Sundance, San Francisco, Aspen, New York Underground, Long Island, Palm Beach, Independent Feature Film, Wine Country and Angelciti. Mr. Blair's film and script awards include two CINE Golden Eagles, four Tellys, an ITVA Bronze Reel, two Silver International Cindys, two gold and four Silver Medals from Worldfest Houston, and the Washington Peer Awards for Best Director and Best Scriptwriter of a narrative film less than 40 minutes.

In addition, Mr. Blair has been a professional photographer, television programming consultant, and the owner/manager of a group of commercial radio stations.

98301023R00241

Made in the USA
Columbia, SC
23 June 2018